for Grace

STEPHEN O'BRIEN

'Britain's brightest young medium . . . Power
seems to radiate from his fingertips. These
eyes can see beyond the grave'
Daily Star

'It's hard to be sceptical of the psychic world
when a stranger tells you precisely what you
were doing that morning, and even days before. I
was startled, almost shocked'
Liverpool Echo

'*In Touch with Eternity* contains many fascinating
glimpses of life in the spirit world, including a
vivid account of a visit to the Higher Realms with
his guide White Owl'
Psychic News

'There is no doubting his sincerity or his honesty'
Girl About Town

ANGELS BY MY SIDE
The Psychic Life of a Medium

Stephen O'Brien

BANTAM BOOKS
LONDON · NEW YORK · TORONTO · SYDNEY · AUCKLAND

ANGELS BY MY SIDE

A BANTAM BOOK : 0 553 40718 X

First publication in Great Britain

PRINTING HISTORY
Bantam Books edition published 1994

This book is set in 10pt Linotype New Century Schoolbook by
Phoenix Typesetting, Ilkley, West Yorkshire.

Corgi Books are published by Transworld Publishers Ltd,
61–63 Uxbridge Road, Ealing, London W5 5SA,
in Australia by Transworld Publishers (Australia) Pty Ltd,
15–25 Helles Avenue, Moorebank, NSW 2170,
and in New Zealand by Transworld Publishers (N.Z.) Ltd,
3 William Pickering Drive, Albany, Auckland.

Reproduced, printed and bound in Great Britain by
Cox & Wyman Ltd, Reading, Berks.

To the Freedom of your Spirit,
which is its Origin and Destiny . . .

Acknowledgements

For the kind reproduction of extracts and a photograph, my thanks to *Psychic News*, especially its editor Tim Haigh, and Rita Smith; and also to fellow-wordsmiths Brenda Kimber, Jackie Krendel and John Jewsbury.

As always I express my love to all my friends and followers everywhere.

And I'm also grateful to all the journalists and their publications, plus the media people and my many correspondents across the world whose kindness, gifts and prayers have been, and still are, so very much appreciated.

And thanks to Dylan Bowen Williams and his camera.

Not forgetting, of course, everyone who has so kindly and willingly contributed their personal evidence of survival plus similar related material for this book, so that others may experience, enjoy, and hopefully benefit from the sharing of it.

I also thank God for the life of Sooty and the joy of her companionship.

And my special love and gratitude will always go

To Snowy
whose shining eyes
and gentle heart
lit up my darkness

Contents

Introduction: Angels by my Side   xii

1   A Candle in the Dark   1
2   Disembodied Voices   27
3   Medium Wave   41
4   Psychic Signs and Portents   59
5   The Silver Cord   81
6   Beyond the Veil   99
7   White Owl Speaks   115
8   'O Great White Spirit . . .'   137
9   Farewell to a Chocolate Soldier   143
10   Chuckle-Muscles   165
11   What Awaits Us Beyond Death   181
12   Questions and Answers   197
13   Journeys of the Soul   225
14   The Living God   229
15   Heal Yourself with Light and Colour   253
16   Ancient Wisdom   281
17   Silent Sentinels   299
18   Psychic News   317
19   'I Heard a Voice from Heaven Say . . .'   323
20   Wee Willie Winkie   349
21   'Willowtrees'   361

Unconditional Love
is the greatest power in the Universe.

I can't grieve for the 'dead',
for they are most certainly alive;
my heart is sad for the so-called 'living' –
those billions of people who are blindly wandering
in the deepest darkness of ignorance,
when they could be feeling utterly secure,
as free men,
basking in the effulgent light of spiritual truth.

Stephen O'Brien
'Willowtrees'
Wales, 1993

Introduction

Angels By My Side

Though I'm but a man of flesh and bone
which soon must fade to dust and die,
  the thought of death disturbs me not,
  it simply passes by
  receiving little heed –
    for no-one yet has ever died,
    and I have seen a host of angels
        standing by my side.

Whenever I pass through valleys dark and grim,
feeling so utterly lost within
that I stumble at ev'ry shaded hill,
  I need no place to sigh,
  for a secret lamp lights up my soul,
        illuminating angels
        brighter than the sky.

Then though I may not always find
        the right words to say
        to express my mind as clearly as I may,
        or loose my tongue when it is tied,
        I never fear,
          for hidden wisdom flows to me
          from invisible friends
            at my right-hand side.

And even when my actions
fail to ease another's burdens

which press them to their knees, then crucify –
  I'm never dismayed;
    instead, from deep within my soul
      I beseech a Presence High:
        'Send your gentle angels
          to free the souls of those who cry.'

And when heavenly voices from eternity speak to me
  (which others cannot hear
  and therefore they deride)
  their lack of understanding grieves me not,
  for behind it – fear hides.
    But *I* am not afraid,
      for softly moving through my mind
      are ancient sounds which cannot be denied:
          these are the silent whisperings
              of angels glorified.

Then when my days on earth
are thankfully over and done,
and my spirit drops its body
when its course is run,
  I'll breathe a breath of pure release . . .

  and after your tears for me have flowed and ceased,
      in the stillness of a quiet night
        perhaps you'll hear my voice upon the breeze,
      or even sense my presence
          or my peace
      within your spirit's inner tide:

      as through the shimmering veil,
        next to your bedside,
          I'll gently kiss your forehead
            and caress your tearful eyes,
              then speak again my love for you
            to show it hasn't died –

          and I will be a Starbright Angel
            standing by your side.

1

A Candle in the Dark

The television studio fell absolutely silent; you could have heard a pin drop amongst the two hundred nervous people sitting in the audience, each person full of expectation, all waiting for me to start relaying messages from the next world . . .

Suddenly, the bright lights dimmed and a powerful spotlight picked me out in my armchair, and three big television cameras glided quietly into position, like silent robots.

Then, all at once, I broke the tension with a short explanation of what I was going to attempt, while every word was being recorded:

'Thank you for participating in this experiment, ladies and gentlemen,' I said warmly, 'and I hope we'll get the results we're seeking, because no medium can command anyone in the next world to communicate with us . . . '

Then out of the blue, somewhere deep inside my mind, I heard a young lad's indistinct spirit voice piercing the silence of death, psychically speaking to me.

'All right, my son,' I acknowledged out loud, 'just

step in,' I suggested; and then he drew close enough for me to hear him much more clearly.

'I've got a young man with me,' I announced, 'wanting to get through to someone in our audience.' And before I could say any more, he gave me a sudden psychic glimpse of exactly how he'd met his untimely death: it was a tragic car accident.

'Yes, I saw you: that's all right. He's just projected an image here, and he's saying he passed over into the world of spirit very, very quickly: he was involved in an accident. And he talks very plainly of Paul and Robert,' I relayed.

Suddenly, an attractive young woman right at the front of the fascinated studio audience started waving her hand to get my attention.

'Do you understand this?' I asked, and she nodded enthusiastically as two cameras turned in her direction. 'Just a minute then, I'll get – oh, all right, son,' – the lad was quickly interrupting again with more evidence – 'he was dead on arrival at the hospital,' I repeated.

'Yes.'

'Who were Paul and Robert? These are people you know?'

'Yes, Paul is the chap who went over, and Robert is his brother.'

'OK. If that's the case you've been speaking to his brother about him recently.'

'Yes, I have; *yes*.'

'And this young man was standing listening to you.'

2

Obviously thrilled, the young woman was eager to know more; but unknown to her, I could hear Paul gently sobbing at my right-hand side, for he knew we'd found his special lady and his emotions had overcome him.

'All right . . . he's crying,' I reported softly, 'because you're the one we want. You love him and he loves you – and he wants to get through to his loved ones. "I love my brother," he says, "and he's never got over the shock."'

'No, he hasn't,' she replied positively, as Paul was urging me to state he was often with Robert, and wanted him to know he'd tried to personally contact him.

'All right, Paul, I'll tell her: I heard that so clearly. He said, "Tell my brother his best mate speaks to him." He says, "They placed some flowers for me, but I don't want them to go there; I want them just to think of me and send me their love." Do you understand that?'

'Yes, I do,' she said knowingly, after which the lad went on to mention some earrings and a place called Station Road, and that there was another person involved in the accident. His lady confirmed to the audience he'd lived just near Station Road and said she understood the mention of the earrings, but wasn't sure about the third party involved in the tragedy, but that she'd check this out.

'"Tell her I followed her here," Paul said, "and it's time she tidied up her shoes!" He's getting good

3

at this now,' I announced with a smile, asking the young woman: 'What does this mean?'

'Oh yes, I have lots and lots of shoes and they're in a big pile, and I *have* to sort them out!' she grinned, later informing me that she'd made that *very same statement* just a few days previously.

Then Paul delivered two accurate statements which, looking back on them, show that he'd cleverly prepared his spirit message, long before it was to be transmitted; and his facts proved all the more evidential because of their intimate nature. In speaking of his roadside death, and of his precise words to his mother on the day that he died, he drew immediate confirmation from his girlfriend.

'He's saying that two people rushed and tried to resuscitate him, but they couldn't resuscitate him.'

'Yes, that's right,' said his startled lady, her eyes glinting.

'And he also tells me, "I used to go out and say to Mum: tarrah, Mum" – but he never said it on that day.'

'No, he didn't,' she agreed.

'Oh, you knew?'

'Yes, I know,' she said. Then Paul continued:

'"I never said it on that day, Stephen, and I've waited now to say: it's not goodbye, Mum; it's not tarrah, Mum – I'm all right, and I'm with Bill and Annie" – these are probably friends or relatives – ' I interjected – '"and I'm safe, so don't cry for me."'

I took an emotional breath for all of us, smiled at

4

his girlfriend, then gently asked: 'Now, will you tell Robert he's been?'

'I certainly will, *yes*!' she beamed from ear to ear. 'I'm seeing Robert tomorrow and I shall *certainly* tell him!'

It was so lovely to see the young lady's happy smile that I almost forgot to let Paul finish his contact, which he did with a final flourish of: '"God bless you, my darling – and tidy up those shoes!" Thank you very much,' I said, completing my mediumship with a smile as big as that of Paul and his lady.

'Thank *you* very much,' was her warm and bright reply.

Millions of television screens across central Britain, which were flickering like candles in the darkened corners of living-rooms, then suddenly switched pictures, as the station ended this video-recording and immediately went live to the studio, introducing *Central Weekend Live*'s popular presenter, Linda Mitchell, who addressed my recipient:

'Can I ask your name, please?'

'Andrea.'

'Andrea, who exactly was contacting you there?'

'My boyfriend.'

'And what was his name?'

'Paul.'

'How close were you?'

'We were engaged. He'd asked me to marry him the night before the accident.'

'When you hear those sort of things what's your reaction?'

'I'm happy, *elated*, knowing that he's still carrying on.'

'Don't you feel a bit creepy? I mean, he died – how long ago did he die now?'

'Two years this January.'

'And you've had this message from him . . . '

'Yes, I'm *happy*. It's not creepy at all, because it's Paul. How can it be creepy? I know him so well, why would he want to frighten me now?'

'Are you a believer in Spiritualism?'

'Yes I am.'

'Do you regularly go to Spiritualist churches and meetings?'

'Yes.'

'Has Paul spoken to you before?'

'He's impressed people, given them similar situations as to how the accident happened, but he's never come through with such positive evidence as he did with Stephen. He's never come through like that before.'

'Really? What was it about what Stephen said that impressed you so specifically tonight?'

'My shoes, my earrings, his brother, his mum – his mum still does get very upset. Just everything really, and I know he'd come through with things like this, you know.'

'OK. Thank you, Andrea. Well,' said Linda into the camera, 'the question is simple: can Spiritualists contact people who have died and put them in touch with living relatives? Leading medium Stephen O'Brien regularly fills town halls up and down the country with people who are eager to know if the answer to that question is yes.'

She then turned towards the colourful set where I was seated with two others (ready to do battle).

'Stephen, that's quite an amazing thing, isn't it, to talk to somebody who's been dead for two years? I mean, you said that you felt emotionally wiped out by this.'

'No, it's not unusual,' I answered brightly, 'it's quite a commonplace occurrence for me as I go around the country, but it didn't emotionally wipe me out,' I gently corrected Linda. 'The link was much longer than that; Central TV have edited it down. What happened was: my communicator began to cry, and because he was in attunement with me I sensed that very strongly.' Linda nodded understandingly as I finished with: 'But I tried to sincerely deliver what he had to say to his fiancée.'

'And you've never met Andrea before tonight?'

'No, I've never met the young lady before,' I said. In fact, that was the first time I'd heard her name, and her intimate relationship with Paul had only just been revealed to me.

Linda then brought into the discussion the celebrated illusionist Mr David Berglas, President of the British Magic Circle, by saying: 'David, isn't this proof that there is something in Spiritualism?'

'I have to say: no,' he replied – which came as no surprise because he'd been engaged to place a counter-viewpoint – but he then went on to try and systematically destroy the evidence I'd given to the elated young woman, after which he had to confess to viewers that he'd spent the previous forty minutes since the link was recorded in defending me backstage, because, as he admitted about Paul's spirit evidence I'd just delivered: 'You got an amazing degree of accuracy.'

And then he offered the rather meagre sum of £10,000 to myself, or any other medium, who could prove to his satisfaction the reality of a life after death – I say 'meagre' because before then I'd turned down £250,000 from sceptics on TV!

'I'm not one bit interested in your money,' I instantly replied – and I wasn't. A great part of my current work is to bring comfort to, give hope to, and also help people to be more aware of the undying nature of spiritual love and the continuity of life, plus the fact that soul-liberating spirit teachings, guidance and inner strength are available to every one of us, transmitted by discarnate loved ones from an eternal world of spirit beyond what many still consider to be 'death'. For the last two decades I've tried to publicly achieve these objectives by consciously joining two worlds together as one, as best as I could, and often under some very difficult psychic conditions.

But I don't think sceptics want to accept that the purpose of a medium is *to serve*: we're not out *to prove* anything. Sensitives help people on both sides of the thin veil called 'death' to contact each other.

Common sense tells us that after telephoning friends in a distant land, you don't then ask the handset, 'What did you set out to prove?' It has simply provided an invaluable service – and even then many electronic and weather conditions may have adversely affected its clarity of transmission and reception. Roughly the same problems can hinder psychic communication, except that mediumship difficulties arise because of inharmonious mental states and the sensitive's lack of sufficient soul-sensitivity.

But let's get back to *Central Weekend Live*:

David Berglas was still stating his case against mediums, and there now came what was intended to be a stunning showstopper but, unknown to him, and everyone else, my spirit friends had warned me of David's 'secret' intentions while I'd travelled to the Nottingham studios on British Rail – so it was no surprise at all! He served his volley by announcing:

'As a magician I can always duplicate what any medium demonstrates, which I've often done.'

To which Linda replied: 'I'd like to see you do that, David,' – but the whole exercise fell flat because I instantly scotched it with:

'Maybe you *could* get up and mimic a link like that, but yours would be trickery, and mine is Reality – and that's the difference between us.'

There was immediate, spontaneous applause from the audience, and Mr Berglas stayed firmly in his seat, my comments later being branded as 'good TV'!

Then Linda threw some red meat to a pack of wolves, so to speak, by opening up the discussion to the ever-eager-to-argue audience – one of the show's trademarks. Or, to put it another way – she might as well have said, 'Let the bun-fight begin!'

Suddenly, a whole basketful of bread went flying, and a barrelful of hoary old chestnuts which the sceptics usually throw at sensitives whizzed past my head, all flung in quick succession, during which a rather pious Christian gentleman said: 'Regarding people on the Other Side, I don't feel we have a *right* to contact them' – which I instantly corrected with:

'But *Paul* contacted *me*, sir. *I* didn't contact *him*, he contacted *me*,' drawing more hearty, spontaneous applause from the studio audience.

After this, Linda brought in another contributor, Jean Bassett, an official of Britain's Spiritualists' National Union.

'Jean, you're an ordained minister in the Spiritualist Church, people are talking of charlatans and frauds: how do you deal with that big credibility gap which a lot of sceptics in the audience don't seem able to bridge?'

'We can only work through it with sincerity,' replied Jean, warmly. 'Everybody's entitled to disbelief, this is their prerogative – but we can then come in and prove to them that survival is a fact,' she went on, truthfully adding that hundreds of genuine mediums visit small Spiritualist churches up and down Britain each week, being paid only their travelling expenses and not personally knowing

10

their audiences, and yet they are regularly able to offer accurate spirit messages to the public.

Then Linda quickly changed tack:

'Stephen, why does it always seem to be pretty minor information? If we're hearing from the spiritual world why do we never hear the answer to the AIDS problem?'

'If anybody would care to look at his life, Linda, it's quite mundane,' I said. 'These messages may sound trivial – but *not* to the one sending them, and *not* to the one receiving them.'

'So you're saying it's a way of proving the link?'

'Yes. This young lady's man isn't going to come back and talk about Einstein's Theory of Relativity – he's going to talk about her and him.'

It's worth mentioning here that spirit links are often full of personal information meant solely for the ears of the two parties involved, which is why other witnesses can never truly judge the meaningful nuances hidden within them.

And so the studio argument raged on for a good twenty minutes or more, coming to an end with resounding applause as we all trooped off to the green-room for coffee and cakes, where David Berglas made a special effort to congratulate me on my work! 'Oh well, Stephen,' I thought, '*c'est la vie!*'

But it was all worthwhile in the end because the programme caused quite a stir and I received much favourable mail from viewers who, after enjoying it, were now interested in investigating the paranormal.

Television, of course, instantly makes one's wrinkly old face a piece of living-room furniture – like a well-worn squashed sofa! – and to my great dismay this means I am now often recognized in public, which – quite frankly – has been one of the biggest blights of my private life. Such embarrassing intrusions, however, can be made much more tolerable when they serve some greater purpose, as one did quite recently.

I was coming out of a marketplace and had just gathered the folds of my voluminous mackintosh about my quivering form, while stepping through a set of those terrifying lightning-fast automatic doors – I'm positive they'll one day shut too quickly and slice me completely in half. I gingerly emerged into the bracing air, when suddenly a loud male voice called out behind me, 'Excuse me!'

I quickly swivelled on my heels, rather startled.

'Pardon me, but you *are* Mr O'Brien, aren't you? Stephen O'Brien, the medium?'

Standing before me was a tall swarthy-looking man in his mid-twenties. He looked rather worried. Although wrapped up warmly against the chilly February winds, his face was reddening in the breeze as I studied his smarting eyes – and even then I didn't know what to expect; strangers can deliver any kind of unwelcome surprise these days.

'*Are* you Stephen O'Brien?'

'Yes, I am.'

'I thought so; I've seen you on television. I hope you don't mind me stopping you like this, but

I've been worried sick. Can I ask you a question, Stephen?'

Suddenly, there was a note of genuine anxiety in his voice: this young man needed help, so I nodded and he spilled out his sad story.

'You see, I lost my father this year, and when he died I was completely devastated. He was a great bloke and it's the worst thing that's ever happened to me,' he said, pathos filling every space of the atmosphere around him. My heart went out to him when I acutely sensed the grief of his great loss.

'What can I do for you?' I asked, pulling my scarf around my neck against the sharp air.

'Well, the problem is I'm a Christian, a Catholic, and my people were very unhappy when I told them I'd been to see a medium. Actually, it was after I'd read your books.'

'Oh,' I said, keeping an even tone when, in fact, I'd already sensed what was coming next. 'Look, I'm sorry about your father,' I added sympathetically, 'but as you've probably found out by now, there's no such thing as death.'

'Oh yes,' he replied enthusiastically, 'your books have been an enormous help to me; and the medium I saw gave me an excellent message from my dad at the Spiritualist Church, proving his survival. She told me things that only he and I knew. It was a magnificent moment, and I can't tell you what it meant to get word from him again, Stephen.'

'That's great,' I said, 'and you're very fortunate to hear from him so soon.'

'Yes, but my problem is my family: you see, they're good people, but they're born-again Christians and . . . well, now they won't even speak to me. They've cut me off from the fold, and told me Dad's message had come from the Devil who was impersonating him, and that now I'd be damned in hell-fire for eternity, for trying to contact my father . . . '

His words trailed away helplessly as he deeply furrowed his brow, and I couldn't believe my eyes when I saw strange psychic shadows fall across this young man's face as he remembered his family's fearful threats and the painful withdrawal of their love for him.

'Please,' he pleaded, rather like a lost child, 'can you help me, Stephen? What do you think of it all?'

'It's absolute rubbish,' I said reassuringly, amazed that his relatives seemed to care more for their religious dogma than they did for the heart and feelings of one of their own bereaved. 'Look,' I began reasoning, appealing to his religious sense, 'Jesus told his disciples to seek and they would find. Well, you went out seeking for your father, and you found him. So you've done nothing wrong at all. If God had thought communication was evil, He would never have allowed His chosen prophets to speak to the so-called dead, now would He?'

'No, I suppose not,' he agreed, brightening a little.

'And the Bible is a book packed with psychic and spiritual experiences, miracles, healings: it's crammed full of spirit messengers – angels from the next worlds – sending help to Earth, and Jesus Himself spoke to the "dead" Moses and Elias on the mount when they appeared to Him.'

'Yes, He did, didn't He?' he said, his whole face lighting up for the first time.

'That's right; and the Master's message was all about Love, as well as promising that we would do much greater things than Him, because He ascended to the Father. Do you remember that text?'

'Yes. That's right,' he enthused, 'He did.'

'Well, there's your explanation. And remember: your dad, just like everyone else who's ever passed on, is still alive in another world. So don't take your family's views too much to heart; I'm sure they don't really mean to hurt you – they're only speaking from their own understanding, you know,' I said honestly, and with as much compassion as I could muster under the circumstances.

'You know, at the end of the day, this is *your* life, my friend, not your family's; and it's you who must live it, breathe it, experience it and seek out its meaning for yourself, in your own unique way.'

There was a pause, and I lifted my collar against the cold wind as I watched this young man's face registering the new thoughts our shared conversation had brought him.

'Stephen,' he said, at last, 'thank you . . . But tell me, why on earth would my people claim communication is evil?'

'Probably because of fear,' I replied. 'Fear of what they think is the unknown – when, in fact, the next

15

world has been well charted for anyone who wants to learn about it. And perhaps your relatives have misinterpreted certain of their religious sayings,' I added. 'And it's worth remembering, by the way, that Christianity isn't the only faith in the world. There are other beliefs which are much older. Besides, all roads lead to the Godhead in the end, so no one Church can possibly have all of the truth – but each faith might have its own small portion of it. And as for the so-called Devil – I don't believe in him.'

A sharp, smarting gust of February wind arose, catching my ears, so I pulled up my scarf and went on: 'My own spiritual faith is built on direct knowledge and experience of the God-force. It's man who draws upon this Power of Life and then wickedly twists and contorts it, using it to say and do ignorant and unkind things. Man is the only Devil I know,' I concluded.

The stranger's face now perceptibly changed: he was psychically beaming out light, and for the first time his eyes regained their youthful sparkle.

'Listen: do you love your father?' I asked.

'Oh yes, very much.'

'And do you think he still loves you?'

'Oh yes, with all his heart; he told me so before he died, and afterwards in that medium's message.'

'Then that's all that matters,' I returned. 'Never forget that love is stronger than death.'

'Stephen,' smiled the young man, reaching out and warmly clasping my hand tightly in his, 'I feel so much better about it all now, thank you very much for talking to me. It's been a great privilege to meet you and I think your books are marvellous.'

'Listen, don't be too hard on your people,' I advised. 'They're only doing what they think is right. Why don't you pray for them and do your best to help them understand, and then share in what you've found; what, in your soul, you already know.'

'I will,' he replied.

'And the greatest thing of all, of course, is: if you can learn to forgive them, maybe they'll accept you again – not for what they'd like you to be, but for what you really are and for what you truly believe,' I said, and he shook my hand again.

'I'm really grateful. Thank you.'

'My pleasure,' I said, calling out as he went on his way through the crowd of cold and busy shoppers, 'and if you continue seeking, you'll find much more.'

But I couldn't help thinking as I wended my way home just how deeply some careless words can hurt, more than those who speak them may ever know; also, I was conscious of the Nazarene's mission which, after all, was based on loving others as we ought to love ourselves.

As readers may be aware, like this young man, over the years I've suffered from similar narrow-minded bigotry, and not just from born-again Christians either (who I regret to report have been the most forceful and violent of all my critics). Even some sceptical scientists have been willing to have a go at me! So I've now come to the conclusion that some people lead such sad, inadequate lives that I'm obviously their principal amusement.

Poor souls.

Still, I've become quite philosophical about it: they also serve who only stand to be humiliated.

You name it and it's been hurled at me. In fact, I'm now so proficient at ducking, I've got a crick in my neck! But the public haven't been one bit deterred by any of the 'professional debunkers', and they still attend my meetings in their thousands each year, in spite of the crippling economic recession in Britain of the early 1990s; a situation so bad that many household-name stars were forced to cancel several of their performances through lack of ticket-sales – but, though attendances at my meetings were lower than normal, none were cancelled, and all seemed well received.

Such public interest in the paranormal under-lines the fact that man is slowly entering a new phase of consciousness, a New Age of Awareness where materialism is on the down-trend and matters of the body, mind and spirit are rapidly ascending.

Over the years, the public have given to me something more precious than their welcome encouragement: they have given me their love.

And they still send small gifts through the post: this year someone even had a tree planted in my name on Holy Island. But most of all, I get sackfuls of letters each year in which people continue to express their condemnation of my noisy critics and ought-to-know better bigots for exhibiting bad behaviour in public. But to me, the people have pledged their undying support.

I hope that doesn't sound arrogant; I didn't mean it to, but it's absolutely true. I've received letters from nearly every country in the world, encouraging and thanking me, and asking that I share more of my life and the spiritual teachings I've received.

Letters have come from places where my books haven't even been published, so it seems many a battered copy has gone 'on holiday'! Funnily enough, an English woman wrote recently that she was reading my last book, *In Touch with Eternity*, on a sun-drenched Spanish beach when suddenly she was first 'accosted, commandeered and then avidly chatted to' by two sunburnt *senoritas* who'd recognized my face on the cover, declaring they'd seen me at one of my meetings!

It certainly is a small world, and it seems my book got a suntan, even if I didn't!

Most of the thousands of letters I've received have been so very touching and emotional, full of sincerity and sensitivity – and others have positively glowed with such effervescent compliments and praise for my mediumship that I'm far too embarrassed to share them here; if I knew you were reading them I'd be mortified, and would probably end up *sending* messages from the next world, instead of receiving them!

Nevertheless, I'd like to thank everyone whose

kindness, thoughtfulness and sincere prayers have indeed strengthened, uplifted and encouraged me to continue sharing the spiritual truths I've found with millions of souls eager to hear them. I still read every single letter, and my personal prayers immediately go out for all correspondents and their loved ones.

And thank you, too, for being so patient in waiting for your replies. My wish for you all is that you may find true peace of mind, especially the correspondent who felt inspired to ask: *'What has developing your sensitivity given to you, and of what use is it?'*

Such a questioning spirit will no doubt lead its possessor on to an exciting path of inner soul-discovery; a road I feel privileged to have walked, and which I'm still dutifully treading. Mind you, it's been a very tough, yet paradoxically marvellous, spiritual journey, a personal quest well worth the effort.

What has unfolding my soul-awareness given me? Well, so many remarkable and comforting things I'm delighted to share with you.

It's revealed to me what awaits every sentient creature after death, and how the incredible Universal Laws of Predestination and Free Will fit into and control every facet of our lives.

It's brought me a more profound understanding of who man truly is, where he comes from, and what will be his ultimate destiny, and the fate of all other souls.

Awareness has engendered great inner joy and made me conscious of each being's unbreakable link with the One Living God, and how, through man's hidden psychic powers and connections with this Supreme Power and Great Light, he can heal not only his own body, mind and spirit, but also the tortured souls and hearts of others.

My increasing depth of awareness has indicated to me the true nature of the Infinite Great Spirit, in all Its pristine beauty, supernal magnificence and spiritual majesty.

Sensitivity has fanned within my spirit the radiant lights of soul-knowledge and eternal spirit truths which I can now, in my own small way, shine into the darkness of other people's lives, into the hearts of souls so desperately dissatisfied with the greed of acquisition and the all-consuming lust for materialism.

By developing a responsiveness to the inner things of the spirit, all people who are craving knowledge of spiritual realities, and seeking the inner peace that passes understanding, can experience these indescribable joys for themselves – and also benefit from the power of unconditional love, when it enriches their lives.

My personal awareness has helped me to link with developed minds dwelling deep within realms of brilliant light far beyond Earth, and I've been able to receive, and then share, some of the wisdom of the ages, secretly revealed to me by these souls whom I consider to be spiritual masters.

My quickened psychic senses have revealed to me angels by my side.

There have been so many innumerable blessings:

Now, when I stand on a summer riverbank and look into the rushing stream, I can feel its spiritual source and power.

In the glinting eyes of an old woman I've seen a shining, bright soul-light; and within the breast of a young man, the true nature of his loving heart has shone forth, openly before my vision.

Nothing can hide from the soul who can truly see.

On many quiet Sunday mornings when drifting breezes carry the resonant peals of church bells across a tranquil valley, their music strikes its harmony deep within my soul.

In so many things, I've intuitively felt and heard the rhythm of life.

At violet twilight when, on the warm breath of night, silent voices come speaking to me from another world, or the radiant forms of people who have long forsaken this cold earth for a much brighter land appear before my eyes, their vibrating peaceful presences are so very real to me that they may as well not have 'died'.

And when I now gaze into the heart of a perfumed flower, I can appreciate its unique beauty in fullness: I don't have to analyse it, or consciously think about it – it isn't a sense experience – it's a spirit-to-spirit link. In the gazing I seem to become a part of its being, and it blends with mine.

The unfolding of soul-sensitivity has opened for me doors to luminous inner worlds which, if they were ever to close again, would leave me bereft of any real meaning in my life.

Greater heart-realizations have also confirmed that war and hunger, hatred and tyranny burn all the love out of the breast of humankind and serve only to increase man's poverty of spirit.

Such inner revelations have urged me to choose the much gentler, more spiritual pathway of trying to practise and make known the benefits of unconditional love, harmony and brotherhood between all life-forms.

These noble thoughts have been so easy to accept, but sometimes so tremendously difficult to enact in daily life – but they form the core of what I've tried to share with as many millions as I could, in the living hope that, one day – even though it may come gradually – peaceful toleration will fully establish itself on Earth.

I realize that every voice for peace is important; and each life expressing it must lead the way, one step at a time.

Looking back on my spiritual journey so far, no-one on Earth, or in heaven, could ever persuade me to forsake one jot of the sensitivity I've gained through the many hardships I've experienced during this personal soul-quest. So I shall continue to seek out, and do my best to express, the powers of truth and love.

As this inner awareness continues to unfold, it seems to me now – as I look around at what often seems to be a mad and rushing world, still bereft of peace — that through my subtle spirit senses I may have experienced more of Actual Reality than some, and probably a good deal more of Spiritual Truth than most.

Passing By

feathered birdwings arc a brilliant sky
  and kiss me quietly
    as they fly,
      stirring my sleeping soul
       like a lover's sigh
        as they pass by

mother earth
  blesses me,
    as I tread her soil
    she tries
      to energize my thirsty spirit
       passing by

tall trees swaying way up high
  draw their veil across the sky
    and shadow youth with coolness —
      many times they sang their sigh
       but my eyes were deaf
        and I passed on by

summer sun lift up your voice
  so I can lift up mine
    and fly —

how many years have I rushed along
without a second glance
and passed you by?

sparkling eyes of the hungry children
shining bright and making me cry –
can you still love me now?
will you open your hearts
and try?
that I might easily forget
the burning shame
of ignoring you
when you passed me by

my dearest friend with the golden heart
you loved me once –
I was special, set apart –
but time was nigh:
and now I'm old
and soon must die,
like a loveless child
passing by . . .

2

Disembodied Voices

The atmosphere in the theatre auditorium was electric: it had been quite a good public meeting, one where the audience had provided just the right kind of psychic conditions to make clear spirit communications easier to get, by radiating their loving thoughts into the atmosphere, and many voices had come in thick and fast.

Grateful husbands had successfully returned to their wives, children had relayed lovely memories to ease their parents' grief, and lovers had comforted their best friends. They'd all done remarkably well to get me to hear their sometimes faint voices clearly enough to faithfully represent them. Their messages had been sprinkled with special thoughts and evidential, quirky turns of phrase which had sent us into stitches of laughter, and also provoked a few quiet tears when their most personal and poignant last moments on Earth had been remembered.

And now time was swiftly passing us by, nearing ten o'clock and the end of the demonstration, something which can be heartbreaking when I'm conscious of many more invisible friends praying for a chance to speak. But the clock had nearly beaten us and I was just going to finish – when I suddenly heard a woman's urgent disembodied voice calling out from behind my chair. Terribly anxious and excited, she seemed desperate to make her special connection.

In an instant, I 'knew' she wanted to reach her two daughters seated in the crowd. But where? I hadn't the faintest clue. Unless I'm told where people are sitting, I just have to call out the facts and hope the link will be placed. It's almost impossible to pinpoint recipients with phrases like: 'This message is for the lady two rows from the back of the upper circle; she's wearing a green coat.' Sometimes I can't even *see* the audience because of bright spotlights, and people underneath deep galleries and in mezzanines are usually shrouded in darkness; that's why I simply offer out the spirit information.

I quickly sent a thought to the worried spirit mum, 'It's OK,' I said, 'don't worry about the clock: I'll *make* time. I won't turn you away,' I said, after which I located her two girls, who quickly stood up and shouted back their replies in loud, excited voices.

This spirit mum's link seemed quite evidential and comforting, containing the kind of love any devoted mother might send to her adored girls. But afterwards, her daughters surprised me by revealing the hidden significance of their mum's clever final phrase, 'You see, girls! I came here anyway!' which had thrilled them and made them 'float on cloud nine' because, as one daughter – Alison – explained:

'It was absolutely *amazing*! Our mother only

passed over last Friday. In fact, we'd bought her a ticket and she was supposed to be here tonight at this meeting. She really believed in you, Stephen, and was so looking forward to meeting you. So when she said, "I came anyway!" we were thrilled. We couldn't believe it was happening! To have a message like that from mum was incredible. Thank you so much.'

Then Alison and Jan threw their arms around me, kissed and cuddled me, and all of us were stunned at their mother's evidential remarks. And later, Alison wrote saying, 'You brought me a fabulous message from my mother last year at the Middlesbrough Town Hall, and it's helped keep me going.'

This kind of spirit message should remind us mediums of what our calling is all about: a sharing of mind-liberating knowledge and spiritual truths, as revealed to us by compassionate inspirers in the Beyond. Communications can bring such comfort and hope to those who mourn, or who feel lost in a seemingly senseless, purposeless existence since 'death' robbed them of their special people.

Mediumship can remove the dreadful fear of annihilation inherent in the mind of man, by unveiling 'death' as nothing more than a false shadow: in all the universe there is only life. God alone knows, this sad old world of ours needs some greater spiritual revelation, as well as a constant reminder of what the power of unconditional love can achieve when beating in the hearts of men and women everywhere.

Unconditional love is the greatest power in the universe, and this alone will help man to save himself from his own all-consuming greed and selfishness. I can't grieve for the 'dead', for they are most certainly alive; my heart is sad for the so-called 'living', those billions of people who are blindly wandering in the deepest darkness of ignorance, when they could be feeling utterly secure, as free men, basking in the effulgent light of spiritual truth.

Spirit – your true essence and mine – can never die: it's eternal and everlasting, and some communicators are very good at reinforcing this fact with clever evidence of their survival. A spirit dad did so at one of my recent London meetings when addressing his daughter:

'Your father wants me to tell you, "I'm still alive! And I'm going to make an appearance on the next wedding photograph when it's taken!"'

'He's done that once before!' was the astonishing reply.

'Well,' I rejoined, 'he's going to do it *again* – complete with a red carnation in his buttonhole!'

The audience was much amused and intrigued, and so, indeed, was a London journalist who followed up the evidence, obtained the wedding photo – complete with this spirit dad's 'extra' image on it – and an interesting article subsequently appeared in a popular women's glossy.

But other spirit links, delivered at my live theatre meetings, have frequently drawn quite different, and often very emotional, or serious responses – like the message linking together two British soldiers, one soul from each side of life:

'I have a Tony here,' I solemnly announced, 'speaking of Bill and Brian, and I'm sensing the presence of a soldier whose life was tragically lost in an Irish sectarian killing. He says, "I was blown up – the IRA murdered me," and he's repeating two Irish place-names: Ballymena and Belfast.'

Before I could get any further, a well-built, mature, grey-haired man in the front stalls quickly, and somewhat emotionally, claimed the contact.

'Yes, it's me,' he said, 'I know him.' And through the glaring lights I could see his eyes glinting with emotion, as I went on:

'Well, he tells me: "I was really bitter when I first came over, but I'm learning to understand now, Corp."'

'Yes, I was his corporal. As a punishment I sent him out on jeep duty in place of myself. He was travelling from Belfast to Ballymena, the places you mentioned, and terrorists bombed the vehicle . . . It – ' and here his voice suddenly caught with tears as he placed a trembling hand over his mouth – 'I'm sorry,' he apologized, 'but it should have been *me* who died, not him.'

There was a stunned silence in the auditorium.

The air became very still, and not a soul moved.

'No, please,' I said reassuringly, breaking the tension while mentally re-establishing my contact, 'please don't be upset; he must have been ready to go,' I added, trying to comfort his ex-corporal by

31

stating the spiritual law that no-one crosses over before their time, no matter how they go.

But then I heard the murdered soldier venomously seething at me through his teeth: 'Those IRA bastards killed me; I'll get my revenge on those bastards' – which I didn't publicly transmit, of course. However, I did feel a gentle spiritual lesson was in order – so I told the audience, and his friend:

'I'm afraid I can't tell you he's one hundred per cent happy on the Other Side because he's just said something unkind about the people who took his life; he's still very angry with them.'

And then I spoke directly to the spirit soldier standing behind me, gently counselling out loud: 'It's no good feeling such bitterness, you know, son; it can't change what's happened to you and, at the end of the day, you should try to forgive them – that's the only way to progress.'

The spirit lad obviously appreciated my remarks and privately replied, 'I know you're right, mate; but I think I was too young to go,' after which I continued the rest of his message to the corporal:

'He says, "Don't worry about it too much, Corp – this is a much better world, anyway,"' I said. 'Oh, and he's sending his regards to "Taff, Smiffey and Smellie!"' I laughed.

'Yes – they're some of the boys he knows.'

His corporal was visibly relieved when I ended with more comforting words from his once-thought 'dead' colleague:

'"No more guilt, sir,"' I conveyed, then adding

from myself: 'because your friend is still alive.'

It was plain to see the ex-corporal had been spiritually moved by the entire experience, and this message, I believe – judging by the way it was received and sent – will undoubtedly have changed both of their lives for the better, which must surely be the true purpose of any spirit contact.

Such a candid link also underlines that peace of mind can never be ours unless we personally attain it; the young 'dead' soldier obviously still had much soul-growth to achieve, even though he'd arrived on the Other Side.

But then, *death doesn't change us, and spiritual progress is gained only through self-mastery of the character, mind and emotions.*

However, not every spirit connection I've given has been so gratefully received, or even placed at the time of its transmission. There are dozens of valid reasons for non-acceptance of messages, but the fault mostly lies with recipients who won't, or feel they can't, publicly speak up and claim their links. This was illustrated when I relayed another tragic passing which, at first, went unaccepted, but was later fully verified, highlighting one of the many difficulties encountered when working with large audiences.

The rather poignant tale had been unfolded by a young lad called Anthony who was killed outside a nightclub. The youngster specifically told me, 'I was stabbed through the heart, died at hospital, and three people attacked me.'

Unwilling to publicly mention his manner of death because such descriptions can be traumatically received by sensitive relatives, I soon had to relent, because I was ordered to do so – by Anthony himself. He commanded me to 'Give the message exactly as I said it' – so I did; but not a living soul claimed him in the silent theatre.

So I gave a few more names which Anthony assured me were his 'workmates', and then went on:

'Look, he's clearly telling me his friend is in the audience,' I repeated again. 'Please speak up. Where are you?'

Utter silence; not a sound from anyone . . .

'Well, he won't give in and go away, ladies and gentlemen,' I persevered, echoing Anthony's determination, 'and he's adamant I must state, "The man who killed me only got a manslaughter charge, that's all; and he's just come out of prison after serving only eighteen months of a two-year stretch" . . . Where am I going with this contact?' I spoke through the microphone, peering into the dark theatre, shading my eyes from the glaring spotlights with my free hand.

But still the link was unaccepted; so all I could do was be faithful to the boy and quickly do my job: I gave the lad's link of love and survival, plus his warning that his assailant was 'out and about in town again, so be careful,' and then reluctantly, and rather sadly, moved on to the next message.

With such large audiences I can't wait forever –

it simply isn't fair to the rest of the communicators or to the people who'd be more than happy to acknowledge their loved ones.

However, it came as no surprise that after the meeting, during my autograph session, a blonde teenage girl, about seventeen, fully acknowledged every detail of Anthony's message as perfectly correct.

'Yes, I know him,' she admitted, her remarks being witnessed by a long queue of people plus two hall stewards. 'Everything you said was right, Stephen: his name, the stabbing, the three attackers – *everything*. But I was too overcome to speak up.'

Such circumstances render me powerless to make communication successful.

Then Anthony's friend wanted to know, 'Did he say anything else to you?'

'I'm afraid his contact was only brief,' I explained again (having already taken great pains to previously state this to the audience), 'and I can't just click back into his mental wavelengths. It's very much his personal effort at the time which brings the connection.'

She said she understood, and I followed on with some more helpful advice. Then later, after everyone had gone, one of the stewards asked, 'How do you feel in situations like that, Stephen? It must be very hard to stand on stage in front of hundreds of people and look a complete fool because of somebody else's reticence.'

'Well it isn't very pleasant, and I know full well the Press were in tonight and they'll probably report Anthony's message as a load of rubbish because no-one claimed it. But did you hear the young girl's acceptance?'

'Yes, I was gobsmacked!' he gushed. 'But the sceptics won't be, will they!'

'Oh, they'll think whatever they like, anyway,' I rejoined.

'But doesn't it annoy you like hell?'

'Let me tell you something,' I said, with quiet conviction, 'when I go to bed tonight I can sleep with a clear conscience because I represented that boy faithfully. I listened carefully to everything he said, gave his message, and provided a service. I know that, God knows it, and he and his friend know it. Two souls were brought together by the power of the spirit, and the truth has touched them – and that's all that matters.'

Realizing I have no control over who'll attempt or accept spirit messages has made me philosophical about seeming failures. Indeed, one never knows who'll communicate next, and one night a rather famous spirit visitor made a guest appearance at a Manchester Free Trade Hall meeting, when I was contacted by the celebrated 'dead' poetess Sylvia Plath, who had apparently committed suicide years previously. Strangely enough, I wasn't even aware that she had 'died' (I can be such an ignoramus sometimes!)

However, I was quite specific when stating her

identity, for she surprised us by giving her full name.

'Oh, I have Sylvia Plath here, trying to reach a gentleman. She says she's been regularly contacting him with inspiration and poetry.'

From up in the circle, a surprised young man in his twenties took the link. 'Yes, Stephen, *here*! She contacts me a lot,' he shouted out. Ms Plath then gave him some personal, very sound advice about his future, which flummoxed us listeners, but he said he'd understood it all 'perfectly'! The poetess showed intimate knowledge of this man's life, and then promised her guidance whenever he might need it.

Such comforting connections reassure us that our spirit friends are often so very near to us, each day of our lives, and that they're caring not only for all our close family members, but also for our animals and household pets, too – and even wild creatures. This has been proven to me many times.

I remember one day, while returning from shopping, I found a wild sick pigeon crouched outside the block of council flats where I lived, and a gentle spirit voice asked me to, 'Please look after her; she's awfully tired and ill.'

The poor dishevelled bird gave no resistance when I quietly lifted up her thin and bedraggled form: she seemed nothing more than protruding bones and feathers; there was very little healthy flesh on her gaunt frame; it was so sad.

'You must have flown an awfully long way, my lovely,' I quietly whispered to her, gently smoothing her feathers while carrying her home, where I tenderly placed her in a warm upstairs room, on some cosy woolly jumpers. She slowly blinked her deep nut-brown shining eyes as I caressed her tired, emaciated body. Even though she was so utterly exhausted, I made sure she felt safe with me.

'God bless you,' I said. 'You sit here quietly, and I'll get you some corn from the town.'

Then I settled her down and walked two miles to get the food, just as the kind young RSPCA man had instructed me on the telephone. But as I walked along, I couldn't help feeling disgusted when thinking that some nasty person must have kicked the poor creature, which probably explained the dents I'd felt in her tiny breast. How wicked and cruel some people can be.

With my mind full of these thoughts, I made my way home with the special corn and vitamins, when – such an odd thing happened. Out of the blue, the wind blew one stray, mud-caked pigeon feather right across my path on the street. I suddenly stopped dead in my tracks, and felt my heart sink, immediately recognizing this as a psychic omen. It was then that a disembodied voice stated, 'The bird will pass.'

I was so hurt and concerned by the news that I rushed along the roads, running as fast as I could all the rest of the way home. I dashed upstairs, and was instantly greeted by the smell of death. My new friend's soul had quietly left this world; her little body was already stone-cold; her silent head resting way back upon motionless grey wings; and her half-open eyes were staring up at the blue sky through the open window, as if gazing, almost forlornly, into heaven itself, where she must have longed to have flown.

The poor bird had died like an angel with gracefully folded wings, just as the disembodied voice told me that she would.

My only consolation was that in my heart I'm positive my spirit friends had helped her to die with the least amount of pain and as much spiritual healing and dignity as possible.

'She had called out within her soul for kindness and rest,' revealed the voice again, 'and it was given.'

Although feeling sad, I thought that at least her last memories of man were, I prayed, ones of brotherhood and thoughtfulness.

Over the years of our association, such predictions given to me by the spirit people have usually come true: they've rarely been wrong. For instance, they'd correctly foretold that because of my mediumship millions of souls would be touched, through television appearances and public work, the written and spoken word and, of course, those mysterious airwaves people from all walks of life avidly tune into each day – the radio.

I hope my broadcasts have helped many thousands of people seeking knowledge of an afterlife to realize there's life in the Beyond awaiting all of us.

But I still find it quite a spooky thought to picture

countless surprised men and women sitting in taxis, at home, or working in factories or offices, suddenly stopping what they were doing when my voice came out of the radio at them, saying things like, 'You will live after you die; and it's not something I believe in – it's something I *know.*'

And this could still happen to anyone, at anytime – just as it did in early 1990, after the release of my first autobiography, *Visions of Another World*, when I was invited on to the following two major radio shows.

3

Medium Wave

Edited extracts from BBC Radio 2's Anne Robinson
Show: *nationally broadcast live from London on
Saturday 3 February 1990.*

*Anne Robinson: Do you believe there is life after
death? Do you, furthermore, believe that when a
loved one dies it's possible for them to speak to you
from the dead?*

*Indeed, is it right or proper that we should even
attempt to contact those we've laid to rest?*

*My guest this morning is a psychic and medium,
and he claims to regularly make contact with those
who've passed on; and he does it, he says, because
he's found he has the power. He does it, he says, not
for profit; and he's about to embark on a nationwide
tour. Stephen O'Brien, good morning.*

Stephen: Good morning, Anne; thanks for inviting
me in.

*Oh, it's a pleasure. I think most people are fascinated
by clairvoyance, fortune-telling, and mediums. Can*

you start by explaining how you discovered this power of yours?

I think I was born with it. I can remember when I was a young boy sitting at the bedroom window just twisting my hair on hot summer nights and watching the strollers go down the road – and some of them, when they approached the brow of the hill, would just vanish or fade away, while others carried on walking.

Of course, being a lad I·didn't question that at all.

But I think the most important event happened when I was ten: it was about two o'clock in the morning when I was woken by hammering on our front door, and I woke up, startled.

At that time I slept with my brother and I tried to wake him but he wouldn't move – he was sound asleep; and so was my uncle who slept in the same room with us, because we were quite a poor family. And my mother and father next door were sleeping, too: no-one woke, bar me.

I even pinched myself at the time to make sure I wasn't dreaming.

That eerie phantom hammering went on for so long that, being young, it did frighten me.

But now I know, after having developed the power of mediumship and now being able to hear the Other Side, the people Over There who work with me have since said, 'Behold, we stood at the door and knocked.'

*But it was when your mother died that the power
came to the fore, wasn't it?*

Yes, I think so. I absolutely adored my mother
– you couldn't find a nicer woman: she used to
help old people in the town; she was a lovely
soul.

But she died when she was forty-nine, of cancer.
And we all felt so desperately, desperately helpless,
as we had to watch the light of this wonderful soul
go out.

But three months after my mother's death I came
home one night to an empty house, turned the key
in the lock and I heard my name called from above:
'Stephen! Stephen, come up!'

And when I turned around I saw my mother in a
brilliant blaze of light, standing at the top of our
staircase and beckoning to me. When I went up
to meet her, she came across and kissed me on
the left-hand side of my face, just as I'd done to
her when she was lying ill with cancer – and she
laughed; as good as to say, 'Well, what are you
all worrying about? I'm OK.'

And from that moment on I remember thinking
to myself, if *she* lives, *everybody* lives; that's
something I must tell the world.

And that's what I've been trying to do for many
years now.

*So what form does your getting in touch with people's
relatives and loved ones take? How does it work,
and where is the setting for it?*

Absolutely anywhere. For example, your listeners are hearing our voices through a receiver which is tuned to a certain frequency or wavelength, and it's exactly the same idea when we contact the world of the spirit.

The message I've got is that we cannot die: we take our last breath here, and our next breath in another world which vibrates at a higher frequency than this one.

What they've got to do from the Other Side of life is tune in to our world, attune their minds to the wavelengths or frequencies of our minds. And once they do that, contact can come anywhere – either as a sighting through the ability to see clairvoyantly, or perhaps we might hear or sense them.

When I take my public meetings around the country, as I stand on the platform there could be any amount of people present – up to a thousand or more – and I listen to the call that's coming in and say to the caller:

'OK, I'll now try and place you with your loved one.'

And once we get the right call with the right recipient, hopefully the messages will start flowing and give that great comfort which says: 'I haven't died; I love you.'

That's spine-tingling, Stephen. I want to ask you a million more questions, and a couple of things occur to me immediately. The first one is my feeling that when we lose a loved one we need to practise

44

some acceptance that they've passed on, and whether what you do is really preventing us having that experience?

I don't think that's the case. Grief is a perfectly natural process and people *will* grieve when they miss the physical presence of someone they've lost to the world of the spirit.

I don't think that what I do stops that grieving process, because people *have* to accept their loved ones are no longer with them physically.

But I get sackloads of mail – I received about three hundred letters this week as a result of a tabloid feature – and people write saying: 'I've lost my child; my mother; my father – can you tell me, is there any word from them? Are they OK? Do they miss me? Will you tell them that I love them?' And they don't realize they can send their own thoughts out to their loved ones on this wavelength we've been talking about.

What I do doesn't stem or stop grief, it adds knowledge to people's faith.

A lot of religions take one to the graveside and say, 'Here we leave you with love and faith.' But what I do takes people one step further and says: 'If you're willing to search and seek, maybe to that faith you can add some knowledge and comfort.'

My lovely mum died three years ago and I think if you got her on your magic telephone I know what she'd say – she'd say what she told me for forty years: she'd tell me to 'Sit up straight and hold my shoulders back.' She'd tell me to 'Wrap up well' when I'm going out, and to look after myself and, 'For goodness' sake, put some money in the bank for a rainy day!'

Don't we all know what our parents would say? They're like long-playing records we've heard so often!

Yes, but supposing you and I were total strangers and you came to one of my public meetings in response to an advertisement, and I got a contact from your mum, who might be able to give her name (and describe) the way she died, or she might even call for you, giving some kind of clinching detail that would single you, alone, out of the crowd.

A radio-mike would go to you and I'd start a three-way connection.

Then, if she *does* say those very things, that's exactly my point: no-one else *could* say them, bar your mum; you'd go away saying, 'My God, she's still alive.'

As indeed, your dog will be – I know you're an animal lover.

Well, I'll tell you what, Stephen, when my dog gets up to those Great Kennels in the Sky she's going to be very uncomfortable – because it can't be as good as she's had down here! (both laugh)

Oh, I think it could be better, you know! But animals do survive, and they're loved by friends on the Other Side.

There's a current trend at the moment in many religious quarters to say that animals do not have a soul: but I can say that they do. That, I know, will comfort a great many of your listeners.

I think it's just because we're often in so much need of comfort, Stephen, that I fear the sort of powers you and others claim would be very attractive to the vulnerable.

As you know, not everybody has really got the powers they claim, and it's an area where I feel the vulnerable could be 'taken', emotionally or financially.

I agree with you, which is why I say to people who are investigating whether or not life continues after death: read and be as educated as possible. And when they see a Stephen O'Brien meeting they mustn't come thinking, this is going to be good: people shouldn't pin their hopes on me, or on anybody else.

They should wait for the message to come.

They must take with them all their reasoning powers; they must sift the evidence, and it needs to be specific.

But my meetings are not held purely to dispense comfort, they also educate people as to what lies beyond death, as well as presenting some specific evidence to show we survive beyond the physical, which is just a world of illusion.

You know, as broadcasters, journalists and producers we all have good days and bad days, tell me: what if it's one of your not-so-hot days, Stephen, and there you are with a hall booked, there are thousands of

people coming to see you, and you're really not terribly
switched into your telephone line to Them –
– Oh yes: that happens –

– do you say, 'Go home and have your money back?'
No, I explain the meetings are experiments in
communication. In *Visions of Another World* I
wrote a chapter called 'Behind the Scenes' which
outlines the fluidity of communication, and how
sometimes I can mishear something or not quite
'see' it correctly.

Like you and your colleagues I do get off-days, but
the people just bear with me and appreciate that at
any one given time I'm trying my very best to help
them.

Though, sometimes, I do feel inadequate when
someone, for example, has lost a child: a man
recently wrote to me from Merseyside – his son
was killed on a motorway and he was absolutely
desperate to know if his boy had survived. Now,
when someone pins all that hope on you, I think
it can hamper communication because then they're
sitting there waiting for what *they* want to hear –
and, of course, I can't command what the spirit
people want to say.

If your mother communicated –

– She'd be frightfully bossy, Stephen! (both laugh)
I was reading in your book, Visions of Another
World, *which has just come out and in fact has had
to be reprinted, that you mention one incident where*

you connect somebody here with somebody 'up there'
and they were suggesting this person 'down here'
was going to have a baby –
– That's right –

– and it was completely wrong!
Yes, I remember that! Someone from the world of spirit, an aunt who contacted her niece, said to the girl, 'You are with child; we're delighted!' and the girl had only found out about it that morning herself.

Then the aunt predicted it would be a boy, but nine months later this woman came to me at a public meeting and said: 'I had a girl! What does it mean?'

I said: 'It means your aunt was quite wrong!' (Anne chortles)

You see, when we die we're not infallible: death doesn't confer upon us any abilities we don't have now.

When we take our last breath here, we take our next breath There, and we take with us everything we've earned for ourselves: the growth of our mind, our spirit, our soul, our education, our morality – or lack of it.

This Earth, in my view, and the viewpoint of the spirit people working with me, is a schoolhouse – a grounding-place where we learn about consciousness, self, emotion, feeling, and where our minds can expand through experience.

And then death is nothing at all; it's just a hiccup in the line of life.

So are our loved ones on the Other Side growing still, and becoming more experienced?
Yes, progression is the law – a natural law, not a man-made law, but a God-made law, if you like: the Law of the Great Spirit that fashioned this universe. The eternal law says: progression is open to everyone.

We're all progressing, there is no going back.

Wouldn't we be better staying at home and just saying a nice prayer to our loved ones that have gone?
Of course you can do that: love is the link – that's the link that joins the two worlds together.

Stephen, do your powers also extend to meeting someone and being intuitive about what's going to happen to them?
Yes, that's what we call a psychic level; psychic coming from the Greek (meaning: soul). So psychic powers are soul-powers. Everyone has a soul, I believe, and therefore we're all psychic and we can meet strangers and think: 'I don't know what it is but I just can't take to you at all.'

But about others you might say, 'What a wonderful soul.'

I believe that this is a part of the soul – the auric fields of electromagnetic energy-wavelengths which surround us, and which have been photographed by people – 'picking up' these impressions.

And would you say that quite a lot of us are probably psychic if we ever 'tuned' ourselves nicely?
Oh yes. At my public meetings when I ask the audiences how many have had various psychic experiences, usually over seventy per cent of the hands go up, and then I say: 'You see! I'm not the only strange person here!'

Now you say you haven't made any money out of your powers –
– Yes, I've helped charities, over the years –

– but in fact you're going on a nationwide tour from February to June, and you will be charging for that?
Yes, today the cost of venues – and advertising which is so desperately expensive – has to be made back, or I can't get to those areas to serve the people.
  I did do an extensive nationwide tour last year – after which I thought it was time for my own funeral, I was so physically exhausted – and I didn't get a penny for that. In fact we helped nineteen childrens' hospitals across the nation.

It's been a great a pleasure to talk to you this morning, Stephen – thank you very much indeed.
Lovely to meet you, Anne: it's been delightful.

*   *   *

*Extracts from an interview with the usually turbaned
author and TV personality Molly Parkin: nationally
broadcast live to Wales from St David's Hall, Cardiff,
on BBC Radio Wales* Level Three Show *in March
1990, in the presence of a live audience.*

*Molly Parkin: It's an absolute pleasure to see you,
Stephen.*
Stephen: Hello, Molly.

He's young, isn't he? (laughter from audience)
Well, doesn't she look young herself? Doesn't she?
(audience agrees vocally) She looks lovely.

*Well, I've got no hat on today! I've bared my head in
your presence!* (more laughter)
   *Now, an old lady told you when you were young
that you would become a medium. How did you react
to that as a young boy of ten?*
Well, I didn't understand what she meant, really.

And yet, in a sense, you kind of did?
Yes: I've always felt ill at ease in this world, as
though I was in the world, but strangely not of it.

   When I was a boy I used to hear voices and
see people, and have psychic experiences which
my peer group didn't have.

   I remember waking up one morning just before
dawn and I heard a choir of schoolchildren – I must
have been younger than ten – and they were singing
'All Things Bright and Beautiful', and I suddenly

realized – 'I'm in bed! This is silly!' And it stopped.
Then I got up and looked out of the window, but there was no-one there.

It's a wonderful enrichment of a childhood, of course.
Yes.

I think more and more people are getting interested in the spirit world. But back to you: you went into rather boring jobs when you left school.
I did, yes – I've never really been happy in this world, Molly.

But you're happy now, this minute!
Yes: I'm happy to be here – but there's an inner longing, a yearning. The real person is within –

– Yes –
– and this physical overcoat is just a shell, a vehicle of expression for the mind and soul, given for an allotted time. And then you drop this body and the true person, within, goes on.

You believe that of everybody?
Oh yes.

And the fact that you're a medium means you're able to express it because your conviction is so strong.
Yes: I've seen, heard and sensed so many people from the Other World that I've come to realize my true place is not here at all; I belong, I believe, in the

eternal world, and I think I'm just here for a time.

Just like the rest of our audience today, we're here to achieve something: to grow and to learn –

– And to help each other –
– that's it.

Then at the point of death we'll take all that with us into the next stage of learning – into the junior class; this is the infants' class.

So this life isn't a haphazard occurrence, but the first step in a growth process.

I accept all that; I believe all that.

When you have your very large audiences, of course, you're very eloquent when you talk about these matters and you have a great stage presence: how much do you think going to a drama school – after those other boring jobs – helped you with all that?

A lot. It gave me confidence to face an audience and project whatever little personality I have. It gave me an inner certainty of knowing that although I was standing before anything up to a thousand people – not knowing who was going to communicate, or where the link was going – I could confidently say to myself, 'Stephen, if you don't get anything it doesn't really matter, you can still talk to the people.'

A few years ago I studied to try and develop my own psychic powers because, at one point, I thought I might go in that direction myself: to become a medium and a healer – and I know you're also a healer.

Did you have any training of that sort? You went regularly to a Spiritualist church – and I say that because other people might like to develop their gifts.
Yes, that was where I found people who understood the powers of the soul. The people who understand these are the people who've already developed them, and they are within psychic centres or Spiritualist churches.

What was the reaction of the Spiritualist Church when you became a professional medium and you had your larger audiences, because there is a view that if this is a gift from God then you shouldn't really commercialize it.
I agree with that.

So some cynics might say you're in this to make a lot of money for yourself; but this isn't the case, is it?
(awkwardly) No . . .

At the risk of embarrassment I'll announce it on radio: I've just recently fought a case for the repossession of my council flat . . . for non-payment of rent, because the money went into last year's United Kingdom tour.

But I've won it; so I've still got a roof over my head!

Well, we're very glad about that, aren't we? (applause from audience)

What do you say to people who say that visiting a medium, or dabbling in the occult, may be dangerous?

I would say: believe nothing, and test everything.

If you consult a specialist about your health you're not obliged to accept his opinion: you can get a second opinion.

If anybody's going to see a medium, sensitive or psychic then they should accept only that which appeals to their intelligence and makes sense.

May I give an interesting example?

Yes.

One of our well-known mediums, Estelle Roberts – who's now passed over – once, during a private appointment with a woman who'd lost her husband was able to tell her: 'Your husband is here. But I'm very sorry I can only hear him saying something rather silly, and that's "Rabbits, rabbits, rabbits".'

To this the woman replied: 'Mrs Roberts, when my husband was dying he took my hand and said to me, "Look, love, if there's another life I'll come back and I'll give you a code-word, and the code-word will be *rabbits*."' (Molly gasps)

So you see, it's only the recipient who understands the full import of the message that's being given.

Talking about rabbits, animals do survive in the spirit world, don't they?

Yes, they do. Are you an animal lover?

56

Oh yes: I'm a lover of everything.
Are you?

Yes!
Oh, *that's* interesting to know, isn't it! (Molly chuckles wickedly, and the audience joins in)

Regarding animals, I remember once giving clairvoyance in the Midlands and there was a blind man at the back of the hall with his guide dog at the side of him, and a message went to him from his people on the Other Side.

But as I was working with him I saw in a silver/golden light that at the *other* side of him was a spirit guide dog, sitting at his feet.

I was told its name was Sandy, and when I gave that to him he started to weep, because this was his previous guide dog which had died.

Sandy proved that loyalty persists, and that love is stronger than death.

Oh yes, and most enduring – that's in your book Visions of Another World *which was published in 1989 and did very, very well, and continues to do well.*

Your audiences are packed, I know, Stephen; is the tour going well?
It is.

And I see you're on in London at the Wembley Conference Centre; that's a very, very big venue, and I know you're going to fill it to capacity.

I'd like to go on and on, but we'll talk to you again later on in the programme.

And we wish him luck, don't we everybody? (the audience applauds)

(over the clapping) Thank you very much, Molly – it's been lovely today.

4

Psychic Signs and Portents

Just like the millions of listeners who have tuned in their radio sets to pick up my broadcast interviews, so the spirit people have to attune their minds to approximate to the wavelengths of our thoughts on Earth, in order to contact us. And some communicators are expert at doing this, especially when they need to give an urgent psychic warning.

One such memorable spirit sign was given to me on a swelteringly hot summer's day in June 1985. It happened while I was ambling through a musty antique market in Swansea, my home-town, idly gawping at ancient clocks and other Victoriana but not really concentrating on them because I was in such a turmoil.

As readers of my previous three books will know, I'd received a baffling prediction from my spirit guide, friend and teacher, a splendid North American Indian whose tribal name was White Owl, in which he foretold I'd move away from Wales to live in North-East England. In due course, exactly as predicted, I received an offer of a council flat in Gateshead, a small windy town on the banks of the River Tyne, and then I didn't know whether to obey or ignore White

Owl's advice to move. 'Should I, or shouldn't I go to England?' I questioned, over and over to myself.

Then I asked my spirit guide to prove this traumatic wrench would be worthwhile: 'Let's have a bit of indication from Up There!' I quipped. 'Do you think I should I go to Gateshead, or not?'

Several days then passed by in Other-Worldly silence, and now here I was browsing amongst the Victoriana and antiques when suddenly I stopped near a box of battered sepia photographs, pictures taken in the early 1900s. 'These look interesting,' I thought, noticing there were about a hundred postcards, all bunched up like a dog-eared pack of cards. Quite at random I idly divided the deck once, and there in front of my eyes was something which made me gasp.

It was a snapshot of the main thoroughfare of a northern town with rusty tramcars trundling along beside busy shoppers to-ing and fro-ing, many of whom were women with long black dresses trailing in the muddy road. And underneath was a printed caption: *Gateshead High Street, circa 1901.*

I was flabbergasted! But being a wily old critter I spent the next five minutes scrutinizing every single picture, and – as you've probably guessed – there was only this *one* of Gateshead in the box.

This was undoubtedly the psychic sign I'd asked for.

'Well, it seems I'll be moving,' I acknowledged loudly, much to the amazement of a passing wide-eyed toddler, who nearly dropped his sticky lollipop when he craned his neck to find my invisible companions. 'Now, don't you worry about me,' I said to him, 'I'm not right!' And I patted him on the head and we both had a good laugh.

And that's how I ended up living in England for two years, during which time the spirit people planned I should meet and help several new mediums to firmly establish their psychic talents; and we all still keep in touch today. Some of my best friends are living in Tyne and Wear, and that clever spirit sign brought us all together – rather like the reuniting of a spiritual family, a long-separated soul-group (which is what I'm sure we all were in the Beyond, before our present incarnations).

Over the years I've received several strange psychic warnings which are worth recalling; you might get some similar happenings yourselves. (Who knows?) One of mine was quite unusual. When my grandmother, Polly, lay dying in the hospital, the doctors kept insisting: 'We don't know how long she'll be in a coma like this. We're not God.' But because of their special vision the Other Side delivered their own peculiar prediction one cold December evening, just as the sun was sinking in the frosty skies. At the time, I was alone, taking off my slippers and putting on my shoes, when suddenly I caught sight of something odd: on the beige-coloured wall right beside my head, five jet-black houseflies had appeared from nowhere. They'd settled themselves down and were merrily fanning their wings, as if it were a bright summer's day, instead of an icy December evening.

Just like one of the Keystone Cops in a silent movie I did a classic double-take, baffled as to what these flies were up to: they shouldn't have been alive, let alone sunning themselves on our cold wall. I even blinked, but they were still there; so I glanced away and tied my shoelaces. But when I looked up again – they'd vanished.

Now, the average Welsh housefly – a creature of no great intelligence – many of whom often plagued our humble dwelling, usually buzzed about for hours in a most infuriating manner – but not these little blighters: they'd completely buzzed off.

At the time I didn't make the connection between these five phantom insects and the fact that I was getting ready to visit my grandma at the hospital, but much later, it dawned on me: *five* flies had appeared on the wall, and *five days later* Polly's coma suddenly ended, and she passed away peacefully in her sleep . . .

Of course, it wasn't easy to know if my father, her eldest son, was upset by her death, because it was always difficult to gauge just how deeply, or superficially, he felt anything. My mother, however, had no trouble in clearly reading Dad's mind, though not while she was alive on Earth – she developed this telepathic skill only after she'd 'died' and passed into Spirit. My mother then used it to deliver a pointed psychic warning.

I recall it was the mid 1970s and Dad and I were living under the same explosive roof, frequently raised by our daily personality clashes. Mam had been 'gone', as we say here in Wales, for about two years before she displayed her uncannily accurate mind-reading. By then, of course, temper-flares between my father and me were so bad that we couldn't be in the same room without the wallpaper catching fire. Our personal relationship had always been stormy and lamentably predictable.

'Oh, why won't you leave me alone?' I'd pitifully moan.

'Because you're a lazy good-for-nothing swine, that's why!' Dad would shout back, furious because I was then unemployed, and he wasn't. But try as I might, he wouldn't listen, and I didn't care, which is why my mother had felt it necessary – as she lay semi-conscious, shortly before she died of stomach cancer – to clasp him tight and plead, 'Ron, promise me you'll take care of Stephen . . . Promise me . . . ' Dad said he would, but after her death, matters just got worse and worse . . .

Then one day I came up with an ingenious plan: 'I'll kill him with love,' I reasoned. (Don't we think silly things when we're young?) Anyhow, I gave this my best shot for months. Whenever he bawled his lungs out at me, I refused to retaliate and just sat very quietly, perfectly relaxed, ignoring his angry and rude remarks, keeping absolutely still and thinking, 'No comment;' and it worked.

It was a truly brilliant plan. 'He'll soon be quiet,' I thought, 'because after a while all he'll hear is his own loud voice, and that'll shut him up.'

Incredibly, I was right. My young logic proved more than effective and an unearthly silence, like that of the grave, fell eerily about our house, turning life into a weird slow-motion nightmare. Dad glided in and out of the rooms like a zombified dumb spectre, seeking some kind of mortal energy to inject his mind with consciousness, while casting sideways glances at me (as if I'd gone completely off my head).

But, oh joy! The blissful peace was heavenly and golden, and I gratefully drank it in like a thirsty cactus deprived of water for months on end. My plan of silence was pure magic, I thought, and I felt very proud of myself, until . . . one night I received a spirit sign from a medium at a public meeting:

'I've got your mother with me, Stephen.'

'Oh,' I said, rather surprised.

'Yes, and she says: "Don't think the current trend will continue."'

'Thank you,' I replied, with not a sausage of a clue as to what Mam's words might have meant. (I'm so incredibly dense sometimes, readers. I'm sorry, but I am.)

My mother's psychic warning was given on a Saturday night, and it materialized itself early on Monday morning when the balloon went well and truly up! Quick as a flash, Dad suddenly bounced back to life with a vengeance, starting his usual shenanigans. So, true to plan, I sat silently on the settee and maintained my deathly hush. But he suddenly slapped the kibosh on that and everything backfired in my face. In the twinkling of an eye, my mother was proven correct: *Father went completely berserk.*

His loud voice just kept on screaming and rising higher and higher in pitch, until reaching its maximum decibel effect: a frightening squeal beyond which it was fatal for the victim to move a muscle without getting clocked by two shovel-like hands – and I was helplessly trapped on the settee between the madman in front of me and the wall. I couldn't move. 'My God, he'll explode in a minute,' I thought; and I wasn't disappointed.

Suddenly he yelled: 'You're no bloody good! You sit about all day without a job! What the hell are you doing with your life? You . . . *You* . . . *You lazy*—' and in the next second he shot out of his chair, pounced over to the sofa, yanked me to my feet by the scruff of my neck and then, his face white with rage, pulled me to the floor by my hair and delivered a few deft kicks into my ribs . . .

So much for my 'killing him with love'.

However, I made no effort to retaliate – he was far too strong and frenzied; besides, he was my father, and I'm a pacifist; also, Dad had been a powerful amateur boxer in his younger days when he'd broken all his knuckles in fights.

After venting his spleen, he stormed angrily upstairs, huffing and puffing, spitting and grumping away to himself, and I was left huddled in a ball, on the floor.

How desperately sad and pitiful that someone could feel he possessed the unchallengeable right to inflict such pain upon another. Some may be shocked to know I was twenty-two when this happened.

My mother's psychic warning had come true. 'The current trend' (of peace and quiet) had most certainly 'not continued'; and her spirit message also proves that our Reality is Thought – she'd clearly seen what was in Dad's mind, as naturally as we'd watch a brightly lit movie on a screen.

The devastating accuracy of this type of easy telepathic reading of our thoughts by the spirit people was once confirmed to my first mediumship tutor, Mrs Palmer. Her main guide – who, when in life, was an Arab horseman called Ahmed – shocked her to the core of her being when he told her: 'Your mind, to me, is as open as the Sahara Desert.'

'Good Lord, just imagine that, Stephen,' she gulped, awestruck by the embarrassing implications. 'There'd be nowhere to hide in the Sahara, would there?'

'No,' I replied timorously, remembering some of my own dubious thoughts, and thinking of the Bible being right when it says, 'nothing is hidden, all is known.'

Startling psychic signs and portents are quite common occurrences throughout the world, as many people know. One mum told me that as she was washing the dishes, one night during the Second World War, quite out of the blue she suddenly reeled backwards, clutching her stomach as if she'd just been kicked in it, announcing, 'Arthur's been killed.' This was her beloved son, on active service, who – it was later confirmed by the War Office – had 'died' at the very moment his mother had received her psychic shock.

I believe Arthur, himself, had transmitted this paranormal signal, his traumatic and powerful emotions being instantly received by his mam, the dearest object of his thoughts – sent to her through the mighty power of his love – just a few seconds before he died.

Many thousands of people have experienced similar 'spooky hunches' or 'intuitions' like this, and the solar plexus area (just above the navel) is one of our main psychic registration points. It's often been medically referred to as 'the second brain of the body'.

But animals possess this type of acute psychic instinct much more so than modern-day man. Although still operating, our psychic senses don't function as strongly as they must have done in ancient times when prehistoric hunters needed to 'know' when life-threatening danger was approaching, even if they couldn't see it with their eyes. On dark moonless nights this sixth sense would have been needed to protect each precious family unit.

My grey-and-white (with black stripes) female cat, Sooty, exhibits these remarkable psychic instincts in abundance. When she was recently ill and had to be spoon-fed a course of chalky tablets, it became very evident! Medicine is anathema to Sooty, and

the minute I nonchalantly saunter off to get it
– her psychic senses are immediately activated,
sending her whizzing through the hall at forty
miles an hour to hide herself in some inaccessible
corner, all hunched up and clamped to the ground,
totally immoveable, ready for battle until the
danger passes! (Only it never did because I'd usually
winkle her out with a strategically placed broom-
handle!)

And her sensitivity also extends to music, it
seems: on some days when I play the piano she
miraculously appears from nowhere and drapes her
luxurious (but flea-ridden) warm fur coat around
my neck and purrs away merrily for all she's worth.
'Oh, I'll play well today,' I muse to myself – and
invariably I do.

But at other times, when stress makes me hit
more cracks than notes, suddenly she vanishes –
I'll just catch a quick glimpse of her fluffy backside
scooting up the stairs to bury herself under a sound-
proof duvet. She seems to 'know' when there's a
monstrous cacophany of music coming! And she's
particularly 'aware' in the evenings, when she
squints her yellow peepers into slits and shiftily
'eyes up' invisible spirit friends whose presences I
haven't even sensed.

'Do let me know if it's anyone important, madam,'
I often say.

'*Miss*!' she seems to reply haughtily. 'Do you
mind!' (I don't think she's ever forgiven me for that
operation, but I'm afraid her unearthly caterwauling

knew no mercy, readers: so neither did the vet's scissors.)

Soul-sensitivity seems to be on the increase these days. In fact, since the 1950s there have been countless strange psychic signs reported by people claiming to have sighted Unidentified Flying Objects (UFOs) in the skies. All over the globe ordinary folk say they've seen them, and I'm afraid I'm no exception.

One evening, after Dad had expertly waltzed me around the room again, I hurriedly left and took refuge on a bitterly cold park bench. Miserably numb, sitting on an inch-thick frost and forlornly gazing heavenwards, I was trying to lose my anger in the incredible beauty of the dark night sky. It was then that I spotted the pulsing silver light. I'd seen satellites like this one many times before: they look just like fast-moving stars as they arc the black sky in a perfect curve. But this one was different; it was particularly bright, and an entrancing sight, until – it unexpectedly changed direction!

Then I realized it was a UFO. Dumbfounded, as I tracked the distant shining ship, I watched it swivelling in the high atmosphere before it quickly shot into space, away from Earth, in completely the opposite direction to its previous path, and then it vanished out of sight . . .

Friends were suitably amused when I quipped: 'Mind you, if the saucer had landed, I'd have been up inside it like a bat out of hell – no messing about!

Well, there's got to be something better than this, hasn't there?'

And more laughter followed when I added: 'But as soon as they realized who they'd picked up, with *my* luck, they'd probably open the rubbish chute and drop me into the sea!'

But more seriously – even though there are many theories about where these space visitors originate, I believe a great majority of them are human, and come from our own future where time-travel has been perfected to such a degree that they can, and do, visit the Earth's past: us. But I also think strict regulations have probably been fixed, instructing them not to land or associate with us, for fear of causing a tremor in the time-stream. Though, of course, many reports of such important face-to-face meetings (close encounters of the third kind) are firmly on record throughout the world.

It's easy to dismiss other people's stories, but not when you personally know these folk and their honest characters. One very sensible colleague of mine, Lin Martin, encountered a spacecraft close up; and her experience proved to be a remarkable psychic sign, for, after it – and she thinks probably linked with it – much wider psychic powers unfolded within her, and today she's a public medium. She says she's been sensitive since childhood, and that this awareness seemed to burgeon following her sighting. Strangely enough, recognized authorities have now collated much similar evidence: after contact it's claimed many percipients often develop heightened telepathic powers, or can somehow have their psychic faculties boosted. In my last book, *In Touch with Eternity*, an artist's impression in pastels, of myself and my spirit guide, White Owl, was drawn by Lin, who has now extended her talents to encompass the rare skill of psychic portraiture: the sketching of invisible spirit communicators.

Here's Lin's verified description of that fascinating sighting which boosted her psychic powers:

On the day it happened the sky didn't have a cloud in it, but a certain coolness had descended over Corby, in Northamptonshire, early on that June evening; not enough to give a chill, but just to be comfortably pleasant after a hot summer's day.

I was eighteen at the time, in the early 1970s, when this sighting took place on the common which my then boyfriend and I had chosen for our walk. The grass was dotted here and there with other couples also enjoying the pleasant evening.

Visibility was very good: it was a clear summer's night, with just a few trees around, as we walked.

Then, for some inexplicable reason both my friend and I were oddly compelled to simultaneously look upwards, and there – about 50 feet directly above us – was a strange object hovering in the sky.

We were both taken completely by surprise.

To this day, I couldn't be sure of its exact size but it seemed a little bit bigger than a helicopter, though, of course, it wasn't one.

Our first reaction was one of utter fright – and to run away as fast as we could, but we seemed to be transfixed to the spot: neither of us could move; we were just motionless, staring open-eyed at the spacecraft up above us.

We also lost all sense of the passing of time – for all we knew we could have been standing there for hours, yet it may have been just a few seconds. Unfortunately, we didn't think of checking the clock afterwards.

The hovering craft was saucer-like with a dome-shape on its top, and large windows extended all around this dome – and an orange luminescent light seemed to be vibrating or pulsating from within them, rotating and circling at high speed inside the ship.

I didn't register the colour of the craft itself, because the bright orange light commanded all of my attention. It was as though I was mesmerized by it.

And another odd thing was – there was *no sound* coming from the object. I couldn't hear any motors or engines.

The silent spaceship was tilted towards us at an angle, so we couldn't see its underside. And even though the windows were quite large neither could we discern anything inside them – yet we both *sensed* that we were being watched, somehow observed.

After what seemed like an eternity, the spacecraft quickly moved vertically upwards – shooting off on a zigzag course at high speed, right across the evening sky – and then it disappeared from sight.

No words were spoken between my boyfriend and me, we simply exchanged disbelieving looks in silence, as we made our way back to the house where we were staying.

We were only young, and discussed nothing whatsoever, not until we felt completely safe behind locked doors – and then it emerged that we'd both seen exactly the same thing.

All mediumistic people, like Lin, radiate an abundance of psychic energy into the atmosphere around them, and spirit intelligences can utilize this to move objects in our world. This frequently happens to another acquaintance of mine who's both a healer and clairvoyant, and who has remarkably vivid dreams which often contain psychic warnings – something I'm sure many of us have experienced.

One of his more notable warnings involved the recently deceased filmstar Marlene Dietrich, who, in her latter years, had confined herself to a Paris apartment where she died peacefully, aged ninety-one.

He was an avid fan of hers, having written to the screen legend for over twenty years and having regularly received personal notes and signed photographs from her. He also telephoned Marlene, but she became a trifle eccentric towards the end, not allowing herself to be seen, interviewed, spoken to, or photographed by anyone. Living as a recluse, she discouraged visitors and all personal publicity, and made the telephone her single lifeline to the outside world.

Sometimes when he rang she'd be quite lucid and able to hold short conversations, but at other times – probably because of her age – she'd act most peculiarly. Once, she answered in an atrociously bad mock-French accent: 'Zees eez Madame de Pompadour! You 'ave ze wrong nomberre. Please 'ang up and do not call zees nomberre again!' – and then she clomped the receiver down!

Another time, she used one of her frequent ploys: because her initials were MD (medical doctor), she rattled out in gutsy German tones: *'Der Doktor ist aus*! The doctor *ist* busy: go away!' And click went the line again!

Poor Marlene. However . . .

About a week before she died on the couch in her Paris flat, my acquaintance, who lives in Wales, says he heard an almighty thud from one of his upstairs rooms: 'I ran up and found Marlene's latest signed photograph, which she'd just sent me and I'd framed, had crashed to the floor. The frame was all smashed but the glass was still intact, and I immediately felt something was wrong, taking this as a serious psychic warning.'

Straightaway he telephoned Paris to check on the actress, but I'm afraid she gave another of her amusing 'performances'. There was loud Italian music playing in the background, which he commented on. 'There is no music!' blurted back Marlene. 'Music is not playing! This is the maid, and the doctor *ist* out!'

Then click – and she was back in blissful seclusion again. But, within the week, the psychic sign proved quite correct and the screen legend passed away, peacefully . . .

Often a highly controversial celebrity, Marlene's openly bisexual lifestyle gained her much unwanted publicity, as did the fiercely guarded privacy she imposed upon herself, when she locked the doors of her life, rejecting attention from the world's Press for most of her latter years.

Readers will remember that Marlene and I met in Cardiff in the 1970s, after one of her world-famous and impressive cabaret shows, when she kissed me on either side of my face. I never dreamed we'd speak again – but we did; only this time it was after her death, while I was undergoing one of my out-of-the-body experiences. I was doubly pleased to see her, especially as Miss Dietrich was firmly on record stating she didn't accept or believe in an afterlife.

Miss Dietrich and I met in the astral world – those planes of thought nearest the Earth – in a large and airy, peach-and-beige-coloured apartment with huge picture windows overlooking deep green fields and extensive parkland. There were bright flowers everywhere in the grounds outside, and inside, too, in large pots, tubs and vases. It was a stylish, lovely home.

In the spirit world Marlene could now walk properly, all signs of her difficult leg problems resulting from the nasty fall off a stage in Washington had vanished in her new body. She was a radiantly beautiful woman in her prime, at the height of all her personal charm: her skin was exceptionally clear and she looked about thirty years old, possibly a little younger. She was wearing a neat black backless dress on her small frame, and there was a delicate gold bracelet on her wrist and some kind of gold locket adorning her slender neck.

She was a glowing picture of loveliness – her features were nicely rounded and not sharp or angular – and she carried with her, as all true celebrities seem to do, a remarkable sense of her own presence.

Seated with her legs folded underneath her, she was reclining on a hugely padded peach sofa. And when she spoke in those famous husky tones, her voice and mind generated a great magnetism.

'My dear, I didn't give a damn about what people thought about me: I did what *I* wanted to do,' she said, 'because I wanted to do it.'

I nodded and sunk down into a nearby plush peach armchair, asking whether she remembered our brief meeting all those years ago. She said she did, but when I tried to make some small talk about life, she rapidly interrupted with:

'Life!' she huffed, stretching her famous legs from underneath her and crossing them, a little provocatively I thought – 'I lived my life to please myself, not others. Life is for living, and I lived it to the full, and I won't stop now.

76

'If I felt attracted to someone, gender didn't matter at all, you see. I made love to them, and loved them completely, because I followed my true self, not convention. But,' and she waved a slim, be-ringed, cautionary finger in my direction, 'although I was highly sexually driven, love mattered the most, my dear.'

I smiled, agreeing with her sentiments.

'Gender doesn't count: love the person; celebrate the body and the mind. What are the alternatives?' she asked. But I didn't have a chance to answer before she carried straight on with: 'Indifference, or hate; and who needs those?'

'No-one,' I said, at last. 'If more people loved each other the world would be a much better place to live in, that's for sure.'

She looked across at me, as if recognizing my intelligence for the first time. Then she half-whispered, quietly:

'That's right; that's right, my dear . . . ' and I sensed her thoughts becoming more contemplative during the short pause which she gently ended with: ' . . . but my social conscience has been pricking me lately, just a little. If I can think of anything to help the idea of love on Earth – lovingness – I'll do it.'

The actress then gracefully rose out of the massively padded sofa and moved, almost regally glided as if in a costume drama, towards the picture windows, where she thoughtfully looked out at the magnificent grounds, before continuing:

'But first I have to learn how to throw my thoughts into another person's mind, people down there on Earth. I've tried a few times with my family, but I haven't had much success.'

'Have you been back to see them?' I asked brightly. And then there was a sudden flash of anger across her eyes as she swivelled to face me again.

'They photographed all my private things, my stuff! I was annoyed. It made me really angry, at first – but then, what the hell? I can't hide forever – no-one can.'

'No,' I agreed, knowing full well the inquisitiveness of the voracious Press, ever-eager to buy exclusive stories about the rich and famous.

'My dear, the public wanted *glamour*,' she emphasized, with both arms opening wide – as if to silently indicate that this quality was now filling every available space in the room – 'and I gave it to them. They wanted to laugh and cry, to feel emotions intensely, and I gave these gifts; and that's why they'll remember me.

'But in the end my own image trapped me, my dear. My people were the most important, but the legend had to be kept alive, even if I was dying a little bit more each day.'

Then she slowly dropped her arms to her sides, turned away, and began staring rather vacantly through the windows at the distant trees, a woman deep in thought.

'I never believed in surviving death, you know,' she said, casting me half a glance over her bare shoulder, then resuming her passive coolness, gazing once more at God's country. 'But we live and learn. Now . . . only now I think . . . there is a growing belief in a God within me; an overseer . . . '

She gently inclined her shoulder-length golden hair outwards towards the fields and the pageant of nature, then sighed to herself and folded her slender arms; her back was towards me.

'Of course, I realize now – now that I've had a lot of time to think – that real beauty, true beauty, is something within a person, and not on the skin's surface,' she said giving me another momentary glance.

'But when I got older, everything sagged, my dear; so I had to hide myself away . . . '

She wasn't looking at me now, and perhaps not even speaking to me any more, as a marked tenderness crept quietly into her thoughtful voice:

'The picture of my face will remain, I think, but I'll be doing some hard work here, groundwork, to promote the idea of love . . . true love in all its forms, just as soon as I settle in . . . '

5

The Silver Cord

Some people share Marlene Dietrich's earthly disbelief in an afterlife, but innumerable others have been forced to accept the reality of a hereafter, especially when they've undergone a sudden out-of-the-body experience (an OOBE).

It stands to reason that if we can exist outside of our physical bodies, as complete entities with established memories and personalities, then survival after death is most certainly assured. But is there any evidence to support this theory?

Just take a look at the following emotional and quite touching account from a young man in his twenties, describing a typical OOBE. But is it genuine, or just a dream, or maybe wishful thinking, rather than a real journey into the next world?

What do you think?

As a child I spent a considerable time with my grandparents, especially 'Bamp', my grandfather, whom I'd see twice a day on my way to and from school.

Years later, when both of them had gone, I was

especially devastated by Bamp's death, for we'd always been close: I was heartbroken.

But about a month or so after he'd died, one night I was asleep and dreaming that I was returning home from one of my regular jogging runs on the street, when on the way back I thought: 'I know, I'll go and visit Bamp.'

So I ran faster and faster, gaining great momentum as I reached the door of his house, and I burst through it – then suddenly, from out of the kitchen, came my grandfather.

I can't describe the emotion I felt when I saw him, and we hugged and hugged each other for an age. I was so happy and overjoyed to be with him again.

'There's a letter from Australia in the front room,' he said. (We have relatives there.) 'Go and sit down and I'll make a pot of tea,' and then he went back into the kitchen. I was incredibly happy, but at the same time I couldn't understand why I hadn't seen him for so long.

I went across to the table, and as I picked up the letter I instantly 'remembered' that Bamp had *died* a couple of months back, and an icy feeling suddenly gripped me when I realized I must be standing inside his home in another world.

I immediately panicked in sudden fright and fled from the house – but all the time I was trying to get away I could feel his strong hand gripping my arm and hear him saying: 'It's OK to stay awhile!' – but my fear got the better of me and I belted through the door as fast as I could go, and ran and ran and ran.

Then I woke up in bed with a start, feeling completely drained, as well as being drenched in a bath of sweat, and for a short while I was sure I could still hear Bamp calling to me.

But after a while, I settled down a bit and realized how silly I'd been, because Bamp would never in the world harm me, and so I chided myself for being so stupid in running away from him.

But then I was upset, and I cried to myself.

Looking back now though, it was a remarkable experience – so clear in my mind – and I truly really know my grandfather has survived death, and this visit to him showed me where he is. I've been there for myself, and I've met him in the next world.

At first glance this seems like a touching reunion between a grieving grandson and a much-loved relative, but whereas many could accept this young man's experience as a genuine OOBE, others might seriously question it; and some psychologists would probably have a field-day explaining it all away.

As for myself, I fully accept it as authentic, for this man is well known to me, as indeed are all the other excursionists we'll soon meet, whose identities I've withheld for privacy, and for whose mental stability and sincerity I can personally vouch.

But what of the experience itself? Does it offer any conclusive evidence that an inner spirit body, and therefore a consciousness, exists 'somewhere' in 'some place' outside of, and apart from, a physical body? What do you think?

Before passing judgement or taking a critical look at these phenomena, here's another interesting case, but this time from a man in his thirties who shares with us an unusual journey undertaken, he claims, while he was lying fully awake in bed, and in which he experiences a deep sense of soul-peacefulness – something reported by countless percipients. But is the following a real occurrence, or just fantasy?

When I was about ten, and even when I was younger than that, I used to leave my body at night; on many memorable occasions I knew I was slipping out of it, at will.

While still fully awake, but with my eyes closed, I learnt a clever trick of sinking down through the mattress – in my other body – and then going further down again, right through into the small confined space between my bedroom floor and our kitchen ceiling beneath.

While there, I could clearly see all the thick, grey, plastic-covered electrical cables, and plenty of fluff and dust, running along the wooden support beams.

Then I'd make myself fall further down again – right down through the floor and into the kitchen – until I could see the kitchen ceiling directly above me.

But I was always horizontal and looking upwards, never looking down.

Then, whenever I decided I wanted to get back to my bed (and this was also a conscious decision), I'd simply reverse the falling process – and I'd suddenly be back inside my physical body. However, it was always so much easier to float down than to go back up; funny that.

Much later, as an adult in my twenties, I can also recall finding myself travelling upwards through space, very quickly, right up into the night sky. This happened quite often, and, when I realized where I was, I'd think: 'I've got to get back,' at which point I'd return with such incredibly fast speed that I'd actually bounce on the bed when I woke up, as if I'd hit it with great force – and my heart would be thudding away.

But on every occasion when I existed outside of myself like this, whether as a boy or a man, I was always struck by the tremendous sense of peacefulness within me, and I was really happy to be light and floating.

The problem raised by these two gentlemen is that because they were the *only* ones to report their experiences, they're purely subjective accounts: no other objective witnesses can confirm them. OOBEs, if verified as genuine, would undoubtedly prove that because excursionists are existing outside the body, the seat of consciousness cannot possibly be the brain. If such astonishing trips can really be made by astral projectionists, have we any objective evidence, any previously unknown facts, that were gained by these travellers, and which were later discovered to be correct?

With these criteria in mind, does this next fascinating account help us? It's given by an intelligent self-employed businesswoman, approaching her late thirties.

When I was nearly fourteen I fell in love and was totally besotted with my first real boyfriend and expected to meet him every day.

Unfortunately, one week he had influenza and I didn't see him for three days, by which time I was convinced he'd decided to drop me for someone else. In this state of anguish, I found it difficult to sleep at night, so I tried a relaxation technique I'd seen on TV, where you concentrate on your feet, imagining them getting heavier and heavier until totally relaxed – and then you move on to the next bit, etc.

By the time I got to my shoulders I was wallowing in a state of deep calmness, but my mind was still very alert. (I now call this state 'twilighting', where I'm fully able to hear a telephone ring but simply can't be bothered to make an effort to do anything about it.)

Lying in bed, naturally I was thinking of my boyfriend and wondering if he really did have a bad cold, or whether he was just making excuses not to see me, when I suddenly found myself standing in the hallway of my home and I was dressed only in my night-wear. The walls around me seemed sort of indistinct, shadowy even.

86

I walked downstairs to the back door and went through into the yard, pausing at the gate because I knew it was old and rusty and would probably make a tremendous noise if I opened it. I was in a dilemma because just standing there in my nightie and bare feet there was no way, I thought, that I could climb over it. But while looking up at the big gate I instantly found myself on the other side of it, out on the roadway.

(At the time, and even now, nothing seemed extraordinary to me: I just accepted it.)

My boyfriend lived about half a mile away so I began to walk towards his house and, as I did, I took more notice of my surroundings. It had been raining and the tops of the nearby hedges were being bent by a strong wind, but I felt nothing of it at all, not even the cold October night air all about me. Although I knew it was late at night, there was enough light for me to see every twig and berry in the hedgerow, so I gazed upwards to see if there was a full moon, but there wasn't, because the sky was deeply overcast. And yet there was this mysterious, hazy grey-blue light all around me which didn't seem to have any source at all.

When I eventually arrived at my boyfriend's place, walking towards the back door I wondered how I was going to get inside, and then how I'd be able to find his bedroom. I'd never been there before. So I closed my eyes to think more clearly, and when I opened them again, I discovered myself sitting on a window-sill on the inside of his room!

The place was strangely lit by this same blue-greyish light and I could clearly see my boyfriend moving fitfully in his bed, coughing and sneezing as he tried to sleep. I was looking at a room I'd never seen previously, and as I gazed around me I took particular note of the wallpaper pattern, the dressing-table and his wardrobe. I also noticed there was an unfinished letter resting on his bedside table.

Then I became scared of waking him, so I didn't try and read the letter but instead admired the deep blue colour of the curtains and carpet, and then realized it was the first *real* colour I'd properly noticed. (In hindsight, I suspect that this colour's intensity prevented the grey light from diffusing it.)

I don't remember returning back into my body, in my own house, but the following day my boyfriend turned up, still sneezing, to say how much he'd been missing me; and when I told him what had happened the previous night and fully described his room exactly as I remembered seeing it – *my description turned out to be perfect in every detail*. But instead of beaming with the delight I'd hoped for, he looked very dismayed and seriously asked me if I was a witch!

(I was only fourteen!)

The accuracy of my description, even down to the unfinished private letter on his night-stand, had given him, he said, 'the shivers', just to think that I'd 'wandered in a dream' inside his own house and 'right into' his bedroom. And being young he quickly made me promise never to tell anyone else, or I might get 'locked up, or something'.

Does this incredibly detailed excursion provide sound evidence for the separate existence of our projectionist's mind from her sleeping body, thereby indicating her soul will survive death?

Many would think it does, but the ladies and gentlemen of the famed Society for Psychical Research (SPR) would strongly disagree, declaring that a portion of the 'traveller's' mind possibly engaged itself in 'distant telepathic contact': that the girl had 'seen' the appearance of her boyfriend's bedroom by linking her mind with his thought-images, distantly. Then the SPR would produce volumes of similar cases from their extensive files, supporting this theory.

(By the way, let's keep in our minds that odd 'grey-blue' light our last projectionist mentioned, because we'll meet it again shortly.)

So where do we go from here?

Well, if we could only find *one* occurrence of a physical object being physically moved or dislocated by an 'ethereal' projectionist's hand, while at the same time being witnessed by people who were consciously awake, we'd be on much firmer ground.

And here's exactly such a remarkable case, related by a man in his mid-forties:

One bright summer's evening I went to bed for a rest. The bedroom was quite light, and I must have fallen asleep quickly.

All at once I was aware of rising up off the bed, fully conscious, then I realized I was standing at the bedside looking down at my physical body which was fast asleep next to me. For all the world, even though *I* looked as if I were dead, I wasn't frightened; I felt great: at peace with myself and as light as a feather. But my bedroom was now much darker, sort of shadowy and a kind of misty grey-blue to my sight.

I left the room and went downstairs in the usual way, where I knew I'd left my mother and father watching television. At the bottom of the stairs I naturally opened the living-room door with my left hand – to about two feet wide – and both my parents were startled: they turned round to see what was going on, but the look on their faces told me they couldn't see *me* at all. Even our old black dog lifted his head and crooked his neck to look in my direction.

I can't remember if anyone spoke, because it's a long time ago now. But what did strike me as odd was that when I'd gone to bed, the living-room had been quite bright (the electric light was also still on), but now, during this experience, it seemed to be dimly lit; shadowy again.

Both my parents, who were staring at the empty doorway, had their mouths wide open and looked dumbfounded, so I shut the door, turned, walked back upstairs and went over to my body in the bed, and simply got back into bed. I think I must have just slipped back inside my body, and then I must have fallen fast asleep again.

But the next day, my mother told me about the door opening on its own and there being no-one in the hall outside.

This man's amazing experience certainly indicates that the seat of consciousness cannot be the brain, for his brain was 'fast asleep' upstairs while his personal awareness functioned in another dislocated vehicle of expression – another body just like his physical one – called by many paranormalists the astral body.

The fact that a separate conscious witness reported the same physical event as experienced by the 'sleeper' rules out hallucination, and strengthens this case considerably. It now defies any reasonable scientific explanation other than a genuine out-of-the-body experience.

It's also interesting to note that most percipients report the same unusual sense of lightness and peacefulness while functioning in their soul-bodies. And when our last excursionist speaks of the rooms being 'light' upon retiring, and then much 'darker' when seen by his spirit vision, his observations tie in with the previous sighting of this same 'grey-blue' light; a phenomenon which has been quite commonly, and individually, reported by countless astral travellers.

My spirit guide, White Owl, explains:

The atoms of physical matter which make up the physical body are vibrating at much slower and lower frequencies than the atoms constituting the spirit body, which are vibrating quite fast; therefore, when a person is conscious in the spirit body, the physical world, to their perception, will be a very slow-moving place.

To an astral traveller, the Earth environment appears grey-blue, dull, shadowy and sometimes lightless, because the slow-moving particles of physical matter create a 'denser', 'thicker' or 'foggier' atmosphere to his spirit vision, which is fast-moving and 'finer' and 'lighter'.

When innumerable, unrelated projectionists experience broadly the same related sights and sounds (as they do when vast numbers of cases are studied), this becomes a valid source of evidence in itself.

Several noted clairvoyants have claimed that the astral body is connected to the physical by an ethereal silver cord or lifeline, which attaches the two vehicles of expression to one another. Just as a baby is linked to its mother by the umbilical cord, so it is claimed the astral and physical bodies are similarly joined by a power-link. When this 'cord' dematerializes, death occurs and the physical body starts breaking down into the chemicals from whence it came.

However, in my experience the silver cord isn't a cord at all, but a fine magnetic energy-link which sometimes manifests itself as light, and there are many of these links constantly moving between the two separated bodies during an OOBE. When your astral body returns to its physical shell after travelling, just like lightning which jumps from one heavily charged rain cloud to another of lower potential during a thunderstorm, so the astral body's cosmic energies 'jump' to the physical, and it is these fine power-lines which are often seen as silvery threads. But they can also appear in other colours.

Some have said the silver cord emerges from the solar plexus of the astral body (just above the navel) and enters the physical through the base of the brain – but it must be remembered that energy can cross at any number of points. Incidentally, I've also clairvoyantly seen the astral forms of physically alive, sleeping people whom I knew, while their OOBEs were taking place, and *no cord or threads of light were visible to me at all*.

We're all linked to one another by numerous psychic connections, no matter what world we live in, and it's along these power-lines that telepathic messages can be instantly transferred. Take the case of my Aunt Charlotte, for example. Her elderly mother lived in Germany while she and her family lived in Wales, hundreds of miles apart, but one night while my aunt was socializing, out of the blue she clutched at her blouse in irrational panic.

'What's wrong?' asked my uncle.

'It's my mother,' she said, psychically disturbed, 'I've just heard her calling to me: "Charlotte! Charlotte!" twice.'

My aunt became so feverish that no-one could placate her. Then later, the family received a telegram to say that her mum had indeed died at the very time her supernormal voice was heard by her daughter. Just by thinking about someone we immediately transmit fine psychic energy-links, projecting them towards the object of our thoughts, and distance is no obstacle.

Now here's another account involving strange telepathic powers operating between individuals. It's not an OOBE, but this time our percipient, a sensitive businesswoman in her sixties, raises intriguing and unusual implications in the light of her experience.

I was a newly appointed lieutenant of a Sea Ranger Crew and we were at summer camp just outside the old town of Brecon in South Wales, years ago now. I'd never been to Brecon before and, as far as I knew, neither had most of the girls in my crew.

It was a lovely sunny morning and, after inspection was over, the captain called us together and said, 'I have business in town today so I've arranged transport to take you all to the river where you can hire boats and canoes. I'm putting the lieutenant in charge and I want you all to assemble at the photographer's in the town at 5 p.m. on the dot for a group photograph.' We were thrilled, and all piled into the back of a lorry and were soon paddling our way down the river and having a marvellous time!

At 4.15 p.m. I blew my whistle and we went back on to dry land. Then I thought: 'Where do we go from here?' because not one of us could remember the name of the photographer's we were supposed to meet at.

'Skipper didn't tell us the name, or the street,' said the girls. Youthful panic started to set in, so I asked a passer-by about photo shops in the town and was told there were four, but some only worked part time!

Then suddenly I felt very calm and immediately and confidently took charge saying, 'Follow me, girls!'

And I led them through the town, winding my way past shops and houses – purposefully – and trooping them in and out of small, quaint old streets. Then I turned a corner and there it was!

Skipper was waiting outside at exactly 5 p.m. 'Thank goodness!' she said. 'Do you know, I couldn't remember if I'd told you the photographer's name and address!'

'*You didn't!*' chorused the excited girls.

Now, years later, as I look back on that odd event, what puzzles me are three things:

1. How could I possibly have known exactly where to go in that unfamiliar town, getting there so

purposefully and calmly, without the slightest hesitation?

2. Could it be, I wonder, that I knew the old streets because I may have lived in Brecon before, in some 'previous life'?

3. Or is it possible that my mind, or some part of it, somehow travelled ahead of me and the girls, and then 'guided' us all to the meeting place?

Each of our lieutenant's explanations is a valid possibility, but I've included her account because it may indicate some others:

She could have been astral travelling on the previous evening, while her physical body was sleeping, and she may have planned the following day's events with 'Skipper'.

Or perhaps both 'Skipper', who fully knew what she intended for the girls, and her lieutenant's minds had been in some kind of telepathic contact during the previous night's sleeping hours, or even somehow imperceptibly linked on the very day of the trip.

But, whatever the explanation, it certainly seems some psychic sense had been active, some power outside of the lieutenant's head had been operating.

If only *one* of the above cases defies rational explanation — and I think the witnessed account from the man who opened the door with his spirit hand does — then the massive edifice of survival evidence, painstakingly built up over the years by millions of dedicated spirit people must stand intact.

Our projectionists, being fully able to exist as complete individuals 'outside of' and 'at a distance from' their physical bodies in another plane of being, have demonstrated to us that *the seat of consciousness is not the brain; and therefore, when the brain (with the body) dies – we will stand unscathed, surviving the transition known as death, complete as conscious, thinking individuals.*

But where exactly is this Other Side of Life which our astral projectionists have briefly visited? And why does it so frequently elude the physical senses of millions of people, this ethereal realm which contains the so-called 'dead'?

Is it possible to locate the spirit world?

I believe it is . . .

6

Beyond the Veil

. . . I was all alone in a deserted lecture hall in which I'd earlier been teaching mediumship, and now I had an hour free. Upstairs, directly above me, the continuing seminar was being listened to by sixty-odd students from around Britain.

More than grateful for my break, wandering on to the empty platform, I lowered my weary body into my big armchair; everyone had always thought of that seat as mine because I'd preferred it when publicly working there. It was so welcoming, as comfortable as a favourite old coat, that I quickly relaxed. Gently closing my eyes to regain some of the vast amounts of nervous energy teaching burns up, I revelled in inner silence, wonderfully liquid and golden, punctuated only by the muffled sounds of a distant tutor's voice coming from the room above.

Entranced by the shining darkness behind my eyes, I began to wonder what occupied the immediate space directly around my chair in the spirit realms. Although I was seated in a deserted small hall, about 30 feet wide by 100 feet long, I knew that within this area many invisible dimensions might exist. Then it happened, all at once:

Without warning my psychic vision opened up and before me was revealed an utterly different world. Instantly I found myself somewhere near a very real and dusty street, full of old-fashioned wooden buildings, resembling a country settlement in the America of the 1930s. In amazement, my spirit sight drank in the stained slatted buildings with their hand-painted signs swaying gently and creaking in the breeze, and all around me was the bustling sound of hurried activity.

It was high noon and the blazing sun's shimmering heat was reflected everywhere. The humidity was palpable. And although I didn't see many people, I knew most of them were sheltering from the heat inside the various quaint shops.

Then my attention was caught by a nearby rickety old Ford car: it was shiny black with large wheels and it came chugging along the street right in front of me, spluttering and shaking, leaving little dust clouds hanging in the air as it passed by. It was perfect in every detail, not a shabby replica but the *genuine* car itself.

I was fascinated; and I remember thinking, this world I'm seeing must be far removed from the hall I'm sitting in on Earth. And this earthly thought, of course, brought about an immediate change of scene: in the twinkling of an eye the dusty road and car vanished like a burst balloon.

And next I found myself seated in a similar high-backed leather armchair – in exactly the same spot – only this time there was no sign of the empty lecture hall back on Earth. Instead, I was now inside a vast amphitheatre with quite a high ceiling. There were brown oak-panelled galleries all around me, as well as circle seats, whereas the hall on Earth only had seating on the ground level and a much lower ceiling.

I noticed some of the upper-gallery chairs were occupied, several people of varying ages were grouped here and there, all watching me on the platform, almost as though they were waiting for me to start speaking or take some kind of service.

It then occurred to me that what was happening was a live event, and they were actually witnessing my experiment.

But I foolishly made the mistake of quickly opening my eyes to compare the two different places, and this instantly brought my consciousness back to grey Mother Earth – and I was once more seated in the quiet lecture hall, all alone again, right back where I'd started.

But I knew exactly what had happened: I'd experienced two very brief existences in the astral worlds, those shining planes of illusion which vibrate very close to Earth.

I was then struck by the incredible realization that in just one small space there are probably millions of different worlds all existing simultaneously – each plane of thought separated from its neighbour simply by the rate at which it exists, or vibrates. But for the most part, the inhabitants of each sphere are blissfully unaware of their neighbours; unless someone breaks into their consciousness as I had just done.

There are countless worlds within worlds, within worlds, all co-existing together, but *interpenetrating* one another.

The experience I've just described might help us to locate these worlds of spirit, which we can visit when out of the body; but before we can get a firmer grasp of their reality we need to consider some simple ideas which explain, for example, why 'ghosts' can walk through walls and we can't.

Science tells us that physical matter is nothing more than an open network of atoms all vibrating and circling one another so fast that they give 'the appearance' of being solid: and it's the speed of their particles which make them seem so.

Everything is constantly moving and in a state of vibration.

The spaces between these active atoms are relatively vast: if we imagine the distance between our own sun and the Earth, this gives a rough idea of the immense gaps between the vibrating atoms that are making up and 'materializing' this book you're reading, which may seem 'solid' enough – although it isn't.

To help us locate the worlds of spirit we need to understand that, generally, atoms vibrating at slower 'physical' speeds make up the the physical, or material, objects we can see and sense in 'the physical world' – and these atoms cannot pass through any other material objects because the speeds of the two sets of atoms are fixed at roughly the same rates of vibration.

For example, if you were to throw this book at the nearest wall (quite a common pastime, incidentally!), it wouldn't go *through* the bricks, but would bounce off, because the atoms of the book are vibrating at roughly the same rate as the atoms of the wall, within a small waveband known as 'the physical world'.

Furthermore, physical matter, so the spirit people tell us, is simply spirit matter (or high-frequency spirit energies) manifesting at lower 'physical' wavelengths.

Here's a helpful example: let's imagine that Spirit, or life-essence, is like a fine morning mist, then as it condenses into heavier rain, and afterwards becomes ice, this might well represent for us the physical world. The basic life-stuff or essence is the same – water – but it's materializing itself in different states or densities, according to its rate of vibration.

This is why 'ghosts' can walk through our walls, because the ghosts are vibrating at higher frequencies than the particles of the walls, which therefore can't prevent their passage.

'Life is Spirit, and Spirit is Life,' says my Other World teacher, White Owl, 'but Spirit functions, or manifests itself, in different worlds or planes of thought – plus in multifarious life-forms, and also in other universes.

'Man foolishly assumes he is a body with a mind, whereas his essence is pure Spirit, registering through a temporary vehicle known as the physical body; but even this is Spirit, existing at a much lower frequency than his mind.'

Here's another allusion to help us grasp why we can't see the spirit world with the naked eye: suppose we boil a kettleful of water until it becomes steam which we can see and feel. By quickening the vibratory rate of the water molecules we've simply changed its state from liquid to gas. But if we then heat it up much more (further increase its vibratory rate), it becomes supersteam which you *can't* see, but it still exists and will burn off your flesh if you put a bare arm through it.

The spirit worlds are like this: they can't normally be seen by our earthly senses because they're existing, or vibrating, at faster frequencies than the atoms of our physical eyes. This difference in vibration came about as a result of evolution: the next spheres formed themselves in early times when the newly born, hot planet Earth started to cool down, becoming denser and smaller. The denser, slower matter gravitated to its centre, while the finer, quicker and lighter matter cooled around the central mass in successive layers upwards and outwards into space, creating several spheres, or circular planes of life all around the Earth, just like the many skins of an onion.

So Earth's core and crust vibrate at the slower rate, and each successive sphere (manifestation, or spirit-skin) exists at gradually higher frequencies. The atoms of each layer, outwards from the Earth, are moving faster than the layer beneath it; and the natural divisions created between these layers are similar in appearance to fogbanks. Fog is made up of two streams of identical air, but one is cooler than the other, or vibrating slower than the other – and where they meet, they manifest in our atmosphere as fog.

Interestingly enough, the spirit spheres contain similar fogbanks where each fast-vibrating etheric atmosphere meets the much slower vibrations of the layer beneath it; the spirit people often refer to these clouds as 'the mists'.

The spirit planes of thought aren't easy to locate geographically because the more evolved realms – and therefore these are the 'older' spheres – extend outwards to beyond all known time and space, and aren't just circling around our small planet. The spirit worlds are thought-worlds, and occupy, as such, all space and time at once; they aren't bound by Earth's gravitational pull, and this explains why there are so many realms in the Spirit: 'In my Father's house (kingdom) there are many mansions (planes of life).'

The spheres nearest to us are called the astral worlds – derived from the Greek word *astron*, meaning a star (or starry), and they're so named because of the shining light in which they exist (fast-moving particles emit greater light and heat). Owing to their nearness to us, these astral planes of thought are naturally inhabited by recently 'deceased' persons; and recent can mean a few centuries in spirit. The people living there have frequently proved their

105

awareness of what makes up our lives here on Earth. One such spirit newcomer even made a surprising appearance in a cemetery as I conducted her own funeral service!

Hannah, and her daughter, Jenny, had followed my calling right from its beginnings and were often seen in the crowds, lending their emotional support at my public meetings. Hannah, very petite and in her seventies, positively adored me ('I think the world of that little boy,' she used to say), and she wouldn't have a thing said against me. Despite the fact that she was small-boned and under five feet tall, she'd been known to stand her ground against a number of six-footer brutes when vigorously defending my reputation. 'They're only jealous people, out to belittle you,' she'd say, poking a lethal finger in what I assumed was their imaginary eyes!

When Hannah passed over, and Jenny asked me if I'd conduct the interment of her ashes at the family grave, I agreed without hesitation, and about fifteen people assembled on a grassy slope one freezing cold November morning. The wind was bitter and cutting, and during the personal service (I never follow books or manuals) suddenly the heavens opened and icy sleet came pelting down on the already-numb mourners.

Apart from the atrocious weather, everything else had gone fine: I'd read a poem and spoken some comforting words to everyone gathered around the graveside, had said prayers of thankfulness for the gift of Hannah's life, and then we'd paid our respects by dropping small white flowers into the grave, to symbolize 'that another soul has risen into freedom,' as I remember saying. After that, we sent out silent thoughts to our friend.

This was the moment that Hannah chose to make a surprising and unannounced appearance to my psychic vision. She stood on the opposite side of her burial place, as large as life, leaning on the gravestone as if nothing at all had happened to her. With pitiful eyes, she looked across at me and around at the blue faces of the elderly mourners – it was such a cold day – and then spoke to me with typical concern: 'Oh, God help them,' she said. 'God love him, too. Thank you all very much,' she added, in obvious gratitude for our presence and the kind words I'd spoken; all so naturally.

Such an occurrence underlines the nearness of the next planes to Earth, these astral thought-worlds in which our thinking has a more direct effect upon the ether around us than it does here on Earth.

Thoughts create every circumstance and condition which touch and affect our lives.

It was such thought-power that drew Hannah to her graveside service.

I believe we should monitor our thought-patterns, and be very wary of them, too; for my spirit work, and the assistance I've given to the patients of psychotherapists in the past, has taught me that old habits die hard and can effectively trap us in thought-cages of our own making if we're not careful.

If a man lives in a certain kind of house all his life and then he 'dies', he'll naturally gravitate to a plane of thought (a world of spirit) where similar houses exist, and then probably continue living there until he thinks he no longer needs such a life style: his Thought will have 'controlled' and 'conditioned' his existence, both here and in the Beyond.

The immense power of negative thought can cripple a soul's psychological progress, and its penetrating effects should never be underestimated. My own father was a man who, I believe, was trapped by a self-created thought-prison. He was a person by whom you could set your clock: he went to exactly the same places every day, met his usual friends for a drink, ate at the same café (a regular order), and then came home like clockwork. With no offence to Dad, this daily routine could hardly be described as exciting or living life to the full; these habit patterns and mind-tracks made his life listless and unprogressive.

Such an abject lack of variety would either throw me into an apoplectic fit of the screaming hab-dabs – during which I might do something rash, like pay a few bills – or else I'd be a zombie in a week! Yet untold millions exist like this each and every day of what I consider must be their sad and only half-lived potential lives.

The trouble with Thought is that it's capable of easily creating illusions: it can fool us into feeling psychologically secure by imbedding regular but stifling habits into our minds, and unless we

108

make conscious efforts to break these, and change such crippling, negative patterns, we'll suffer the unfortunate consequences.

How many lives, I wonder, are only partly lived because of the illusions of Thought? How many unfortunate souls are daily existing in a 'waking sleep', barely conscious of the great pulse of life? I think they would number more than the grains of sand on a beach.

But change we must – it's absolutely inevitable. So why waste any more time? Let's all start now.

It's from the astral worlds that a great majority of spirit people relay their messages at my public meetings, of course, and because these communicators are relatively new arrivals in the spirit world, they will not have had the time to acquire more wisdom – and this should be remembered when considering any advice these personalities might offer.

Astral levels of consciousness are the easiest for us mediums to contact; but communicating with advanced, progressed souls is much more complicated because they exist deep within the inner realms of spirit and are infinitely more difficult to reach, requiring a refined sensitiveness and a highly developed psychic awareness on the medium's part in order to be successful. Our physical sensory equipment is quite unsatisfactory for registering such subtle vibrations. Slow-vibrating physical eyes, for example, can only perceive light existing within very limited wavelengths.

We can see the brilliance of a golden sunrise, but its 'secret' vibrations of ultra-violet light, given so freely, remain hidden from us.

We can watch the lightning as it flashes through the heavens on a dark stormy night, or be entranced by the sparkling flames of a crackling forest fire; and yet we're unable to see the X-rays penetrating right through our bodies when we're being examined for illness.

As mere physical machines, we're very limited in what amounts to our minuscule range of sensory perceptions; some animals can hear the ear-piercing sounds of dog-whistles which woefully (or thankfully!) escape us.

I often have a chuckle when sceptical academics reject the mind as being a separate vibrating entity from the brain, and state there can't possibly be a sphere in which it functions after the body is 'dead': we can't see the air we breathe but it certainly exists.

Just because something is 'invisible' to physical sight, doesn't mean it has no reality. Just think about the ordinary sound waves of next-door's TV coming through the wall when you don't want to hear them: they penetrate the bricks and travel in the atmosphere, right through to you and me. They undoubtedly exist, but we can't see them with our naked eyes.

And what about the powerful forces of love and anger? We'd be hard-pressed to slap hatred on a dinner-plate for scientists to dissect it.

I once flummoxed a rather confused sceptic on radio with: 'If one of your ardent admirers declared, "I love you" – how could you see it, believe it, or even prove it, I wonder?'

He was cornered into silence.

(By the way, no helpful suggestions on postcards, please readers!)

It's also illogical that sound and light vibrations pass through an empty nothingness; all energies must surely be carried by a medium of some sort, and the spirit people tell us this universe is filled with invisible ether – yet another vibrational aspect of an Infinite Spirit – and this ether is the vehicle or medium through which all energy vibrations are conveyed.

When contacting us, by lowering their mind vibrations, the Other Side are very clever at manipulating this ether and drawing power from it, and us, to accomplish seemingly impossible feats. Theories behind the reproduction of matter into clone-like versions of original substances are now being taught to most schoolchildren, but I can cite an impressive spirit-world example.

Someone from eternity must have been very close to me one morning when I had a grumble in the bathroom about the talcum powder. 'The silly thing,' I said, vigorously shaking the sealed can to get the last dregs out, 'it doesn't last five minutes! Why don't they make it everlasting?' I moaned to myself. But little did I know someone in Spirit had overheard this, and then set about doing just that!

The Old Spice talc in its light-proof red tin was used by me every day, but after a few months of usage I began to suspect something . . . 'This must surely be coming to the end by now?' I mused; yet the supply just kept on sprinkling out more and more each day. Eventually, the penny dropped when I heard a young spirit child saying, 'I've been practising my skills in matter-reproduction!' – the talent of multiplying and cloning physical atoms by manipulating spirit vibrations through the ether.

'I *wondered* what was going on!' I replied to the moist bathroom air.

The darkness inside the tin must have provided the perfect conditions for such physical manifestations to occur, for the Old Spice carried on serving me each day for no less than an incredible *eight consecutive months*, after which the powder suddenly disappeared and I had to buy some more. (Now that's what I call value for money!)

Later on, of course – now thoroughly intrigued – I tried the same experiment with my Brut 33, but alas to no avail!

The ether and the spirit worlds are all around us:

'Nothing exists without the Power of the Infinite Spirit,' states my guide, White Owl. 'With Spirit there is consciousness and life; without it there is nothing.

'We are all constantly bathed in a vibratory sea of Spirit Power, an indefinable life-energy which permeates every aspect of being: physical, mental, emotional and spiritual. The Power of the Spirit is everywhere, within you and "outside" of you.'

Though in reality, of course, as I'm sure White Owl would agree, absolutely nothing can ever reside 'outside' of ourselves, for whatever we're conscious of is a subjective thought and spirit experience.

White Owl has often taught we exist within the Infinite Spirit's Essence: everything in this universe can be likened to a great sea of spirit viewed as an endless vast ocean, and we are like small jellyfish floating in, and being supported by, its power. Therefore, we're made up of the sea-water: it feeds us, it is within us and without of us; we are it, and it is us. And all manifestations are linked to this Infinite Spirit, he says, and therefore we cannot be where It is not. But I'll have more to say on this later, when discussing the nature of the One Living God.

I believe that everything exists because of Consciousness, even the spirit worlds, and other philosophers have stated something similar by declaring: they don't think Earth-life itself is a Reality, but a mere Dream.

I wouldn't disagree.

Life – both here and in the realm of spirit – *is* a dream, but a very real one to the dreamer, nevertheless. Just imagine that one night you experienced a vivid dream and then, in this deep sleep, your physical body suddenly 'died' and never woke up – for you, that lucid dream would now be your Reality, wouldn't it?

Life's like that, no matter where we exist.

113

The next worlds of vibration contain countless billions of such 'dreamers', including White Owl; and, dreamer or not, he's a 'dead' man who continues to receive hundreds of personal letters from people in different parts of *this* world each year!

As a frequent spirit communicator and active teacher of natural law and spiritual realities, it seems he's made a considerable impact on many Earth lives. His teachings are the result of what he claims to be the benefit of a much wider spiritual vision, gained because of his great age and his vantage-point in Spirit.

Perhaps we should question this?

Maybe it's time to place him under the critical eye of a glaring public spotlight. So let's peer now through the divisions between heaven and Earth, those cloudy fogbanks, the vibrating spirit mists, and lift the veil on one of these interpenetrating spirit realms, so that we can take a glimpse into its vast store of wisdom as revealed by my spirit guide's own world of Thought.

Perhaps then we may discover exactly who – or what – White Owl truly is . . .

7

White Owl Speaks
A Guide in the Spotlight

White Owl, who are you?
I am a soul who has undertaken a mission, in co-operation with many other minds more advanced and progressed than my own, to help enlighten mankind and bring his thinking back on to paths of peacefulness and a deeper understanding of spiritual realities. We are endeavouring to spread knowledge of who and what man is, where he came from, where he is going, and why he has incarnated on Earth.

I am a very close friend of the medium.

How old are you?
I am ancient.

Physical age and your timescale means nothing to us here. If I told you I was a hundred years old, seventeen hundred, or even a million years old, would these figures matter? Can wisdom come from the unwise? Can the darkness of ignorance spring from the mind of a knowledgeable being?

If your world judges me by my teachings, by what I say, then I think it will be apparent I have tried to achieve my goals through the power of love. I have never dominated or suppressed my medium's free will (limited though it is).

I have consistently advocated that man should use his faculties of intelligent questioning and reason, and that he should accept only that which is in accordance with the highest principles of wisdom, and of love, one toward another.

Were you a Red Indian only in your last incarnation?
'I' am not a Red Indian at all. The astral body of this balanced personality known as 'White Owl' is just a vehicle for my thoughts and teachings.

I am a much older soul who uses the instrumentality of the gentle Indian, just as the Indian uses the mentality of Stephen O'Brien.

It is like a stepping-down process, a transmission of higher knowledge and vibrations down through various 'transformers' or 'mediums' until it reaches your present understanding.

Neither is my teaching entirely my own. I receive guidance and instruction as to what shall be transmitted at any given time. I, too, am a medium.

Where did your soul originate, White Owl?
Souls do not originate, they are part of the outbreathing of a Universal Spirit; they have always been. There is no beginning and no end to existence, it is eternal.

Here, we cannot say that we had a starting-point, or indeed that our lives will eventually finish.

God is Infinite Being, and such boundaries would demean this almighty power and make of it a mere finite entity, and that is against all we have found.

An end to existence, to God, would be illogical.

Where do you live?
Close by, geographically speaking, and yet, to your slow physical senses, I am sometimes very far away, it seems.

I occupy space and move through time in dimensions beyond the narrow confines of Earth, existing in planes of thought which are inter-penetrating your world at this very moment.

Can you describe for us the sphere in which you normally exist?
I have no adequate words with which to convey to you an exact description of my world. You could not compare it with anything in your physical plane, which is but a very pale shadow, not even a flickering candlelight when set against the radiance and wonder of the realms which I inhabit when in my natural state.

Having now been many years in this world – which you are forever trying to locate beyond death but which, in reality, resides within you – I have earned for myself the right to exist in planes of thought far in advance of this astral world – which is full of mental illusions, and from which I am now communicating.

My true place is a world of indescribable light and

117

incredible beauty. It is a realm where the power of thought instantaneously brings its beneficent effect.

Here, all the finer aspects of the soul are perfectly free to express themselves, within the limitations of the Great Spirit's Laws.

The living and vibrant colours of our vegetation cannot be fully appreciated or captured by you, imagined by you, or reproduced by any means currently at your disposal, for our manifestations are self-luminous and have an iridescent brilliance which lights them from within.

We have animals here, too, but in a progressed state of evolution, and their companionship is wondrous in its innocence and purity.

But this plane from which I am now addressing you is a dark and grey sphere (to my vision), and one very slow in vibration because of the often selfish thoughts and intentions radiated into it by people of the Earth.

Such is the state of the lower astral worlds.

However, the realms I *could* exist in, but have relinquished for the time being to undertake this two worlds' mission with my medium, are filled with unutterable beauty and fineness of spirit.

Because the majority of our loved ones live there, picking up on something you said about the astral worlds being 'full of mental illusions' – what did you mean by that?

Simply that the mind is not the man: it is merely

an instrument which creates a self-awareness of its own reality; it thinks, pictures, and gives life to its own mental images – but it is not the man. The man is the essence, the soul.

Mental illusions operate as follows. When you inherit my world, having left the slow vibrations of Earth behind you, your thoughts will have a more immediate and direct effect on your surroundings here. So if a man 'dies' but still feels he is a very important person and he perpetuates an over-inflated opinion of himself, needing – he thinks – to be regularly told how wonderful he is, then he will draw around him those who will oblige these wishes and convince him of his false 'kindness'.

But this is not Truth. It is illusion, and also far from the real state of that man's soul. He will be living within the illusions of his own making.

Your Earth-plane is full of people like this. Earth is, in many respects, a dream-world full of beings who are building up false impressions of themselves and others within their own minds; but to them these thoughts become very real.

The true inner reality of their soul-state is usually quite different. Yet man's mind – the deceiver and master illusionist – continues to create these supposed 'realities' and stops at nothing to try and sustain them.

But the only Reality is the Spirit, Consciousness, and this can only be experienced when all the mental dross and shadows of illusion have been gradually dissipated and discarded, which often takes a very long time.

But if we are not our mind, then what are we?
You belong to the Essence of the Great Spirit; you are Consciousness, which is the vibrant life-power that your clever mind uses to generate and maintain its Reality, as well as its many falsehoods and delusions.

So when we discard the mind, as you call it 'the deceiver', what will be left?
God-consciousness: a fuller awareness of union with your Originator.

Are you a part of the medium's 'deceiver', White Owl? Are you a secondary personality of the medium, another part of his mind impersonating a guide?
No, I am not 'a secondary personality', though I am a part of my medium's individuality.

What do you mean, a part of his individuality?
For people still registering through the flesh, concepts of the spirit are frequently difficult to grasp, especially when my own vantage-point is significantly different from yours; language often obstructs my meaning.

There is a tremendous difference between 'the individual' and 'the personality'. The personality is that to which you have given a name because it seems to manifest in the physical body you currently use. But your individuality is much greater than this.

I am a part of my medium's individuality.

There are a number of personalities currently incarnated on Earth – and who now have contact with Stephen to support him and his mission, and there are a few more to be introduced to him as yet – plus others here in my world, who are all fragments of the one individual, which 'incorporates' us.

We are all seemingly separate persons, but in fact we share the same common nexus, link, or essence, and this is our individuality.

What happens to our individuality after death? Do we live for ever, or are we to be eventually merged back into God, the whole?

I have been on this side of life for many, many years, as you would gauge time, and I have heard of no-one who has 'lost' or 'diffused' their individuality back into the Godhead from whence it came. Once individuality has been characterized, it seems forever established.

Often I am privileged to take counsel with many great teachers – the Ancient Shining Ones – who are aware of all our thoughts and the work we are undertaking through mediums on Earth. They come to instruct and guide us, and they teach that a greater awareness of individuality will be afforded to the soul as it progresses towards the Light. They do not speak of annihilation, back to a primordial source.

But that is not to say we will always have an outward tangible vehicle of expression, for eventually we will have no need of this. I have communed with some greatly advanced souls who have remained perfectly individual in their essence but who have no outward form of any kind. They are points of consciousness, pure thought and feeling: time and space is open to them.

But I am speaking now of souls who have existed here for aeons, and not newcomers who have been here a mere few thousand years.

We are told that individuals from the Spirit are frequently close by: does the next world guide us daily, White Owl?

Most assuredly, often imperceptibly. We are near your minds, and not only when you are awake. When you are asleep we are also present, at night when you cross to our realms.

Our guidance and inspiration reaches you through the power of thought. We can throw images into another's mentality, for his or her consideration. It is quite easy to do — you yourselves are transmitting these thought-forces every second you exist; but we are specialists at it.

Why are so many guides, as given by some Spiritualist mediums, supposedly Red Indians, Zulu warriors, ancient chieftains or Chinese mandarins and the like?

You have answered your own question: they are not.

Much is relayed through certain unreliable mediums which does not emanate from us.

Mediums are all at different levels of soul and psychic development. Some are more sensitive to our influence than others, but we cannot make our thoughts clearly felt or perceived if the abilities of mediums we must work with are under-developed.

A great musician can play beautiful music on a finely tuned instrument, but the same performer can hardly be blamed for the sub-standard sound if the tools you provide him with at the concert fall short of high quality.

You have to learn to distinguish between what is coming from us, what is coming through the medium from his or her own subconscious mind, and what is pure delusion.

Are you saying we should never trust mediums?

I always advise caution in accepting utterances from any source, in whatever world, without first pitting them against your keenest intelligence.

Surely you would not expect me to say otherwise?

But now let me ask you a question: do you think it important to know who guides you?

Yes, I do.

So you will want to have a recognizable identity, a guide-personality either given or revealed to you by another sensitive?

Yes, I would like to know who guides me.

I must tell you: it is very easy for me to clearly read that thought from your mental aura. Let me now explain what could happen if you keep this idea in your mind.

You will draw to you through the Laws of Attraction someone from my world who would like to work with you, but they may well be hindered by this dominant guide-thought in your mentality.

Your spirit friend will want to get on with the important work, while your dominating desire would be to know your guide's identity. Furthermore, if you wish for a certain type of guide, a colourful personality – such as those already mentioned – then the intelligence working with you will be obliged to meet that powerful desire-force in order that the lines of communication can be opened up and the work may progress.

You mean they would lie to me?
No, they would meet your need: it is you who would lie to yourself.

We are not interested in names, positions and high-sounding titles, we are concerned with helping the Great Spirit's truths to liberate man's mind from ignorance and fear.

But your remarks indicate that mediums may mislead people, White Owl.
Mediums are only human beings, my friend, and quite fallible ones at that. They, like we who are in Spirit, will doubtless make many silly mistakes.

As far as Our Side is concerned, communication is not as easy at it might sometimes appear. We try to blend our minds and personalities with those of our mediums and we are not always as successful as we would like to be, owing to mental, spiritual, emotional and physical conditions obstructing our efforts at the time of contact.

So, are some guides purely thought-forms, or images, created by the minds of their mediums?
Yes, some are just that.

Thought-forms of – let us say – an elderly Chinese mandarin would appear just like pictures hovering within the mind of the sensitive who has created them, created by his desire-force because he wants this kind of person to make contact with him.

These 'images' have no real life of their own, but they can be seen by us, and sometimes psychically aware people on Earth are talented enough to attune their perceptive powers into the mental frequencies of the medium and clearly register that very thought-form –

– Through telepathy?
Yes; and then the psychic describes this thought-image to its own creator – the sensitive.

The medium then goes home believing he has an old Chinaman as his guide, which is exactly what he thought he had, and what he wanted to hear, is it not?

Yes. But genuine guides do exist?
Oh yes; I am one of them!

Can you tell us something about your own guides, your superiors: who are they?
What do you mean by the term 'superiors'?

Those much higher than yourself, those for whom you work.
I am guided by the Mind and Will of the Great Spirit, who is the epitome of all perfection and wisdom.

Perhaps you are referring to the individuals through whom this inspiration reaches me?

Yes, the hierarchies in the world of spirit – we've heard of these.
There are many wise souls, yes, but even they are ruled by the limitless natural laws. We have no governments here, not as you understand them.

Here there is service and a constant search for truth and wisdom, with a gradual unfolding of greater understanding. But most of all, we know the blessings of true friendship, love and service.

It is love and friendship which motivates us, and it also binds souls together.

So how do you reach Earth to guide, exercise 'control' over, or inspire, your medium friend?
First, I must think myself close to the Earth by remembering what the conditions of its slow and ponderously heavy atmosphere felt like to me when

I lived there, many centuries ago now. I then move through the surface of the astral world and descend to Earth.

Upon 'arrival' I am able to move within what is known as the aura of the medium: his electro-magnetic fields of vibration which are an out-picturing of his soul.

By an intricate process of mental attunement I can then gain access to the frequencies of his subconscious mind, and it is from here that I can inspire him with my thoughts.

It is always a willing co-operation undertaken to forward the Divine Plan.

What is the nature of this plan you've so often spoken about through Stephen?
The plan is now in full operation, and will not fail. It is organized by a vast conglomerate group of minds who have taken upon themselves the mammoth task of liberating the mind, heart and soul of man and delivering spiritual light to the human race.

We shall uncover to his gaze his true spiritual nature and his real state of soul-evolution.

Man has scientifically evolved in a technological way, so to speak, but his spiritual evolution has certainly not gone hand in hand with this advancement. Man on Earth remains, in the majority of cases, a self-centred, selfish creature who expresses little concern for the development of his self, the stewardship of the world in which he lives, or the respect he should have for the other life-forms existing around him.

It is this blinkered vision and ignorance which we seek to dispel with our teachings, by always appealing to common sense.

But surely organized religion has undertaken this task for many centuries?
I would disagree with you; you are gravely mistaken. Many organized religions, to use your phrase, have – by setting up their narrow mental and spiritual boundaries, sects, divisions and 'isms' – caused immeasurable strife, hardship, darkness of the soul and hindrance to the light of true spiritual knowledge spreading throughout your world.

Hypocrisy has always dwelt within the earthly mind of man; what he preaches is seldom what he practises.

So we have decided to go outside these organizations, creeds and theologies, and to reach the masses with our spirit teachings through the loving hearts of those who are specially incarnating now, and whose work will eventually lead the human race forward, out of spiritual darkness and into the liberating light of truth.

Will you give your teachings through sensitives other than Stephen, White Owl? Only we've received reports of you speaking in various psychic circles.
My influence is brought to bear where I believe it is needed, but my channel for the spiritual truths

128

which I have promised to deliver is through Stephen O'Brien.

People on Earth, through no real fault of their own (it is just their somewhat restricted viewpoint), do not fully appreciate the many and complex intricacies involved in the processes of spirit communication.

I was diligently trained for this task over a long period of time. I then chose my medium, and he, me. I then had to guide him and gather together the others of our band of spirits. But now we are an established team, a bridgehead, a partnership: and we two, in a wider sense, are one.

After all this time and effort it would be foolish to seek out others through whom to deliver my message.

We understand, but Stephen won't be here for ever.
What I am charged to deliver will be given during his allotted time of service. When the work is finished, the mission will cease: though I am not permitted to state when that will be. After it expires, my Earth-voice will know silence again, as it did before our work began.

But if I decide to go forward and inspire other channels, they would not necessarily know, would they?

Some are already claiming you're working with them while your medium's still alive.

'Test ye the Spirit'; I think you have heard this before. Anyone can call himself a medium.

Are mediums born, or made?
Where any form of mediumship is evident, you can be sure its possessor has earned every jot of that facility through hard work in prior incarnations.

Mediumship, however, functions more favourably through certain physical bodies because of their chemical make-up, which is why the incarnating servant selects a suitable family group and personally decides on its own destiny and broad future upbringing, before its life materializes on Earth.

Mediums are born with a mission, to play their part in the Divine Scheme of things.

Then what, in your view, is the true job of a sensitive, or anyone who claims conscious connections with intelligences in the next world?
Mediums have a sacred calling – but, if you are a public medium, I have a question for you: what exactly are you doing? You are most certainly *not* proving survival of the human soul after death; some of the best scientific minds in your world, and mine, would find it extremely difficult to prove you are now existing in *your* world, not to mention mine.

Ultimate proof of survival comes when you pass from Earth and arrive in my world. Then there is no doubt about your eternal nature.

Then what are all the sensitives in the world doing?

They are providing *evidence* of survival, but not proof *per se*. They are offering a priceless service to those who feel spiritually lost: the lonely, the ignorant and those who mourn and need knowledge of spiritual realities.

They are comforters and educators.

Are there any other hidden purposes behind mediumship?

Those who are serving in this way chose this time to undertake their current responsibilities – it is all impressed within your spiritual nature, in your pathway, and there are far deeper implications to being a living entity who claims conscious links to us than at first might be imagined.

Mediums should not deceive themselves as to their true role in the Divine Plan.

Do mediums require dedication and commitment to succeed?

Yes, for you cannot be a medium once a week on a Sunday, or only whenever you perform public service. As an aware soul you are continually representing God, the Great Spirit, on Earth – in your own unique way, every second that you breathe.

This is an awesome personal responsibility.

So in what way would a medium's prayers affect a guide like yourself?

Your life is your prayer. You are a flowering tree, and by your fruit shall you be known, for a man

131

cannot lie to himself, or to the God within, or to we ever-watchful friends in spirit.

In my world all is known – for here Thought is King – but Consciousness is the great Reality; all else is illusion.

We are totally aware of your innermost motivation for wishing to act as bridges between us and man incarnate.

Do you have access to our intimate thoughts?
If we desire to know something, nothing escapes us; we are alive and monitoring all that touches your lives. We intimately know all those who are co-operating with us.

We know who is with us and who is against us.

Ours is a very organized world. Sometimes instruments for the spirit need a gentle reminder about this law.

Service is a sacred calling and the voice of the spirit has summoned you to go amongst your brothers and sisters and render service to them in whatever way you can.

So what would you say to a person engaged on any pathway of spiritual aid to his fellows?
Keep on serving in whatever way you can. Your life is important and your talents are important, so use them whatever they may be.

Never for one moment forget that you are touching souls, awakening minds and hearts to the Living Power of the Great Spirit and the fact that It resides in, behind and through all manifestations, seen and unseen. You are a spiritual catalyst, a divine channel for the power of God to effect changes for the better in the lives of His children, many of whom are helplessly lost in the darkness of spiritual ignorance and despair.

But you are an ever-burning lighthouse of the spirit; a bright beacon of truth shining out across the storm-tossed seas of life.

God, through His Messengers of Light, has called you to uphold this sacred office of mediumship. Therefore, do not forsake us, for we are doing all we can to uplift mankind from being a beast to a saint, from vile thoughts to purity.

How can we get a closer awareness of your presences? Through silent meditation, and a heart filled with love.

With all of your love and your willing co-operation we can help the human race lift itself from the quagmire of its animal nature and up into the light of its Divine Aspect.

Each one of you is playing his part in this cosmic jigsaw puzzle of certain evolution.

Seek within: speak with us, and become conscious of the greatest power in the Universe – God, the Infinite Spirit.

But remember that by every thought you think and every act you perform you either degrade and darken your own soul, or else transform and clothe it with raiments of radiant light and love.

Can we earn a place in the state known as heaven by following your advice?
You are building your own heaven, right now on Earth, fitting yourself for a sphere of existence in my world, earned by the daily purification of your mind and character.

Heaven is a state of inner being, of mental perception – not a location, but a mental appreciation. In rendering service to your fellow creatures, in whatever form, you are therefore also adding merit to your own evolutionary state. Always it is the motive of each action which is the most important factor.

Do your best to help, you can do no more.

The seeds you sow today, will be the plants you will reap tomorrow. Some leaves, however, cannot be picked until you join us here in the light.

Whatever soul-abilities you are endeavouring to express, remember that as true mediums for the Spirit you are engaged in a wonderful work indeed: you are actively helping the race to advance, onwards through the sea of life, helping it to sail towards the light of knowledge and into a tranquil harbour of peace.

We need you to help us in our task of raising a struggling humanity out of the abyss of cruelty and into the effulgent light of spiritual love.

So must we have faith and keep on working to comfort and uplift humankind?
Yes: keep faith, but base your faith on the spiritual

knowledge which has been revealed to you.

Blind faith is a barrier to the open-mindedness required by servants of the spirit. You must remove such psychological barriers in order to receive your guidance and inner revelations.

Blind faith obstructs; open-mindedness reveals a pathway.

Fear must also be completely eradicated from your thinking for it prevents contact with us because our mental and soul-radiations are so fine and subtle that such gross emotions can easily sweep away our influences.

So go forward and serve; try to be kind and keep cheerful; for we are just a hair's breadth away, guiding as much as we can.

Just call on us and we will respond.

We are standing ever beside you.

8

'O Great White Spirit . . .'

(An invocation delivered by White Owl.)

O Great White Spirit
from hidden worlds within we have come
to bring our truths and wisdom
to all who will listen.

We consider it a privilege
to forsake our right to exist
within shining realms of light,
earned for ourselves
through spiritual progression,
and return to this dark and often grey earth-world.
In a spirit of friendship we make contact
as elder brothers and sisters
seeking to aid a human family
which stands in great need of
Thy Divine Light
and
Thy Divine Love.

Soul-sensitivity and awareness
are the fields within which we stand,

waiting for man
to lift the veil of ignorance
and discover our presence . . .

Within the flowering of spiritual unfoldment
our silent voices will be heard.
Residing in the secret kingdoms of the soul
our tones will resound within
the minds of men and women everywhere –
in anyone who seeks
to know us
and
to love us.

We need only to hear the cry of the spirit
to respond as quickly as we can.
We need only to sense the loving heart
of one who serves
and we are near.

Where two or three be gathered
in the name of Love,
we will also be there, in the midst.

We are ever surrounding the faithful
as
Angels of Light,
ever ready to comfort and guide;
that all men may know
no child of earth is unworthy
of our co-operation:

and when only one step forward is taken in love
a thousand souls from my world
will step behind
to serve.

In the heart which cares,
in the soul which acutely feels empathy
sympathy
and compassion
for its fellows and lesser life-forms –
in such a mind our inspiration
is as a Living Spring of Clear Waters
flowing
through the mists
of earthly consciousness
and out
into the darkness of the earth-world
as a Guiding Light.

For these, our true servants,
there is no night,
no despair,
no loneliness
and no sense of irreplaceable loss:
they know not grief,
or sorrow
or any lasting pain
which breathes within emotion.
They see only
the Light of Knowledge
and

a bright Torch of Hope
burning in the centre of
a Universal Heart.

In the silence of the hushed soul
we are waiting;
in the purest breast we reside;
in the quietness of a sensitive mind
the link with us is made –
for we cannot function successfully where there is doubt
uncertainty
fear
avarice
self-centredness
or a grevious lack of compassion.
But we are ever near
the faithful
and
the kind.

May it please the Will of the Great Spirit
to bless our work
with the fruitfulness and inspiration
of the Shining Ones
above.

Thy Will be done:
Surely, so let it be . . .

A Visionary's Prayer
(Composed and given by Stephen O'Brien.)

May those who feel lonely and unloved
    meet the arms of another
    and be embraced . . .

May those who feel lost in the darkness
    seek the light of truth
    and find it . . .

May those who have plenty
    give to those
    who have nothing at all . . .

May those who are intolerant of others
    learn patience
    and practise it . . .

And may those who cannot see the beauty of the stars
    open their eyes wide
    and be thankful;

    for then their fear may become certainty
    and their vision, clearer –
    revealing each challenge as a friend.

    And may peace live in their hearts,
        Great Spirit –
    if only for the sake of the children
        as yet unborn,
        who are waiting to come . . .

9

Farewell to a Chocolate Soldier

I'd been earnestly sending up prayers for spiritual healing to aid my elderly father, whose ill-health had been getting increasingly worse for some time, when one day my only brother, John, telephoned with some bad news:

'Stephen, Dad's very poorly. You'd better go and see him.'

It transpired that my father, now seventy-one and grossly overweight at 22 stone (140 kg), and who lived alone, had fallen down at home and remained helpless on the floor for over an hour and a half, unable to stand up on his own.

'Oh, I didn't know what to do,' he said, fearfully. 'I was so weak, I couldn't sit up, boy. I laid there for ages before managing to drag myself to the telephone cable, pull it down and phone an ambulance. They busted the door down and put me right. But I don't mind telling you, boy, I was frightened. It shook me up good and proper.'

After this, Dad made a slow recovery, but then just before Christmas 1991 another urgent call came from John:

'Dad's in hospital, Stephen: he nearly died.'

So I jumped into the car again and sped straight to Swansea's Morriston Hospital where he was recuperating.

'I've had a terrible chest infection, boy; it nearly killed me, but they treated it just in time: another hour and I'd have been a goner. I was shivering and shaking from head to foot and burning up like I was in a furnace. They've taken lots of X-rays and blood tests and I've got to stay here for a week or so, they think.'

'Oh well,' I said, 'as long as you're comfortable now, that's the main thing, Dad. Do you need anything?'

'No, I'm OK. All I want is to get out of this place, boy. I can't bloody stand hospitals, they're for women having kids or people who are gonna die.'

'Now come on,' I said, 'cheer up! They'll soon put you right.'

'Aye, I expect they will,' he said, but I could see he didn't believe it; so my brother and I visited him every day: John in the afternoon and I in the evening.

Despite my father's weight, the doctors said he was malnourished, suffering from a protein deficiency. This didn't surprise us because every day he'd eat at a café where the food was nothing but stodge: potatoes and vegetables boiled for so long that, quite honestly, he'd have been better off drinking the vegetable-water. So hospital dieticians immediately placed him on high-protein food, consisting mainly of meat and fish, but mostly fish.

'And how are we today then?' I'd chirpily ask.

'Oh that bloody food's getting me down!' he'd grumble and groan. 'Fish, fish, fish; all the bloody time! Fish every bloody day! I'll grow a set of fins in a minute and bloody swim out of here in the end!'

Poor old Dad always was a bit of a moaner: he'd grump over the slightest thing and was never a pleasure to have around. If my father had a pain in his little finger or a cut on his toe he'd swear he was in dire agony, ready to be carried off to the crematorium. And he was always moaning about the arthritic stiffness in his neck and the fact that he couldn't walk properly – but when the doctor told him to diet, he paid no attention at all: he would much rather eat and drink as much as he liked, and then sit down and grizzle about it.

But soon another complication set in: Dad contracted a blood disorder, the doctors finding salmonella in his blood cultures. They ordered him to keep scrupulously clean and to wash his hands every time he went to the bathroom; something he'd rarely done, in or out of health, and indeed he continued not to do it, despite strong warnings of reinfecting himself and the nurses on the ward, but all to no avail.

There wasn't a man in the world more stubborn than my father: he only did what *he* wanted to do, when he wanted to do it. He was an exceptionally strong-willed man, except when it came to pain – that was another kettle of fish. I vividly recall that while my mother lay dying of cancer back in the 1970s, after Dad had broken the news of her imminent death to me, which I took reasonably calmly, he said, seriously:

'I don't know how I'm going to get through this, boy. Perhaps you'll be the strongest of the lot of us. I might turn out to be a chocolate soldier.'

'A what, Dad?'

'A chocolate soldier. You know: someone who puts on a brave face, but who melts at the first sign of battle . . . We'll see,' he added, solemnly.

And, as readers might already know, my father did turn out to be a chocolate soldier when his wife passed over: the realization of my mother's death was too much for him to bear, and during her last moments he couldn't face it, so he went to a neighbour's and my brother plied him with drink and he fell fast asleep. So as my mother died, her husband wasn't in the same house: he was a few doors away, out like a light.

Anyway, while Dad underwent further hospital tests, in response to our request for more explicit information about his complaint, his female doctor asked my brother and me, 'Could I see you privately?' and we knew what was coming. We'd already been told he had a cancerous growth in the left lung, and it was I who had explained this to him weeks previously. He knew what he was being treated for – he'd been a very heavy smoker in his younger years – but now his consultant informed us:

'It's in a very progressed state. Radiotherapy and chemotherapy injections haven't stunted its acceleration.' Then she paused before adding: 'I'm very sorry, but all we can do is help to control the pain.'

We, his two sons, were silent for a moment.

'My brother John and I have already discussed this,' I replied calmly, 'and we want to know, will you help our father to die peacefully?'

John nodded rather solemnly in agreement, saying, 'We know him so well. He's not the kind of man who'd want to suffer.'

The doctor's eyes gently scanned the floor and then they looked at my relaxed face, as she said:

'No, I'm sorry . . . you see, we don't practise euthanasia: it's not our policy.'

'But we're requesting it,' I added quietly, 'and I know that my father would, too. Why don't you ask him, doctor?'

I particularly noticed that she registered this last pointed remark of mine.

'While I fully understand your feelings,' she continued, 'I'm afraid there's no way we could agree to that.'

There was another silence while I gathered my thoughts, and presumably everyone else did too.

'Doctor,' I said, 'both my brother and I, and our family, are extremely grateful to you for looking after Dad and for promising him such wonderful care, as he's nursed towards the end of his days on Earth.'

At this point my brother's eyes filled up and were covered by his hand. His head lowered a little and the doctor looked at him compassionately, then she turned to me and said:

'You've obviously come to terms with losing him?'

'Yes. I believe in a life after death, so the quicker my father passes, with as little pain as possible, the happier I'll be – especially because he'll be reunited with my mother,' I replied.

'So for you this is just a pause in the journey and not the end of it?'

'That's right.'

'And what about you, John?' she said, turning to my brother whose eyes were still full.

'I don't think like my brother,' he said quietly.

'So how do you feel about your father's passing?' counselled the kindly doctor.

'Well, it's inevitable and I can face that, but I'd like to be able to talk with him, you know.'

'What about?'

'Well,' he answered softly, 'I'd like to tell him that I love him, I suppose.'

'Then why don't you do just that?'

There was a respectful lull in the conversation.

'Who's going to tell my father?' I asked. 'He has a right to know his true condition. I think it's wicked that people are allowed to die without even knowing the crossing is near.'

'Well, if you like,' said the gentle doctor, 'I'll come up to the ward with you today and the four of us will all have a chat together, and that'll give you the opportunity to speak to your father about things you want to discuss before his last days.'

'That's a good idea,' I concurred, and we agreed to meet the doctor in Dad's little side-room in fifteen minutes' time . . .

John and I got a cup of hot reviving coffee in the hospital canteen, and in silence we drank it. I was waiting for him to start speaking, as I sensed he wanted to; and when he did, I felt we were then much closer than the days when, as small boys, we used to whisper secrets together in the old tiny bedroom we shared way back in the 1950s.

'He won't talk to me,' he said sadly.

'What exactly do you mean, John?'

'Well he just sits there and stares into space whenever I visit him. He won't speak, and I've tried to make conversation, but I just can't break through.'

'What would you like him to say?'

'Well, I don't know . . . I suppose I want him to tell me that he loves me . . . '

I gauged this was not the right time for my personal thoughts on this controversial issue, so I withheld my opinions.

'Listen,' I said, 'the doctor's told us we shouldn't expect Dad to change just because he'll know he's dying. She's watched thousands of people die, and they don't just suddenly drop the habits of a lifetime: they usually die with exactly the same character as they had when they lived.'

Inwardly, I wanted to tell John, now just turned forty, what I truly felt about whether Dad really did love us boys, but I let the moment pass; and we finished our coffee and walked silently up to the ward.

Dad was propped up in his bed, coughing, and as we came through the doors he was violently sick. A nurse and I stood on either side of him and John stood by his neck, and we held kidney-shaped, papier-mâché bowls underneath his chin while he filled them four times over with a green-and-brown viscous fluid, the like of which I've never smelt in all my life before: it was horribly pungent and acrid.

When the human body's healthy it's a wonderful work of art, but when it's ill it's horrendous.

I glanced across at my brother, as good as to say I didn't think an animal, let alone a person, should have to suffer these indignities, as our father was obviously doing.

But he never made a sound did Dad, not a moan or a grumble. He just persevered with having his mouth wiped several times, then afterwards when everything had settled down he said, just like a child would, 'I don't know where it's all coming from, I haven't been eating.'

'It's a reaction to the chemotherapy,' I counselled, honestly. And we both sat down as I added: 'We'd like to have a bit of a chat with you today, Dad, and the doctor's coming along in a minute.'

And in that moment, I think he realized his true condition.

Then the sympathetic consultant arrived and after

some very gentle conversation she sat on the bed and tenderly took Dad's hand.

'Now, Ronnie, how do you feel? Tell me.'

'Oh, you know – good days and bad days,' he said.

'Yes; but how do you *really* feel?' she asked softly.

'To tell you the truth – awful.'

'Well, you know we've given you some special nursing, and I did tell you last week that you've now had the maximum amount of treatments. Do you remember?'

'Yes,' he said – and there was, for him, an awkward pause.

'Do you remember, Ronnie . . . when you were first admitted you said to me, "There's no point in going on living like this." And do you still feel like that?'

'Yes, I do,' he replied without hesitation and with deep conviction. Then Dad looked her in the eyes and said, 'You've come to tell me I'm gonna die.'

There was a long pause.

I noticed everyone's eyes glanced downwards, except my own which fully registered Dad's moment of realization.

Then the doctor smoothed the aged yellow hand which couldn't now even legibly sign its owner's signature in his pension book. John and I looked at him and it was just one of those moments when words were inadequate and everything was conveyed in silence. But the wonderful doctor gazed with such tender compassion at Dad, squeezed his hand again and said, so quietly:

'How do you feel about that, Ron?'

And Dad said something which surprised her, but not us because we'd heard it so many times over the years. He said, 'Everybody wants to get to heaven, but nobody wants to die.'

And the four of us smiled at that.

And that was it.

The moment had passed, and there were no violent hysterics from anyone; my father was remarkably brave about the whole thing.

'Well, Ronnie, you know I have very strong links with Tŷ Olwen (Olwen's House) – the hospice just along the road, and there's a private room there for you. If you'd like to come, we'd be so pleased to have you with us.'

'Oh no,' he said quickly, 'I don't want to go there.'

'But it's a lovely place, Dad,' interjected John, 'Stephen and I have been there – it's a beautiful place and the staff are marvellous.'

'No,' he said, very uneasily, 'I don't want to go there.' And he really meant it. 'Everyone's got to die,' he continued, 'We've all got to go sometime . . . I'll just have to face it.'

'Everything that *can* be done, *will* be done for you, and you'll get the best treatment possible,' my brother added.

'Aye . . . ' Dad said, 'Aye, I know that, boy . . . '

So the kind doctor promised him he could stay a

few more days in his little side-room, and then she'd ask him again about a move; but we all knew that now he understood his true condition, he'd simply give up the fight and slowly slip away from us – which later was to prove correct . . .

On the way to our separate cars, walking down the steep hospital steps and out into the bitingly cold and frosty January air, I took what I thought was the right moment to broach with my brother the subject of our father's love.

'You know, John – don't be shocked – but it may very well be that Dad doesn't love us,' I ventured.

'What are you talking about? Why do you say a thing like that?'

'I suppose it all depends on what love means to each of us. But, to me, he's always seemed such an insular, self-centred man. He had a house, he had a wife, he had friends, he had his club, he had his drink, he had his possessions, he had his money and he had his two boys. I'm not at all sure that we weren't just another part of his life, rather than an intimate relationship within it, as two sons who were loved.'

'You're talking rubbish, Stephen!'

'But that's how I feel, you know,' I said honestly.

My brother fell silent for a while, breaking this with:

'So what happens now? How do you think we should treat him?'

'Like the nurses do: to us he's a man with a history – we've shared time and memories with him – but to the staff he's a seventy-one-year-old sick man who's going to die and needs as much tender loving care as they can give him. I think we should give him that too, no matter what the past has been like.'

John listened quietly, as I went on:

'Even though Dad and I have never really got on together, we've made our peace, you know; and these will be his last days on Earth and, come what may, we've got to be kind to him.'

Then we parted company, both deep in thought . . .

Immediately after this, the doctors attached a battery-powered injection pack to Dad's chest, filled with a pain killer and medication to ease his sickness. In the quiet early hours of the morning – between midnight and 2 a.m. when I'd often sit with him while he slept – I could hear the technology gently whirring as doses were automatically delivered, quite frequently.

Sitting quietly next to the sleeping man, I'd send out my prayers to the Great Spirit, then draw upon the Great Healing Light and pass these energies on to my father as he lay still in the bed. This I did on many nights, praying it might help him have a dignified passing; and at such tranquil, early morning moments I was very aware of my spirit mother's presence close by.

'Look after him, Mam,' I said, 'for he'll soon be with you.'

There was no reply, but my inner soul sensed her acknowledgement: the only sound disturbing the quietness of the night ward was the intermittent ticking and whirring of his injection pack as more medication passed into his body.

On several visits during the next few days, John and I would sit at the bedside while our father, now only semi-conscious, struggled for air.

'He won't be long,' I said.

'No: he could go on for weeks.'

'I don't think so, John. He will just be a few more days,' I said.

Then one morning at about 1 a.m., while I sat alone at my father's bedside on one of my night healing-visits, he suddenly half awoke.

'Hello, Dad. It's me, Stephen. How are you feeling today?'

He groaned something inaudibly.

'You know, I'm glad we made our peace over the last few years, and especially these last few weeks, Dad. There's no point in bearing any grudges, is there?'

He shook his head very slowly.

'Since you've been in hospital we've had lots of conversations about the soul, Dad, and the afterlife, and the fact that we don't go into nothingness when we die, remember?'

He nodded again, tired, and then smacked his dry lips together.

'Well, I spoke to help you with the crossing you've got to make. I hope you knew that,' I whispered, as more injections were automatically delivered into his body.

There was silence between us as my father now closed his eyes while his chest heaved for air, spasmodically, every six to eight seconds – interspersed with six or eight seconds of silence and no movement.

'If you like, Dad . . . I can explain what'll happen to you when you pass through death and go to the Other Side. Would you like me to do that?'

And immediately my father's head laid back to rest on the pillow and he nodded once or twice.

'OK,' I said, 'I'll tell you all about it,' – and I did.

I explained death's painless nature and how his spirit would be released from the temple of his body, and then he'd be free – conscious through the vehicle of his spirit body. And most of all I stressed that afterwards, he'd be standing beside my mother, whom I'd sensed at his bedside, waiting for him nearby. This news, especially, seemed to bring him a great deal of comfort as he drifted into sleep again; and I went home more at peace with myself.

The following night, which – as it turned out – was to be my father's last on Earth, John and I concluded our lengthy visit at about nine o'clock in the evening.

Dad had fallen much deeper into unconsciousness and John expressed a foreboding that we should stay because he felt the end was near. However, we didn't. But at the end of the session I stood up, smoothed my father's brow, and leaned over the bed and kissed his forehead, saying: 'Good night, God bless, Dad,' exactly as I'd done to my mother nearly twenty years previously when she was dying from the same horrendous disease. Then strangely I added: 'Say hello to Mam for us.'

John and I walked silently to the doors, stopped, looked back over our shoulders at the old man lying in the bed, and we both knew his hour was near.

In the corridor, we two brothers started up a much freer conversation, beginning with me saying:

'Just now, in the room, I had a spirit vision of Dad.'

My brother seemed intrigued, so I went on:

'There was a field of bright flowers where the hospital wall should have been, and on a small pathway I watched a young couple walking away from me – I could only see their backs.

'The woman had dark springy hair and was wearing a 1950s flowery-print dress, and he was a stocky man in a sailor's uniform from the Second World War – complete with a hat.

'Then they stopped, and the young man turned and looked back, right at me, and it was Dad: but in his late twenties and walking hand-in-hand with Mam, as a young woman.

'They were together,' I said, 'so he's slowly withdrawing his consciousness, and what we've seen of our father back there in the bed is just the last throes of the body's nervous system fighting for life in this world.'

John had listened silently as we walked, but now we stopped and he asked me:

'How long will he be, Stephen? Have you *heard* anything?'

'Do you mean from the Other Side?' I asked, inwardly quite surprised by my brother's keen interest in my mediumship.

'Well?'

'Yes,' I answered truthfully. 'As a matter of fact, a spirit voice clearly told me, just as we were leaving, "He'll remain unconscious now for several hours." They didn't make it clear whether he'll ever regain awareness in this world; but I feel he won't. We shall see . . . '

Well, my father's eyes did remain closed and he slipped deeper and deeper into his comatose sleep induced by illness, disease, age and the effects of pain-killing drugs, and he never spoke to us again on Earth.

Just over four hours later, that very same night, I was visiting a friend when, at around 1 a.m., I suddenly dropped everything and announced hurriedly, 'I've got to go!' I felt impelled to get to the hospital and I belted out of the house and shot into the car and drove like the wind. As I dashed through the ward doors I saw Dad's side-room curtains were drawn, and a nurse came rushing to meet me.

'He's gone,' I said.

'I'm sorry,' she replied. 'It was very peaceful. We've been trying to reach you at home but there was no reply.'

'I felt compelled to come,' I said, 'I knew he'd gone.'

A sad John came out to greet me, and I asked the nurse, 'Could we sit with Dad, please?'

'Of course, please go in and stay as long as you like.'

My brother had already sat with him for an hour and he said he'd recited from the bedside Bible, 'The Lord is my Shepherd', as words of comfort.

We entered in silence and closed the door.

The room was all spick and span: in the peaceful dim light I could see that all of Dad's personal effects had been removed. A small bowl of fresh flowers and a Bible had been placed on his bedside table – and nothing personal belonging to him was anywhere in sight. And there he lay, motionless in death; but, thankfully, at peace.

As soon as I saw the body, I walked over to him, smoothed back the silvery hair on his forehead and said kindly, 'Now you know the truth, old man. God bless you.'

My brother and I then took seats at either side of him and sat and reminisced for an hour about the life we'd all shared.

'It's the end of an era tonight, Stephen. Both our parents have gone now.'

And together we gathered our many thoughts and memories in moments of passing stillness.

'Poor old man,' I said finally. 'I always felt so sorry for him, you know . . . He always seemed to me to be a very sad and lonely person.'

My brother sighed, looking at the body of our father.

'I did love him, you know,' John said.

'I know you did,' I added. 'And in a strange way, my own way . . . I suppose I did too . . . '

It was a very cold and crisp January day when my father was cremated at Morriston Crematorium in Swansea. Everyone was well wrapped up against the sharp wind as they gathered to pay their last respects. And, just as in the case of my mother nearly twenty years before, I'd offered to take the service but the family had again declined, feeling that my place should be seated beside them in the front pews.

I agreed, but as a personal tribute to my father, halfway through the service I walked to the front of the altar, near the coffin, to read a poem for Dad; and, as I turned round, I was more than surprised to see the crematorium was three-quarters full. All my father's workmates and friends from his club had turned up in a minibus.

I gently spoke to the gathering.

'I'm sure my father would wish me to thank you for your presence here today,' I said.

'My Dad believed in the Kingdom of the Soul; we spoke about it many times in the hospital, and now I want to give my one hundred per cent assurance that I know beyond a shadow of a doubt that he and my mother have been reunited in the world beyond this.

'My father told me he'd thought of my mother, his wife, every single day, and that he'd spent a very long and lonely seventeen years without her since her death. But now they're together again.

'In tribute to my father's life, I'd like to read a poem,' I said; and this I did.

Afterwards, in complete silence, I resumed my seat next to Dad's only surviving close relative, his brother Billy, who'd lived with us many years ago when John and I were children. Uncle Billy, moved by the verses, patted my knee in gratitude.

No words needed to be said.

The service concluded, and we all went home . . .

A few days later I unhappily learned that when I'd announced my personal tribute, some people in the congregation had tut-tutted. I was disillusioned and, for me, this highlighted once again just how hard-hearted the majority of people can be.

Glad that my father was now out of pain and discomfort, I wondered for how long he'd remain silent after death. But before two days had passed, I received an accurate spirit message from a young medium who conveyed a clear description of him, and then delivered three pieces of evidence which unquestionably proved his survival, to me.

The meaningfulness of my father's message was concealed from the medium, but from the world Beyond, Dad felt able to transmit the three points he could never have brought himself to say while here on Earth, even though I sensed he might have wanted to speak them on many occasions. These were:

'Tell Stephen: thank you. Tell Stephen he was right. Tell Stephen I love him.'

The first was his gratitude for my fully explaining

to him his journey through death. The second was something he couldn't ever confess to on Earth, even though he knew I was often right about many things. And the third was the greatest of all, for it was something I'd never heard my father say to any living being.

These three statements addressed the three areas I'd often considered to be Dad's weakest character points, and this was highly evidential in itself.

And now, I'm extremely happy to report that since his passing Dad's also communicated his love for his eldest and closest son, my only brother John.

In fact, since then he's returned several times to give interesting and accurate spirit messages, saying that even though my mother has progressed much further into the world of spirit than himself, they're often together and that, 'I'm not the same man you remember, boy. I've changed my viewpoints a lot and I'm learning all the time, quite fast.'

The light of progression bestows its blessing upon us all, thank God, and I've often sent him good thoughts and wished him well in his life on the Other Side.

And now, whenever I think of my father, of all the memories that could spring to mind, the most poignant is the one concerning the incredible courage with which he bore his illness.

Nearly two decades previously, when my mother lay dying of the same disease – cancer – my father had said of himself, 'Perhaps I'll be a chocolate soldier, boy.'

Well, Dad, in your own time of dire crisis, when you stood uncertainly before your mortality and feared its possible extinction – you faced it squarely, without one grumble of complaint.

You were a remarkably brave man.

You were courageous, and strong, Dad – and you were most certainly not a chocolate soldier.

10

Chuckle-Muscles

These days, whenever I remember my father, many odd memories float back to mind, especially those of my teenage years when I was such a home-loving, quiet child, a characteristic that seemed to bother him no end, and which made him issue loud commands like: 'Now, get out *there*! *That's* where life is – outside that window, not in here, boy! Get out there and live it! Shake yourself!'

So one day, when I was about fourteen, I did just that, joining the local YMCA theatre group where I spent some wonderful adolescent years, still fondly treasured as happy memories. Not only did I 'star' in their Christmas pantomimes but I also wrote some of them, and frequently took roles in my own plays, too – many of which were successfully received.

Our pantomimes were very frivolous and most amusing, and one of the funniest laughs an audience got was caused by the front curtain being sabotaged by a jealous cast member. The heavy drapes rose up by means of a manually operated pulley-system – they were yanked up by pulling on a piece of knotted rope! (None of your modern technology at Swansea YMCA in the early 1970s.) But our crafty saboteur had nailed one end of the drapes to the foot of the proscenium arch, and when the overture struck up and the curtain was also supposed to go up, revealing a tap-dance routine – only one end of the drapes rose off the stage. The opposite side didn't budge an inch, treating the audience to the unforgettable sight of twelve, shapely pairs of chorus-girls' legs tap-dancing, with feet clicking away for all they were worth, all bodiless and face-less! There were hoots of laughter from everybody in the hall until some bright spark unhooked the curtain and the show got under way properly.

Incidentally, one set of those legs belonged to the now-established Welsh West End and film actress, the beautifully featured Catherine Zeta Jones! She and I trod the boards together a few times, but she was just a wee slip of a girl in those days.

Following many such jolly times, readers may remember I then progressed to college, from eighteen to twenty years of age, during which time my mother died, and after this I was introduced to the Spiritualist Church where she returned to me from beyond death and proved her survival in a remarkable way, as recorded in my first book, *Visions of Another World*.

The psychic impact of my mother's spirit return quickened my powers of mediumship and finally made sense of the many disembodied voices I'd often heard, and the silent guidance and spirit presences and impressions I'd intermittently received through-out my young life: suddenly everything fell into place and I perceived the visible threads of a spiritual pattern having weaved itself through my days.

Tightly embracing my mediumship with characteristic vigour, I then whizzed off all around South Wales taking public meetings, not only in churches but also in small halls as my work got better known. I soon became 'a special ticketed event', and was instantly and – I thought – miraculously accepted by an often staid, older Spiritualist generation: certain people who'd so bitterly criticized my youth and inexperience then suddenly couldn't do enough to impress me! A modicum of success meant previously officious personalities now wanted to hitch their wagon to my guide-star, so to speak – which first of all confused, and then amused, me.

But thankfully, the Spiritualists, God bless them, have the remarkable gift of being able to hoot with laughter at themselves – as well as at everyone else! – which is just as well, considering some of the antics and performances that went on in some of their regional churches.

Although hundreds of dedicated and sincerely talented mediums present their services with dignity and intelligence, it must also be admitted that there are plenty of eccentrics in their midst! Some are a constant source of merriment, often saying the most amusing things in public, without even knowing it. One such Welsh sensitive is Gladys: to say she's the Spiritualists' equivalent of Mrs Malaprop (the literary character who always chose

167

the wrong words to mean the wrong things) would be a gross understatement.

Glad frequently got herself into a verbal twist, and one night, during one of her public meetings, she made a most unfortunate remark to a very plain woman indeed. After selecting the lady for a contact, Glad started relaying a spirit message in which she'd *meant* to say, 'Do you recognize a horse from the next world?' But instead, what she actually asked the plain woman was: 'Do you *resemble* a horse?'

After an awkward moment's pause, the poor soul said, 'Yes, I do.'

Everyone had an instant fit of the muffled giggles – all except Glad, who didn't have a clue about her embarrassing *faux pas*.

Other witty mistakes tickle me when I recall them, one of which occurred when a rather befuddled London medium pointed to a woman in her audience, announcing during her clairvoyance:

'Madam, do you know a Constance on the Other Side?'

'Yes,' said the enthusiastic recipient.

'And can you tell me, was she a cook?'

'Why yes, she was!' replied Constance's daughter.

'Ah!' said the triumphant medium with a flourish of her hand, 'I *thought* so, because as she made her contact I felt a very strong apple-dumpling vibration.'

I still chortle over that silly phrase whenever I think of it!

And then there was the northern medium who copied Mrs Malaprop (and Gladys) when he got his descriptions mixed up. What he'd actually seen from the spirit world was a small, frumpy woman wearing a pillbox hat, but when conveying this to his recipient he made a funny mistake by asking:

'Do you know this woman who always wore a *pillar*box hat?'

The ridiculous thought of that frumpy spirit lady tromping around the astral worlds, proudly patting her tufts of hair sticking out from underneath a big red pillarbox stuck on top of her head, keeps me cheerful twenty-four hours a day! Indeed, it's such merriment as this that makes life tolerable and well worth the living!

Speaking of frumps, by the way, reminds me of another occasion when such a person came to a sticky end! It happened when a friend of mine drove me to one of my early small 'ticketed do's' at a church right up in the Welsh valleys. The snow was thick on the ground and we didn't think we were going to reach the meeting-place because the road was frozen with ice, and his car kept slipping and sliding all the way.

Then, about a hundred yards from the small church, it suddenly conked out. 'Oh, bloody hell!' he exclaimed. 'Trust the bloody contraption to clap out here. I hope the bloody thing'll start and we'll bloody well be able to get going again afterwards!' (John was very fond of his 'bloody', and still is.)

'Calm down,' I said, 'a man's voice has just told

me there's a wire loose in the front of the engine.'

'Don't be so bloody soft' he returned, 'it's only just been bloody serviced!'

Then he moaned his way out of the car, lifted the bonnet, and the next thing I saw was his astounded face, wide eyes peering over large spectacles, and in his hand he was waving the loose wire. 'Well, I'll go to bloody hell, O'Brien!' he shouted. 'You and your bloody voices!'

It was just then that the 'star' of this memory, a now-deceased but extremely frumpy and officious Spiritualist church secretary, suddenly bustled into view outside the nearby church door. The nosey old dear tottered forward on bandy legs, swathed in thick black support stockings, and came fussing through the porch into the freezing drizzle. Precariously balanced over her head she clutched a battered copy of an old *Psychic News*, looking like a soggy pyramid that barely covered her freshly permed hair, which itself resembled a tight, shiny golf ball of blue-rinsed curls.

For someone well-known for being so bumptious and 'important' she didn't half look a comical sight as she slid dangerously across the icy road towards the car with her newspaper quivering in the sleet until she reached the windows, glowering at the drenched driver as she passed, and then she peered at me through the glass – much as people stare at monkeys in the zoo. (The poor soul wasn't a raving beauty, either; as a matter of fact I'd often heard her unkindly described as having the features of a pit-bull terrier.) Anyway – she suddenly gasped in horror when she saw me (as I'd done when I first saw her), dropped her jaw to her chest, straightened her back, shot over to the church and screamed at the top of her voice as she reached its portals:

'Doris! It's *him*! He's come! The medium's *arrived*!' – immediately after which she promptly tripped over the front step, fell flat on to the polished floor – spread-eagled with spectacles all awry – then performed the singularly remarkable feat of hurtling forwards on her famed features, like a flattened aeroplane, right down through the outer hall – whereupon she amazed the congregation by gate-crashing through the inner doors! The poor soul!

Oh, I know I shouldn't have laughed, but what with the car breaking down and all John's 'bloodys', and then this bumptious woman's fall from grace, I was well and truly tickled. (But then I'll laugh at anything, as everyone knows too well! I even guffawed when the taxes went up!)

It's no great secret to mediums, of course, that members of the public can often lack a good sense of humour, and even seem quite dense and lifeless when viewed from the platform, especially when confused. I had to laugh once, when a rather famous medium visited Wales and couldn't get such an audience member to claim her message. The bemused recipient was wondering why this frowning, silent medium kept repeatedly stabbing the air in her direction, with a maliciously pointed digit, so she kept looking backwards over her shoulder, scratching her head, and thinking the irate medium obviously wanted someone else to respond from the row seated behind her! At the end of her tether, the rather famous sensitive loudly declared:

'No! *You*! Yes, *you* there, turning round! *You* with the silly blue thing on – the *hat*! *You* with the vacant look on your face!'

(Oh dear!) But smiles broke out all around the room, and my terribly overworked chuckle-muscle – my wobbling diaphragm – was certainly quivering away for a good half an hour after that.

Of course, when messages go wrong it can also be very funny. I remember once linking a father with his very elderly daughter who was sitting right in the front row of an audience – she must have been in her late nineties, and, although she wasn't wearing spectacles, I announced confidently:

'Your father tells me, my dear, that your eyesight is rather bad,' to which the dear soul loudly squawked back:

'*Pardon?*'

'Oh, it doesn't matter,' I said, 'I obviously got it quite wrong!' and everyone had a good laugh at my expense.

And now I can't resist quoting the funny story of a mason's silly blunder. A man who loved his wife dearly, it's said, wanted to make her a special tribute when she died after an illness. Having been such a God-fearing woman, her husband asked the masons to provide a tombstone and inscribe it with the inspiring words: *She was Thine*, which they duly agreed to do.

But the following week the man was horrified when he visited the cemetery because the mason had made a silly mistake on the stone and had left out an 'e', the unfortunate inscription now reading: *She was Thin*!

The furious husband went straight to the mason's and complained, but only the young Yorkshire apprentice was on duty because the manager had gone on holiday; nevertheless the young apprentice agreed to visit the grave straightaway and put the missing 'e' on the stone.

But the next day the husband was absolutely livid when he found the apprentice's further mistake, when on the tombstone it said: *E, She was Thin*!

Humour, of course, also has its pathos, a sadder side which was once proved to me by one of the most farcical and ridiculous displays of so-called public mediumship I have ever witnessed. It occurred at a transfiguration service: this is a special seance where a very rare form of physical mediumship takes place in a darkened room while the medium's face is lit only by a small ruby lamp. Under such controlled circumstances, spirit people are able to get so close to the medium that they can withdraw an energy from him, called ectoplasm, with which they try to reproduce their features over the bone structure of the medium's head. The spirit face then materializes as a kind of misty, semi-material skin, or 'mask'.

I've been privileged to witness this genuine phenomenon. However, the meeting I'm about to describe was more of a cheap vaudeville variety act, or perhaps it should have been advertised as a *dis*figuration service; for that's exactly what it was: no-one in the public hall saw any supernormal changes whatsoever on the face of the plump and deluded male 'medium'.

After suffering through his many gruntings and groanings, and pulling of comical grimaces, which alone could have earned him the title of 'Buster Bloodvessel' or 'Britain's Best Gurner', he then (to go out with a bang) proudly proclaimed:

'My dear friends, there's been so much love here tonight that I'm going to allow the spirit people to conduct a Cavalcade of Faces!'

'Oh, my God,' I thought, 'spare us that.'

But he didn't.

'Now, friends, as the faces come rolling through I want you to shout out their names and give them recognition. Welcome them into this wonderful seance tonight. And here we go!'

And suddenly – quick as a flash – nothing whatsoever happened to the medium's features!

But to my utter amazement, the gullible in the crowd started seeing things which weren't there at all, and in a trice I wondered where on earth I was. 'It's like the Nutter's Night Out,' whispered a sensible woman next to me. And she was quite right; people started shouting out things like:

'Oh look! It's Marilyn Monroe!'

'No, it's Winston Churchill *and* Queen Victoria!' – though how those two beauties managed to get on to the same face together, frankly escapes me. Then someone else yelled:

'I can see Elvis, Elvis Presley!'

'No, it's an Indian!' bellowed a woman from the back.

Then to top it all off nicely, the last person shouted:

'My word, it's Bing Crosby! My God, I can see Bing Crosby. That's *amazing*!'

Amazing indeed, for Bing Crosby was *still alive* at the time!

Every *true* Spiritualist in that hall was thoroughly disgusted by this man's ridiculous performance, and he didn't receive a return booking. The Bible says, 'By their fruits ye shall know them', and I couldn't agree more.

By the way, while we're on the subject of 'gurning' most of my public meetings have been photographed for posterity, and Voices Management has had the films developed over the years by a cheeky young chap called Kevin. He's dealt with hundreds of shots of yours truly – but only about eight or nine have proved worthy of public release! After handing back the last batch, Mr Flashlight wittily suggested to my manager: 'You know, Jeff, you could save yourself a fortune on these photos. Why don't you pocket the money and send Stephen for some plastic surgery instead?'

Then thankfully another friend, Lel, tried to

redress the balance with: 'But Stephen looked *gorgeous* on the television last night. He must have been down in make-up for four hours.'

'Listen,' I said, smoothing my features, 'I'll have you know I have skin like a peach.'

'Yes, a thirty-year-old peach!'

Honestly, it's a good job I've got an excellent sense of humour!

I actually learnt the delicate art of 'papering-over-the-cracks make-up' at drama school in my late teens, and also during the long runs of those hilarious Christmas pantomimes.

Thoughts of my earlier days trigger off many other poignant December memories, especially those spent at the Psychic Centre, a society I had helped to found in 1983, and of which I was a vice-president for nearly three years.

Each Christmas I felt the group ought to help physically and mentally handicapped children.

'Let's get a big fir tree, decorate it on the public platform, and collect presents for under-privileged children,' I'd suggested, and this idea was enthusiastically accepted – and each year we did just that.

Every December the Social Services Department sent us a list of over fifty mentally or physically handicapped children, orphans, or sometimes those sadly lacking in parental love and care. Members of the public 'adopted' each child, whose age and background were roughly stated, then bought them presents which were wrapped up beautifully in coloured papers and foil and displayed under the fairy-light tree.

One snowy Christmas, after we'd had a soul-stirring carol concert, a happy Santa Claus collected all the marvellous gifts: dolls, space games, a huge tricycle for some lucky boy, and my own name-sake's present – a woolly hat and scarf specially knitted and embroidered with a capital 'S' for the five-year-old handicapped youngster called Steven, plus an educational game and some colourful books to help him with his reading.

That night at the Psychic Centre dozens upon dozens of people had turned up and gathered around a special altar where they'd placed lit candles, to symbolize the illumination of the world's darkness. Then each one said a silent prayer for their special loved ones who were held in their thoughts at Christmas-time.

It was an enchanting evening.

In flickering yellow candlelight and with a huge wave of love washing over the people, warm Welsh voices sang out uplifting hymns of praise in memory of the Prince of Peace.

Then later, when the last of the public had filed out after being wished 'A Merry Christmas' and 'Peace be with you', Dorothy, one of the committee, said to me as we both gazed out through the big windows at gently falling snow: 'Stephen, those children will be very happy. It was a grand idea.'

I smiled, nodded, and then lost myself in deep, contemplative thought, remembering the many happy Christmases I'd shared with my mother, when I was lad.

'Mind you, Dorothy, I do feel sad,' I said, at length.

'Why?'

'Well . . . I wish I had the chance to tell some of those handicapped children that one day, when they inherit the world of the spirit, they'll exist in a perfectly formed energy-body: a body free of pain, and fit and healthy. Wouldn't it be wonderful to tell them that one day a balance will be struck?'

'Yes,' she said, 'it would.'

We both stared through the misted glass and watched the crystal snowflakes falling on the YMCA opposite, where many such children had attended those Christmas shows I'd performed in as a lively teenager.

Then Dorothy broke our reverie by suggesting something that, several years later, turned out to be quite prophetic:

'You should record a cassette, Stephen,' she said. ' . . . An educational tape, to help all kinds of people, not just the handicapped. It'd be an excellent way of sharing your knowledge, you know. And I'm sure there's a real need.'

For several moments I remained silent, entranced by the swirling snowflakes outside, and watching the bustling to and fro of the scurrying shoppers, dashing across busy twilight roads, hurrying home with their arms full of brightly wrapped gifts, heads

From beyond death, screen legend Marlene Dietrich revealed to
Stephen private thoughts about her life and career.
(The Kobal Collection)

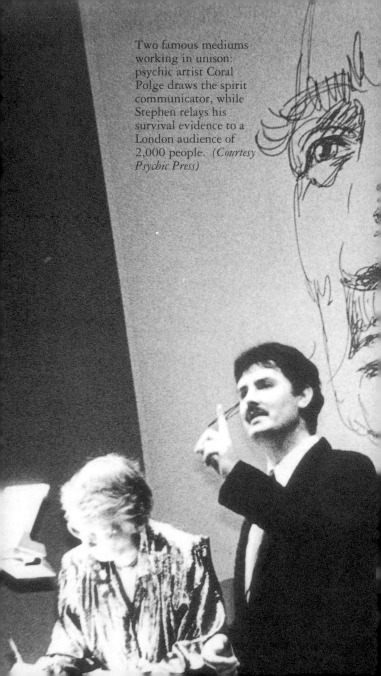

Two famous mediums working in unison: psychic artist Coral Polge draws the spirit communicator, while Stephen relays his survival evidence to a London audience of 2,000 people. *(Courtesy Psychic Press)*

Delivering a spirit message to a recipient in the theatre circle. *Inset:* Stephen's spirit guide, a North American Indian called White Owl.

Queues waiting for an autograph, a handshake and a chat with
Stephen after one of his public meetings.

Two days after his death, Stephen's father, Ronnie, returned to
his son with impressive survival evidence.

Healing by sunlight: a rare moment of relaxation for Stephen. 'A man has time to think in the country, its sights and sounds refresh his spirit.'

STEPHEN ON TELEVISION AND RADIO WITH:

Gloria Hunniford

Michael Ball

Anne Robinson

During his nationwide tours Stephen brings messages of love and hope from the next world to countless people.

'The public have given me something more precious than their encouragement: they have given me their love.'

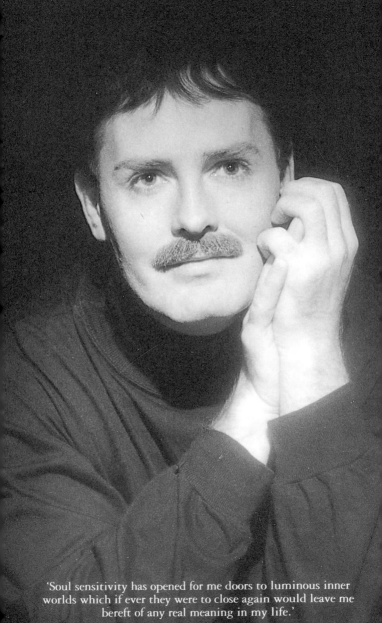

'Soul sensitivity has opened for me doors to luminous inner worlds which if ever they were to close again would leave me bereft of any real meaning in my life.'

down against the cold breeze, and shoes clicking on the hard frosty pavements.

A sudden car horn loudly split the atmosphere and, as the vehicle sped past, a tipsy passenger leaned out of its window and called at the shoppers: 'A Merry Christmas! And good will to all men! And the women!'

Smiling, I gathered my thoughts, turned to Dorothy and very quietly, and rather thoughtfully said:

'Record a cassette? Perhaps, one day, I will . . . '

And we both gazed out at the falling Christmas snow again.

11

What Awaits Us Beyond Death

In November 1990, to meet an ever-increasing demand for me to supply spiritual knowledge, I recorded an audio-cassette which gave many people a basic understanding of what awaits us all after 'death'.

It was an instant success, becoming a best-seller by mail order through Voices Management (the company that arranges all my tours), and it was particularly appreciated by people who found reading difficult, and others who gave it to friends seeking helpful information or a gentle introduction to the paranormal.

By public request, the tape is still available, and details of obtaining it by post, plus other items, can be found on page 369.

Its subject matter remains undated, except that since its recording I've added another two volumes to my life-story: *In Touch with Eternity* and *Angels by my Side*.

Here's the text which many correspondents found 'enlightening', 'healing in essence', and imparting 'many fascinating insights into life in the Beyond'.

The introduction is spoken by James Lewis:

Introduction:
Stephen O'Brien is one of Britain's most famous mediums. He's also a best-selling author and popular psychic celebrity, often being featured on national television and radio shows. Magazine and newspaper articles about him have also appeared across the globe.

His autobiography, *Visions of Another World* is a psychic bestseller, followed by its sequel, *Voices From Heaven*.

On side one of this tape, Stephen speaks about what many people consider to be vital issues in life. And on side two, he answers some of the many and varied questions often put to him by countless thousands of people who have attended his sell-out public tours of the United Kingdom.

So now, let's listen to Stephen O'Brien as he describes for us the soul's journey through life, death, and into the Beyond . . .

Stephen O'Brien's voice:
Before a child is born into this world, its coming is already known. As a conscious mind we have always existed; there has never been a time when we were not in existence. So the soul's journey through its many and varied experiences starts long before it is born of woman into this world.

We are far greater than at first we might think. We are not a physical body with a mind attached –

but we are a mind first and foremost, registering through a body of flesh.

We are consciousness itself, individualized and characterized into our present personality.

The soul's journey towards perfection is a long and arduous one. No soul, no matter how great or insignificant the world supposes it to be, has an easy road to travel. When we come into this life a great many of the challenges, trials and tribulations which we will definitely encounter are already known to our Higher Selves. But through the process of birth there comes a cloaking-down effect which naturally keeps from our conscious awareness who and what we truly are or were before this life.

So we did not begin with our first breath on Mother Earth. We go back much further than that.

Some say the soul chooses its Earth family, environment and physical circumstances before incarnation because these will be necessary for its spiritual progression. Many people find this difficult to accept, but it's certainly worth giving a lot of thought to. And, if we're honest with ourselves, we'll recognize that even though the pathway has often seemed difficult and rough, and we've frequently failed to see the lessons in soul-growth lying behind all the obstacles, we have eventually emerged as much stronger people, with greater experience and more developed personalities.

And so we come to the point of our birth into the Earth-world.

When it happens, it's just the start of another

phase of spiritual growth for us. Sometimes it seems that some individuals are born into highly favoured circumstances, while others inherit abject poverty and cutting hardships. But as passive observers of other people's lives it's impossible for us to know the full extent of stress, challenge and difficulty encountered by another soul on any pathway.

And so birth conveys to the Earth a soul with a mission.

No-one is born without a spiritual blueprint which will broadly direct that individual's life in all facets of its being – physical, mental, emotional and spiritual. The blueprint is constructed by ourselves alone, and is made up of all our experiences.

The inner self knows that life on Earth is a training-ground for souls; a place of learning, growing, somewhere to expand the mind and become increasingly aware of our developing consciousness.

Poets have often referred to Earth-life as a 'vale of tears', but there is also great joy here – and each life-plan decrees we shall taste a wide range of human experiences: lessons of comparison. After all, no-one can appreciate the brilliance and warmth of a summer's day unless they've also known the night. And we cannot truly wonder at the glorious view of the world from a mountain peak, unless we've first dwelt for a time in the shadows of the valley. And similarly, how can we treasure the gift of peace, unless we've known pain and disharmony?

At some time or other, into every life comes the

dark night of the soul; a time when we struggle to find stability, love and contentment, as well as the vibrant joy which consciousness should bring. These inner battles with ourselves are inevitable – no-one escapes them: not rich man, poor man, beggar man or thief.

King or pauper, each of us is a soul on the road of progression, and in order to grow, hardships will be met.

Major soul-growth stems from our interaction of thoughts and feelings within personal relationships and our environment. But there is no force in our lives, no matter how great, which we cannot overcome.

As a wise man once said, 'We are never given a cross to bear, without the strength to bear it.'

Through it all your human spirit can triumph supreme because the mind is master, and the body is servant. By positive wilful thought, each soul governs its own journey forward.

Therefore, challenges should be welcomed as friends, and not enemies, for without them there would be no spiritual evolution.

Meanwhile, as we struggle on, by simply changing our thought patterns we can gain a different outlook which would make our lives much easier.

If a person holds dark negative thoughts and pessimistic attitudes, then the soul looks out into its world through deeply stained glass, and through its own mind sees nothing but despair and gloom.

But thankfully, the reverse is also true.

Bright and cheerful positivity draws to itself a happier quality of life, and the darkened glass is then cleared.

If we think of the soul as a shaded lamp, brightly lit from within by a spark of the Great Spirit's Life-force, it becomes clear that we are personally colouring our understanding and vision of this world. We are continually creating our own heaven or hell, for they are states of mind and not geographical locations. And we can blame no-one for these visions, but ourselves.

Many souls cause themselves untold misery through holding selfish thoughts. These are the people who always want their own way and create havoc when they don't get it. These are the people who are unaware of others' needs, feelings and desires.

The undeveloped soul has thoughts only for itself.

Let's look for a moment at one of the universal laws by which we are all governed: *Like Attracts Like*. Birds of a feather, flock together. We are constantly drawing around us, through our general thoughts and feelings, those of like mind from both sides of life; and it is we ourselves who create harmony or destruction.

In passing, I'd like to say if at present you feel unloved and uncared for, then go out into the world and love and care for others.

And if you feel lonely or uncomforted, then be a true friend to others and comfort *them*.

I think this is what St Francis of Assisi meant

in his prayer, when he said: 'It is in the giving that we receive . . . and it is in the dying that we are born to eternal life.'

And so now we move on to that time which awaits us all – the moment of death; a part of the soul's journey which sometimes strikes fear into the hearts of those who don't know what to expect.

When the physical body takes its last breath and gives up the spirit, life is not ended for the traveller. My conscious links with the Beyond have proven over the years that death from this world means birth into the next. And absolutely everyone survives, no matter how the passing is made – through tragic circumstances, or by natural means, survival is one of the laws which govern this universe, and it's the birthright of all.

And we don't have to hold any particular religious faith to enter the next world. In fact, we don't have to hold any faith at all to inherit eternal life: it will happen naturally.

Having worked with the spirit people for many years as a medium, I've also come to believe that no-one can cross into eternity *before* their time. No matter how near we may be to death, the time has to be right or the crossing isn't made. For instance, I have a dear friend who was once very seriously ill; in fact, she was placed in a hospital side-room to die, after having had an exceptionally large cancerous growth removed from her abdomen. In great sadness all her family gathered around her death-bed, waiting for the end. The doctors held no hope for her whatsoever.

But while she was in her coma she underwent a remarkable out-of-the-body experience. Unknown to anyone on Earth, she floated out of her tired frame and found herself on a marble pathway walking towards an archway, under which she met her mother and father. They had both passed over decades before. Suddenly her mother stopped her and said: 'You've got to go back – you haven't finished your contract yet' – and she immediately awoke in the hospital bed. She was back in her physical body, slowly regaining her health – much to the amazement of her specialists, all of whom had been completely wrong in their prognosis.

At the time of recording, all this happened twelve years ago: so you see, her time to die had not arrived.

This true story also shows that her spirit family knew more of her true condition than the medical profession did.

It's because we're part of the Great Cosmic Mind, that vast Breath of Consciousness known as God, or the Great Spirit, that we survive.

The Universal Mind which placed the stars in the heavens and makes the seasons follow one another in unbroken constancy, is Immortal. And we are forever linked to that unlimited power source, which is everywhere.

God is the macrocosm, and we are the microcosm.

Let's take a look now at what actually happens when we 'die'.

Sudden or 'accidental' deaths sometimes knock the spirit body unconscious, but this type of concussion is short-lived.

When someone's been suffering from a very long illness, however, many relatives and friends from the spirit world are aware of the imminent passing. Then, as the traveller crosses the threshold of death to life, they are met. Sometimes the ill person actually sees those who've come to greet them, and calls out their names. The reason they're present is that they've picked up thoughts – not only from the sick person, but also from the anxious relatives; for when a thought is born, it radiates outwards: just like a pebble dropped into a still pool of water it creates a rippling effect, and our loved ones in the next world home-in on those thought wavelengths.

If an ailing person's been placed on a life-support system, it's possible his spirit may have already passed into the next world. If it has, then, technically, the only thing keeping his body alive is the machinery. But, of course, this is not so in all cases, for some patients recover.

Loved ones who are in a coma and who occasionally regain consciousness are similarly passing in and out of the physical frame.

I'd like to say a few words now about people who have taken their own lives:

Suicide solves no problems, because we cannot die. We simply find ourselves still existing, but in another world. So I must stress, I most certainly am not advising anyone to take their own life; for life is about growth which comes by facing our challenges, working through them, and therefore becoming a more developed soul – and if we can't cope with our lives here in this world, then we shall not be able to cope with them in the next, for we'll take this inability to cope with us into eternity.

So, suicide doesn't solve all our problems.

I'd like to say, however, that these people are not in an outer darkness or in some place of punishment, so often taught by some. They are alive, and still having to solve their attitude difficulties in the next life.

Death itself is painless – in fact, we all die every night when we go to sleep. As soon as the physical body relaxes, the spirit body loosens and departs, travelling out into the next world.

But on some evenings we might not visit the Other Side, but remain close to the earthly body in a state of semi-sleep. Our spirit counterpart then absorbs cosmic energies from all around itself and channels them to the sleeper, who awakes refreshed the next morning.

At the point of death, the spirit body – which is more or less a replica of the physical (but without any deformities) slowly exteriorizes away from the earthly body. At these times clairvoyantly gifted people have seen the two bodies separating and the spirit form linked to the physical by a powerful magnetic connection, sometimes seen as a fine silver thread of light.

When the physical ceases to function, our consciousness then expresses itself through the vehicle of the spirit body. The link between the two forms breaks, and the spirit is then free.

Death can best be described as the releasing of a trapped bird from its cage: the bird is your soul, flying out into freedom and into a world where it can express itself more fully.

In the new body we will have perfect health and a vibrant feeling of youthful strength. And there are many places (or spheres) in which to exist Over There, but those nearest Earth – called by some the astral worlds – contain the counterparts of everything we know here in our daily lives. This is because those spheres have been created by the thoughts of their inhabitants; they've built the kind of world they're accustomed to seeing and experiencing.

'Thought is King.'

'Thought rules Supreme.'

In eternity, there are cities and towns, rolling countryside, flowers and birds, sunshine, water and trees: it's a very real world to those who inhabit it.

The spirit world itself functions or vibrates at a much higher frequency than physical matter, which is why it often remains unregistered by many on Earth. Yet the spirit body, in its own world, has dimension, shape and form and is as real to its possessor as our physical bodies are to us.

On arrival in the next life the soul will eventually take stock of its mission on Earth, asking questions like: 'Did I achieve what I intended to do?' Or, 'Is the Earth a better place for my presence having been there?'

We review our life experiences and, of course, are reunited with our loved ones.

The following words were the conclusion to my book *Visions of Another World: The Autobiography of a Medium*:

And
when we stand
on the shores of eternity
and look back
upon our experiences
in earthlife,
we will notice
how all the things we did
happened
in just the right places,
at just the right times:
And
we shall say to ourselves:
it is good.

After settling down, nearly all spirit people go back and visit the loved ones they've left behind. Many of them even attend their own funeral services. I've officiated at several of these and have often seen the spirit forms of loved ones watching the service, or standing close by their relatives with arms round them, comforting them as best they can.

I've even seen the spirit people *before* their funerals took place. One difficult old lady visited me the night before her service and with her walking stick she poked me in the ribs and ordered me to, 'Get it right, and do it properly!'

We certainly don't change when we die – at least, not immediately.

People who think the act of death bestows upon us untold wisdom couldn't be more wrong. We won't suddenly become the possessors of all the secrets of the universe. Nothing could be further from the truth.

We only take with us ourselves, our minds and characters – everything we've developed during our growth on Earth.

If we couldn't see the future when we were here – then we won't have that ability Over There. Death doesn't confer upon us any skills we haven't already earned.

So, looking to the spirit world to solve our difficulties is of little value. Our problems are our own and therefore we must solve them; besides which, the spirit people most certainly don't have all the answers. They are progressing, just as we are.

Regarding their work in the Beyond – they're very busy people indeed. If they so choose they can follow the arts or sciences, or pursue further education, or perhaps learn about spiritual healing. In fact, anything their hearts desire.

There's no need for them to work for money though, as it's largely unknown in the spirit world. Work is undertaken because to serve others is the best way to progress and gain a deep and lasting sense of self-worth.

In fact, many opportunities denied us in our world, perhaps because we didn't have the necessary qualifications, may now be available in the Beyond because *the inner motive* is the most important thing of all Over There.

Some communicators who've passed tragically young – let's say, in a motorbike accident – often decide to help other youngsters crossing under similar circumstances because they're well equipped to help them understand what's happened to them.

Progress is open to every soul, including the animal kingdom.

So, if you've lost a loved one, remember there is no such thing as death – it's just an illusion. And what seems like the end is just the beginning of a new adventure for the person making the crossing.

And when your own time comes to make the transition, have no fear in your heart.

As I wrote in *Visions of Another World*:

I have stood on the mountaintops of the shining lands and experienced countless visions of other worlds beyond death, and I am not afraid to die; for death is the great liberator, the bright angel who leads all living things into an eternal life, which is their natural birthright.

I'd like to finish now by reading one of my short inspirational poems, taken from my second book *Voices From Heaven: Communion with Another World.*

I think it sums up the message of comfort and hope I've tried to give to so many people during the course of my calling. It's just a few short lines but, as I read it, perhaps you'd like to replace my voice with that of someone you dearly love who's passed into the higher life.

If they could speak to you now, maybe they would say:

Do Not Forget Me

Do not forget me when I go,
For go I must, I cannot stay;
But do not forget my face, my love,
Nor my life, I pray.

Yet, if you should forget awhile
When I am gone — do not despair,
But keep your tears at bay,
For the silver love we shared
Will never fade away.

And one dawn soon,
Together we will stand
Upon some silent mountain, in some silent land,
And gaze into each other's eyes once more;
Then, hand in hand

Along some distant shore,
We'll remember all the times that slipped our minds:

> Our fond goodbyes;
> The times we loved;
> The time we met;

My love, we'll not forget.

12

Questions and Answers

Edited extracts from side two of the educational cassette: Life After Death, What Awaits Us in the Next World. *Questions posed by James Lewis.*

Stephen, I'd like to start by asking you if everybody survives death?
Yes, of course they do: there is no such thing as death. Every soul survives; even animals have souls, and they survive too.

And do the spirit people eat and sleep?
Yes, if they want to. The spirit body is the energy body; it's only the physical body on Earth that needs food. The spirit body draws energy from God, the Great Spirit, so we don't need to eat when we're in the next world – but of course if they want to, they can, because all manner of fruits and foods are duplicated Over There.

If they want to sleep, however, that's slightly different. They can if they wish, but mostly when they want to rest they just lie down on a grassy bank or on a couch, or take up another mental pursuit, because a change of scenery is very often as good as a rest, isn't it?

It is, yes. What about clothes, Stephen, do they wear any?
Oh yes, of course – well, nearly all of them do anyway! Mostly they're clothed by thought, the same as us in this world. When you get up in the morning you take thought before you don your clothes for the day, and it's the same Over There.

If a woman has passed over and she had a favourite outfit, by the power of thought she can clothe herself in that, but mostly they wear spirit robes which are – how can I describe them? – they're a kind of loose-fitting robe or universal garment, and they come in all different colours.

Something I find a little difficult to understand is speech. What language do they speak in the spirit world?
Well, any language they want, but mostly their mother tongue. If a person were French or German, then his mind is ingrained into that way of speaking, so when he passes over he'll continue to use that tongue.

But what we have to remember when thinking of the spirit world is that behind everything is thought, so thought is the reality; and thought can be conveyed from one soul to another – no language is really necessary.

If a mother loves her son and wishes to convey

that love she doesn't have to express it in speech, she can send it to him and he will receive it.

What about day and night?
In the spirit world, you mean?

Yes.
Well, there is no night there, they have an everlasting day.

How can I put this to you?

Mind conditions its surroundings, so there is eternal day Over There. There's no night because the spirit light – the glowing sun that lights up their world – is very, very high in the sky (there is a high atmosphere) so there is everlasting day.

Something which I'm always being criticized for is being late, so what about the concept of time in the Beyond. Does time exist?
Well, if you're late in this world, you know, you'll be late in the next as well!

But they don't follow the clock Over There because they have no day and night, therefore they can't mark out days, weeks, seasons, months and years: there's no clock-time in the spirit world.

They do have time, but not as we know it. Time as we know it is an illusion: we're trying to mark it out into chronological time, and that's an illusion. What they have is the true time which is the Eternal Now – and that's what we've got, too. We're living in the Eternal Now, and even as I say that 'Now' has gone and there is another 'Now' – so it's a succession of Eternal 'Nows': no clocks.

You mentioned briefly before how important thought was. Does this apply to the way the spirit people travel from one place to another?
Yes, it does. We all travel by thought: if we want to make a journey in this world, first and foremost we must think about where we want to go, and then we have to use thought to get our physical bodies on to some kind of transport. It's the same in the next world, but it's more direct.

If they put their mind on a place and home in on it – faster than lightning, faster than sound, faster than light – they will be there, once they've perfected this idea of travel.

Of course, Earth transport is duplicated Over There for those who want it. I mean, if you fancy going down a canal on a boat of a lazy afternoon, it'll be there for you. And of course we'll still have limbs and bodies so we can stroll, walk or run.

Keeping on this subject, Stephen, can you explain to us your thoughts on prayer?
That's a difficult one for me, because prayer is an intangible thing. I would say it's a stream of spontaneous thought, born of desire in the heart of the person praying.

The person doing the praying is opening up his own soul, raising his mind and linking it with Inspiration and the God-force which is waiting to pour into it;

so it's a soul-exercise to get your own guidance, your own healing, and to get your own strength from your Creator. That's the main purpose of it.

Of course, there are also prayers which we send out for others.

Let me ask you a very personal question: do you believe in a God who hears our prayers?
Oh yes, undoubtedly. I believe in God – not as a person but as a Life-force, a Consciousness, a Great Spirit, and I believe that we're all linked to this Great Spirit and therefore we're a part of the Great Spirit. That makes us His children. So we're all God's children and that makes us brothers and sisters.

When we pray, our prayer moves out on this power of thought, and it's usually picked up by other small portions of God's Spirit, that is: our loved ones, the people who care for us and watch over us, and it is they, I believe, who do their best on God's part to answer our prayers.

Let's look at the area of personal relationships now. I'm sure many people would be interested to hear your views on these. For example, if a woman marries twice, which husband will she be reunited with in the spirit world?
Well, it's a bit complicated: the answer is both of them, neither of them, or either of them. It's entirely up to her, because the soul has free will.

One man said, many years ago, 'In the Kingdom of Heaven there is neither marriage nor giving in marriage,' and that's very true. What binds souls together is the power of love, so provided that two souls love each other, they'll find each other in the next world and they'll remain together. So if the lady loves both her husbands she can exist with and see them both.

If she's just drawn to the one she will see the one, or it may be that all three will decide to go their separate ways.

But of course, there's no end to life so they can remain good friends anyway, can't they?

So when we lose a loved one, are they always with us and at our side, and do they know everything that we do?

Oh, no. I know a lot of people believe that, but I have to say from my experience that the spirit people aren't always beside us and neither do they know everything we do.

You see, the world of spirit is existing at a higher frequency, and they're busy Over There, they're working, and if they want to know what's going on in our world, just as the listeners to this tape have had to turn on the machine and listen in, so do they in Spirit have to tune in to our world, and we have to tune in to them.

Provided that attunement is made, each world will know what's happening in the other.

They visit us, but no, they're not always aware of everything that goes on here.

So when they communicate their survival to us, through you at one of your large public meetings, or on a one-to-one basis in a private consultation, are they always successful?

No, they're not. In a great many cases they *are*, I have to say, but contact between two worlds is an experiment: it's a telepathic attunement, a joining of two worlds on a wavelength of thought and love.

It's rather like TV and radio waves which are passing through this world this very second: we can't receive them and translate them unless we're tuned in to their particular wavelengths. We must have a set or a channel to pick up the signals, and mediums are the same; we have to have a medium who can pick up the thoughts, voices and sounds coming to us from the world of spirit.

Also, we must remember that radio and TV sets can go wrong, so it's not an easy job for communicators from the next world. A great many of them are very successful, but for the reasons I've just given, it has to be viewed as an experiment.

Those who push themselves forward to get their message across will do so, whereas the shy ones on the Other Side sometimes stand back and I have to encourage them and say, 'Come on, now, let's have your message, I'm willing to listen to you.'

And, of course, there's the medium's sensitivity: the message is reaching us, but is the medium developed or sensitive enough to pick it up clearly? Do you see what I mean?

Yes I do.

Now, one of the most tragic areas that you must encounter is the death of a child. It seems to make little sense to us here on Earth.

Are you able to give any news and comfort to the grieving parents?

Yes, I am — because as I've already said everybody survives, even miscarried and stillborn children. The spark of Life is there, the spirit body is within them, and although the physical body is lost — even while it's being carried by mum — the child will be born into the spirit world: it will grow and mature.

They're not dead.

The child is still alive. And, you know, a lot of people think that the child has to belong to a particular religious faith, or it must have been christened or baptized into a particular religion in order to live after death, but that certainly isn't true.

We're all parts of God, and because of this, we survive. God isn't going to overlook a little child just because it hasn't been confirmed into a particular faith.

Does the child then still grow on the Other Side?

Yes, right up to the full bloom of youth, to a time of maturity where they feel strong.

And of course they regularly visit their parents, and they never ever forget their mums and dads because of these consistent visits to Earth. In the dream-state when mum and dad are sleeping at night and their spirit bodies move into the spirit world, they can reach their children, meet and love them, and speak to them Over There.

The family in the Beyond takes care of the little ones.

Let's move on to another important area now, Stephen, the area of spirit guides. Do we all have guardian angels?

In a way: yes, we do. I know there's a current trend on Earth to think each person has one particular spirit person attached to them, right through their lives, but I don't know I entirely agree with that.

I believe we're personally responsible for governing our own lives in any world whatsoever.

So I would say: yes, there are many people on the Other Side who are interested in us, attached by ties of blood, relationship, or simply spiritual kinship. We do have people watching over us, but not necessarily, I think, one particular person.

Like spirit guides, an area that's been written about a lot is that of poltergeists. What exactly is one?

(smilingly) Ah well! We're into the area of Hollywood now, aren't we?

Poltergeist roughly translates as noisy or trouble-some spirit. These are people who have passed over and are bound to the Earth by their desires: 'Where your treasure is, there will your heart be also'.

So if someone was very, very materialistic regarding his possessions, then that's his treasure and so his heart will be there: he'll stay close to the Earth, for that's where he wishes to be.

The word poltergeist indicates the actions which some of these people are able to perform. Sometimes they can move an object, but they can't do that unless they first draw psychic power from people in the house – there must be mediumistic people present.

Having said all that, in the years that I've worked as a medium – and with researchers and psychologists – in my experience much poltergeist activity is *not* poltergeist activity at all. In fact, it doesn't even come from the spirit world.

What is it then?
Well, I think it's often a child or young person in the house who has reached the age of puberty. At such times the hormonal levels in the body change greatly, and then the aura – the electromagnetic field of energy surrounding the body – throws off immense psychic energies which can actually move objects.

A lot of poltergeist activity is actually spare psychic energy emanating from someone in the house, and not spirit-based at all.

I'm sure many people out there will be glad to hear that.

Most people have heard of spiritual healing, and of course you yourself are a healer. How does it work? Well this, of course, is one of the subjects close to my heart. Spiritual healing is a spiritual energy and it comes from God, through the healer, into the electromagnetic aura of the patient.

We think of it as a love-force or a correction-force which comes *from* spirit, *through* spirit, *to* spirit: from God the Great Healer, through the spirit of the healer, and to the spirit of the person requiring it.

So it's an exchange of energy, and doctors on the Other Side – plus guides and helpers – help mediums such as myself to transmit this energy to the sick and the suffering, wherever they are.

Incidentally, in recent years there's been some very good news in the healing profession, because the British Medical Association have now given doctors permission to refer their patients to spiritual healers, provided, of course, that the doctor maintains overall responsibility for the welfare of his patient.

Spiritual healing works on Love, and I think it's probably one of the greatest gifts that anyone can possess.

Do we need to have faith for this healing to work? No, no: it works because it's a psychic science, it works because God is there, and we are Spirit, too.

It comes to us through a series of natural laws,

but I'd like to say that if you *have* faith, it certainly helps. Jesus the Nazarene, when he healed people, said: 'According to your faith be it unto you'. What he meant was that if you have faith, if you yourself believe that it's going to work, then you start up a wonderful self-healing mechanism, kicked off inside you: your body starts to heal itself, as well as with the healing coming from God through the spiritual healer.

When people require such help they should really find recognized healers who are registered nationally. That's probably the best way to go about it. Maybe their GP can refer them to spiritual healers.

But it works because of Love and God, and certainly because it's a psychic science – so you don't really need faith.

Supposing then that I wanted to visit a healer. What could I expect?
A natural process. You'd probably meet a very gentle, kind soul whose motive is to serve because of compassion and love for suffering humanity.

They'll settle you down in a chair nicely, talk to you, they may touch your shoulders or hands – that's contact healing – or they may sit (alone or in a group) with you in mind and send out healing by thought and prayer – that's absent healing.

We know there's been a lot of study on spiritual healing, and yet some people don't respond to it and death occurs. Have you any thoughts as to why that should be?

Yes, I believe through my experience that nobody passes until the time is right. So even if they're receiving spiritual healing, if the soul is ready to move into its next stage of development and growth, through the natural laws which govern us, then their time is up and that person must pass.

Having said that, there are two more things I'd like to say. Death isn't the end of life, it's the beginning of life in the next world. And secondly, spiritual healing can relieve pain. It can bestow a more dignified passing on the person who is about to make the crossing.

Staying with the medical side for a moment, what about people who have lost a limb in this world, or who have some kind of physical deformity? Will they still be deformed after death?

Goodness me, no. The spirit body exists in perfect health. Whatever you do to the physical body, you cannot damage or make ill the spirit body. So if someone has lost a leg, for example, it's only the physical limb that's gone: the etheric limb will be unharmed in the spirit body. That's the law.

What about people with mental difficulties and special needs?

The same thing applies: such difficulties arise because there's something wrong with the brain. The brain is the computer that registers the mind through the power of the spirit, which then manifests as action in the physical world.

If the brain malfunctions it doesn't mean that the mind isn't perfect. It's the brain that is the problem; and once the brain passes and the person dies, then a balance is struck and they'll have freedom of expression.

There's a reward at the end of the day for anyone suffering in this way.

We've discussed the medical field in some depth. Let's move on now to an area in which it seems to me more and more people are showing an interest, and that's the area of reincarnation.

This is when a soul comes back to be birthed as a different individual. What are your thoughts on it?
Well, obviously I'm not the Great Spirit, so I don't have all the answers, but, with God, I believe all things are possible. I fervently believe that.

So reincarnation is possible. I can't prove that to you, and I believe that a lot of souls who say they've been reincarnated would also have difficulty in proving it to you, because there are lots of alternative explanations available.

But I think that, for example, Mother Teresa of Calcutta is a wonderful example of an old soul who has taken up a mission to come into the world again and show us what the power of love can do.

Martin Luther King in America – I think he was an old soul who came into the flesh again to take up the job that Abraham Lincoln started, that of helping to free black people.

The soul itself undertakes to incarnate because of its own free will and of its own choosing: no-one Over There tells it to do so. So the souls that come back, are souls with a mission.

You've said that God is a Great Spirit. I'd like to pursue this and ask you why God allows so much suffering in this world?

I don't think God does. I've already said I don't think of God as a person or a vengeful deity who wreaks havoc on those He doesn't like and pours His love on those whom He does.

I think God is a Great Spirit, a set of natural laws that govern the Universe, and one of the most important laws is possibly the law of *Cause and Effect*, which many scientists accept. This means we put causes out through our thoughts, words and deeds, and eventually we reap the effects of them.

I think suffering is the effect of possibly a number of causes that we've put out into the world. So for me, suffering means breaking the laws of the Universe, under the umbrella of which we live.

Through free will we can put ourselves in harmony with these laws of nature, and if we do that we'll gain inner peace and radiant health, and if we don't – we'll gain disharmony and disease. So I don't think suffering is God's fault, it's our fault because we don't align ourselves with these wonderful laws that govern health.

Do you, then, believe in the Devil?
No I don't. I'm often asked that question, and I don't.

I believe man has the power of God in him and through his free will he uses that power to create beauty or to destroy. So I think it's man's free will that perpetrates many of the misguided acts on Earth.

I'm not very happy, you know, about the word 'evil'. I always think about misguided souls rather than evil souls. And of course, like attracts like. So if a man in this world isn't a very nice person – inasmuch as he's selfish or self-centered, or he may commit terrible acts within society – that man will draw to himself people of a like mind from the next world, because *like attracts like*.

So the only Devil I believe in, is man.

If man looks into the mirror he'll see the most cruel animal that ever stalked the Earth.

Or if his vision is different, he could see a wonderful part of God that can love, care for, teach and help others.

Can I take you on to another common subject, Stephen? We have all heard of people undergoing major surgery and being pronounced 'clinically dead' on the operating table, then they suddenly come back to life and report that they've undergone an out-of-the-body experience and either travelled down a tunnel or into an all-engulfing light. What do you think exactly happens in these cases?

212

Quite simply their consciousness has exteriorized in the spirit body; they've moved from the physical body just a little and then returned to bring back the message.

They weren't actually dead, but they moved out into the world of spirit.

The all-engulfing light could be the light of the spirit world which is brighter than in this one. And the tunnel, I don't think anybody is sure of what that is. Some people think it's a mental representation, a symbol. Being freed out of darkness into light, perhaps the mind may be picturing this as a tunnel.

There are many theories and I don't really know how to answer this one, but what I do know is that those people have made a little journey into the next world.

A lot of people who've had this experience come back with the absolute conviction that they are never, ever, going to die, and many of their lives are changed for the better. I don't know if you've ever heard that on television?

Yes, but I've also heard that some people believe it's the subconscious beginning to prepare for death. What do you think about that?
That could be a possibility, except that a lot of people who've had that experience have come back to life in this world, and are still here!

If I came to you, Stephen, and called you a fortune-teller, what would be your reaction?
Oh, I'd say you were in the wrong place because mediums and fortune-tellers are totally different.

In fact I've just read an article which somebody did about me: it arrived this morning out of a newspaper in the north of England, and they've said that mediums look into the future and can foretell your future partners. That's completely wrong.

It's not the first time, by the way, that journalists have been wrong in either quoting me or talking about my life.

Mediums are not fortune-tellers; mediums link to people in the next world. Fortune-tellers have no such link. They are pure psychics and what they do is either read your mind, your aura, or your circumstances. And very regrettably a lot of people go to a clairvoyant, or a fortune-teller, and pay them tremendous amounts of money, which always distresses me, to be simply told all that they already know.

Mediumship means communication – fortune-telling means psychic work.

Many people today are very concerned about the misuse of nuclear power. But supposing full-scale nuclear war broke out, utterly destroying the world which we know. What would happen to the spirit world?
Nothing at all. You can't destroy Mind or Spirit: it's

indestructible, immortal, it cannot be harmed. So the spirit world would still be there.

As you look forward, Stephen, can you ever envisage a time when there will be no more war in this world of ours, and can mankind ever live in peace?
I have to say that only when individual souls birth the idea of peace within their hearts, and then actually live it out with all the love that they possess – only then will peace reign on Earth as it does in heaven.

That concludes the tape, but following on from the wide interest generated by my last book, I'll now tackle some more of the unusual, and sometimes quite personal, questions about myself, my life and work, asked on my public tours.

Let's go live into the theatre:

Does abstinence from sexual activity help the soul to realize its Greater Self? Has it helped you? Are you celibate?
Everything has a purpose and I don't believe we'd have been born with sexual characteristics if they weren't important in helping the evolution of our soul-natures. Abstinence from sexual intercourse is a personal choice. Some mystics have chosen and have publicly advocated this path for various reasons, but I have not. To deny one's sexuality and its obvious impulses could cause deep psychological problems.

I would, however, advise moderation in all things.

So no, I'm not celibate; though there've been times in my life when it certainly felt like it!

What are your vital statistics?
Thirty-eight, thirty – and *never you mind*! (laughter and applause)

In In Touch with Eternity *you said 'people can be irritating': isn't that a rather unspiritual comment?*
No, it's the truth.

What does being 'spiritual' mean? Surely one mustn't be a liar or a hypocrite to be 'spiritual'? To obtain a firm basis for progress, first and foremost we should be honest with ourselves. We can't lie to ourselves.

I can love and respect the God-spark of Divinity within every soul, but the way that light is shaded, or partly obscured, by the personality often leaves much to be desired.

There's a very true saying: it's easy to be an angel until somebody ruffles your feathers, and sometimes, especially if workloads are stressful, I don't think I'll ever fly again!

Stephen, as a devotee I've followed your work and teachings for years now, and gained much benefit from your lectures, discourses and demonstrations, but I'm particularly interested in your growth as a person.

Your three autobiographies have shown three very

different Stephens. Why is this; and which one is the real you?

None of them are the real me, sir. *I* am nowhere to be found in my books because they're just records, memories of the growth of a personality through its life experiences – but *I* am not that persona or 'mask'.

The real me – the soul, the essence of my true self – lives beyond individualization, thought and emotion – and it transcends clumsy words and descriptions.

If you are not a 'who', then what are you?

I'm a part of God, the Great Spirit; a consciously aware reflection of the Universal Mind, just like you. But the difference between us, is that I may have realized this, and perhaps, as yet, you have not.

If you come from God then surely you can convey something more important to the world and its thought than our survival after death?

That's true, but I'm currently materializing a carefully prepared spirit mission which I agreed to undertake before my birth and, at the moment, this part of the message incorporates the teachings of soul-growth delivered through mediumship. But beyond these beginnings lies a much greater purpose, a more profound message which has yet to be delivered.

I disagree with the last questioner, because I've

found many hidden spiritual lessons and deeper teachings about the meaning of life and the pathway of the soul in your books, Stephen. (spontaneous applause)

Thank you; I can only say that there are seeds of truth within my writings, readily accessible to those who can perceive them.

I was most interested when you wrote that within relationships once respect is gone, that relationship is over. What exactly did you mean by respect?

Respect means allowing another soul the time and space to freely express itself, to be given the kind of unfettered freedom that you yourself desire.

Respect asks nothing for itself, because it doesn't give in order to receive.

Making a big show of respect to someone in 'higher' authority over you is nothing but fear or cunning, masquerading itself to gain its possessor future rewards.

In any relationship, real respect means having a sensitive appreciation of the intrinsic right of other individuals to express their feelings, opinions, life styles and thoughts according to their levels of development.

A man with respect doesn't condemn others for being different from himself, so I'd place respect hand-in-glove with toleration, unconditional love and graciousness.

When respect is missing in relationships, what exists in its absence? Surely: turmoil, bitterness, shallow judgement, and a myriad physical and psychological barriers curtailing the free-flowing thoughts and activities of others.

There can be no happiness amongst all this.

It's better to live alone in peace and freedom than to suffer all the soul-crippling indignities that a lack of respect breeds.

If the delicate flower of respect withers away, then true spiritual love couldn't have been living within that relationship – for if love had been there, respect would not have died.

So would you advise couples who are spiritually at loggerheads to stay together for the sake of their children, until they've grown up?
I can't make decisions for others – we're all personally responsible for ourselves – but surely it's better for children to mature with one balanced, emotionally stable parent, rather than exist in a home poisoned by anger or rent with frustration, ceaseless bickering and argument?

Is it right that you teach we know when we're going to die?
Yes, just as you knew when you were to be born, and this information resides in the Higher Self.

But if we know what our future lives will be, having mapped them out during sleep-time existence, what's the point of incarnating when we know the outcome?

Knowing it, and *living* it, are two quite different experiences.

How can people who are trying to be spiritually minded ever be happy in this sad and ugly world, Stephen?

Happiness has nothing to do with the world, or anything or anyone else which seems to be 'outside' of ourselves, because happiness is purely a state of appreciation – it is *within*.

Everything is passing and transient, except *you*, the inner being: your consciousness will remain for ever, so the most important task is to set yourself right, realign yourself with the Universal Laws, emotionally and psychologically.

Instead of building castles in the air and wasting energy chasing fanciful desires – forget all that: stop these negative thoughts from today. Instead, take a long, cold and objective look at what you *already* have around you in your life.

Make a comprehensive checklist: write down and identify everything that's breeding misery and discontent. Then systematically remove all those obstacles (if you can).

After this, you'll feel much better because you'll be subject to less inner stress, and will feel far more mentally free. Removing the misery cleanses the mind, and it's from this stable position we can count our blessings and go forward to build a much brighter future.

Should a person who is spiritually searching for God, and Self, or the meaning of existence, forsake society and the world to become a hermit, or live alone, or go into some sort of closed religious order to find answers to his questions?

Not necessarily, for all the answers lie within the Self; and by this I mean the Eternal Consciousness, that essence of the Great Spirit's life-force which pulses deep within each being: this is where the solutions will be found – nowhere else. Within the Self we can also blend with helpful inspiration and spiritual guidance.

Even during strenuous activities, we can find inner peace. But whether we stay in society or not, we can't escape the fact that we're all very necessary to one another: we like to think we're independent beings, but in fact we're all interdependent.

In the light of this, what does running away gain us? Who was it that built the hermit's mountain cabin? Who formed his steel axe and hammer? Who beat out the nails from hot metal? Where did the recluse obtain his clothes?

You can't deny the material world on the one hand, and then buy your food from the city merchants with the other.

No man is an island; we need each other. The very chair you're sitting on was fashioned by someone's thought, skilfully materialized.

Every problem – great or small – must eventually be faced, challenged and solved through personal effort. But all these solutions are already living within the Self, side by side with their causes – and what the questioner must do, is find them.

So we should remain amongst people while seeking out the Way?
You can be in the world, but not necessarily of it. Surely it's better to give service than to ignore humanity's pitiful cries for help? We have an eternity in which to solve our difficulties.

As one of your followers I was shocked to read some of your tour manager's contributions about your good self in your last book.
Don't be; they're only one man's thoughts.

Stephen, I especially like your spiritual poetry. Are your poems given to you by outside intelligences or are they all of your own making? And will you be publishing them in volume form?
My poetry is inspired and born in many different ways, sir, but generally it springs from my own mind.

I'm pleased you've enjoyed it, and I will be publishing a volume, though I don't have any dates yet.

You talk a lot about loving, caring and sharing, but you don't have children, you say you aren't interested in personal relationships, so what can you possibly know of love?
Please don't assume that by reading my books you now know me, sir; hundreds of correspondents write

saying they feel I've been a part of their lives for years – but this is, perhaps, sentimentalism, an emotional reaction to my life and work.

Only those intimately connected to me might understand me – and only they know who they are.

As a very private man I do find your question rather personal, but nevertheless I'll answer it:

I most certainly know what it is to give love, freely from the soul, unconditionally, with no strings attached. I've also been extremely fortunate to have felt deeply loved in return, and, of course, like many others, I've suffered several losses.

So life hasn't passed me by, sir, and I'm just an ordinary man with sometimes very powerful needs, desires and thoughts, just like yourself.

How Deep is the Night

How deep is the night
how still the air
how silent is the sleeping city
how empty is this room
      since you went away.

     Alone in the silence,
       I remember when our nights were filled
        and the air was living-bright
         and the city's sleep passed unnoticed
         in a dark room, full of light.

But now, you've gone
– I know not where –
      and the night is void with loneliness
      and all that's left
      are flickering mem'ries
      galloping across the lighted hills of my mind
         watering my sight –
      but I'll never be blind.

      . . . Tonight, my breast is still,
               inside a velvet darkness . . .
      deepening the night,
       and emptying the air,
         now that I breathe it alone . . .

13

Journeys of the Soul

A Spiritual Odyssey of Free Will and Predestination

Take an imaginary step with me and, just for a moment, visualize God as a man instead of a power.

God sits down and gathers together one hundred six-inch wooden rulers and glues them, horizontally and vertically, on to a very large hardboard base.

Soon, He has created a solid and very complicated maze: one hundred wooden rulers are joining, interlocking, creating dead ends in an almost impossible to solve puzzle, just like the many famous tree-mazes found in the grounds of English country mansions.

God has now finished His work, fashioned by His own hands under the direction of His own mind, so He then places it on the ground.

Gazing down at it from a very great height, God knows that there is only one entrance and just one exit on the opposite side. From His objective viewpoint He is able to see where any traveller may enter, and also all the dead ends that he may encounter, plus the only possible way forward towards the eventual exit.

Satisfied with His work, and content that the pattern has now been set and placed on solid earth, God sits back and awaits the arrival of a traveller, the first investigator who will try his luck in the complex wooden maze.

A short while later, a little white mouse happens along the road and suddenly discovers the entrance to the maze. But at first he doesn't recognize it as a puzzle, so he steps inside, and after turning a few corners he soon feels hopelessly lost among the high wooden walls.

The white mouse is so very small and fragile that the walls of the maze overpower and dwarf him: he cannot see over them, around them, through them or above them. All he knows is that as he glances forward there appears to be a set of possibilities in front of him, several different roadways from which he might choose in order to escape the complex maze.

So he puts his best paw forward and travels along a selected pathway which, to him, he has chosen with his own free will.

But way up on high, God – the Maker of the maze – gazes down from His privileged position and clearly sees that the road our traveller has taken will ultimately lead him to nowhere but a dead end.

God already knows that the little white mouse will have to eventually retrace his steps and try another pathway until he finally stumbles upon or discovers the correct route forward and out.

God knows that all the effort put into this brief investigation by the mouse will add to its experience of life; but this information is not immediately available to the traveller.

All this while, our little white mouse shuffles along, and turns up into blind alleyways and around corners that seemingly lead nowhere, or into interesting diversions which teach him valuable lessons and keep him travelling forward with interest and vigour.

But then, after many futile attempts and disappointing failures, much anger and frustration, the young traveller suddenly delights God (who is still watching and taking a personal interest) because at last the mouse reaches the pathway which will take him into freedom.

But even as he walks it, he doesn't yet recognize it as the roadway forward and out.

But God, observing from His high vantage-point, sees all and rejoices.

This is the pattern of the journey of your soul.

God is your own Higher Self.

The maze is the tangled web of life's experiences you have planned and set down.

The many pathways may well be different lifetimes.

The solid ground is the Earth-plane in which you now exist.

Our traveller, the little white mouse, is you – but

in your physical consciousness, exercising what you believe to be your own free will.

The way to freedom is your release into Spirit, from whence you originally came.

Now read the story again, but this time with the added knowledge that hidden within it there is an All-knowing, All-powerful unseen Consciousness which created every single element in this spiritual odyssey – including you.

14

The Living God

'Is there some kind of God?' hundreds write and ask, 'and if there is, why doesn't He intervene in times of tragedy, or clearly answer sincere prayers?'

Many seem discontented with their idea of who or what God is, but a more careful investigation would probably reveal their disillusionment is rooted in their concept of a God in which they've been *taught* to believe.

The questioning of orthodox thought is actively discouraged in some faiths, but, in my view, those who blindly follow the dictates of others may never come to realize the true nature of the Infinite Spirit, which – for want of a better name – man has called God; a Power whose Essence, I fully believe, is found within us, and which therefore needs to be rediscovered, unveiled and revealed through a process of self enquiry: *Man Know Thyself*.

Solving this seemingly unfathomable mystery could well be one of the most important steps we may ever take in our soul-evolution, so let's see if we can discover the true nature of God – simply, step by step, through a short investigation. After all, if there is a God who will, as some world religions teach, lovingly 'reward' or cruelly 'punish' us, then we ought to know something about Him, to safeguard and ensure our long-standing personal happiness.

But, of course, such a God might not exist at all. Let's see . . .

To start this journey we must first be willing to surrender any preconceived ideas of what we may think God is, for unless we can release our deep-rooted opinions and personal biases, no fresh concepts will be welcomed.

Another vitally important point to realize is that, in such limited space as this, we're undertaking the immense task of trying to understand a concept which may very well lie beyond all possible human understanding. So many previous attempts, made by the Finite to comprehend the Infinite, have inevitably fallen short of uncovering all the answers.

Perhaps it's for these reasons that God has often been termed 'The Ineffable One': something – or someone – which remains fully inexpressible and defies adequate description in words; a vast *Consciousness* or grounding-place of the soul; *a Sense of Being*, or a state of *Living Experience*, rather than something we can categorize with intellect or mere language.

Nevertheless, even with our limitations, let's go ahead anyway, and see if we can understand this mysterious Sense of Being.

In order to unveil the nature of God, we must surely begin by making the assumption He exists:

this deity has already fascinated billions of questioning minds over countless millennia, creating a general feeling that 'somewhere' there might well be a powerful 'something' or 'someone' that is existing through, or at the very back of, Life itself.

So let's start our quest with a universally fair, generally acceptable statement of what many questioning believers have conceived to be the nature of God. This presents us with a common-ground supposition from which we can work.

And it reads like this:

Somewhere, seen or unseen, there is some kind of Eternal, Infinite, All-powerful Influence, Consciousness, Spirit, or Presence pervading every facet of existence, which seems to have a measure of responsibility for creating, governing and/or maintaining the order and running of Life in this universe.

It is said to express emotion and mentality, and It appears to be somehow personally, or impersonally, involved with Its creations.

We can now investigate these claims by following one prophet's advice to 'seek and find', beginning with some simple philosophical thought.

Down through the centuries many great minds have pitted their intellects against the existence of a Superior Being. For these people, an invisible power of Faith in the deity was not enough, as indeed it isn't for many of today's thinkers who require evidence, reasons and facts to support the existence of a supposed Supreme Power.

Philosophers counter religious assertions such as 'There is a God', with challenging questions like: 'Before you can affirm "There is a God", explain exactly what you *mean* by "God".'

At first glance, 'There is a God' sounds like a simple statement of fact, as though we might be saying, 'There is a tree' – it appears to be a straightforward sharing of information, but is it?

We can see and feel the tree, cut its bark, and obtain enough material evidence to indicate its objective existence. What's more, others can copy our actions and get the same results.

But it might prove difficult to obtain objective evidence of God's existence – and this is where all our problems start.

When believers come up against this logic they sometimes quote religious teachings, because – for them – they carry the stamp of absolute authority. But philosophers challenge again: 'You haven't explained what you *mean* by God' – to which the eventual end-of-argument reply is often: 'A Power in which we must have Faith.'

This, of course, plunges us into very deep intellectual and mystical waters, for what is Faith? Such a question leads us away from objective facts and into the misty realms of inner *Being-ness* and *Living Experience*. And then, when people say, 'Faith in a God is not enough: prove His existence to me' – we are then back into a classic circular argument. But let's see if we can resolve it.

Working from our statement of God's probable nature, if such an Infinite Being exists, He can have no boundaries. His Beingness would know no lines of demarcation, for Infinity immediately becomes Finite once we place limits around it. Therefore, everything that has life and consciousness must be living, or vibrating, within the Essence of what, for want of more adequate terms, we might call an Infinite All-pervading Presence, or Spirit.

Following on: such an Infinite God must also be eternal, because man's measurement of time is a finite activity. An Infinite Presence would also be spaceless, non-physical, and an immortal, everlasting Being.

Something that is eternal, could not have had a beginning and will never experience an end. So the Origin of Everything would have to have been in existence long before our finite selves.

Such a limitless Infinite Consciousness, unlike physical man, would be omnipresent – present in all places at once; omnipotent – all-powerful; and omniscient – all-knowing. These qualities seem implied in the teaching of Jesus that God knows of the smallest sparrow's fall, as well as of the thoughts which make up every mind.

So this God-Spirit, moving through the hearts and minds of His creations, now provides a common link between everything that *Is*. Therefore, each religious belief-system is functioning within the Essence of the

One – and the One is in the All, and what at first seems like diversity of form and belief, would be, in fact, Unity, underlying everything.

This could best be illustrated by a vast symbolic pyramid of Spirit-Consciousness-Being: along its base are found the various diversities of existence, but climb much higher and everything that *Is* originates from, and is linked up to, the summit: *the Many are contained within the One*.

Of course, if such realizations were accepted and then practised, much would be accomplished in sweeping away religious bias, as well as fostering a common respect among all creatures everywhere. But to continue:

We've reasoned that this One Power has no limiting physical person, therefore It Is an Impersonal Spirit: operating without selected favour, minus all petty human likes and dislikes, and not restricted or confined in Its thinking, as many human minds seem to be.

Yet, if we look at one of Jesus's revelations claiming God as 'a Loving Father', moreover 'Our Father', then initially, this concept of impersonality seems directly in opposition to it – for an Impersonal Power must surely operate impersonally, meaning that God would be an objective witness and seemingly beyond the personal decisions and actions of His 'creations'.

But this riddle is resolved by God's immanent omnipresence: His conscious Spirit being everywhere at once and motivating each life-form, a vital link with us is firmly established, and He becomes *personally involved* with each of His creations, even if they've assumed Him to be disinterested.

Furthermore, if God is all-knowing, containing within the Essence of His Spirit the minds and lives of all His creations, He would be fully aware of every emotion and feeling reflected in human nature. Therefore, God must know of, and also possess: *consciousness, sensitivity, awareness, feeling and emotion*. It couldn't be otherwise, for we, who are human (the Many), freely express these attributes, and we couldn't possibly manifest anything which hadn't first originated within our Primal Source (the One).

The Nazarene strengthened this concept in man's mind by painting a picture of the Great Spirit's Feeling Nature as 'a Loving Father', encouraging man to foster a close and loving, intimate inner relationship with his Creator through recognition of the gentler aspects of God's Spirit – those of an elder compassionate parent and a caring Power, rather than the widely taught, old-world concept of God as a wrathful judge who must be feared and appeased.

By further observing the world around us: sentient creatures seem divided into two genders, and this also applies to several forms in the vegetable kingdom. Therefore, if the all-pervading Presence is at the back of every manifestation, perhaps we could consider He might well be an androgynous power – a Power within whom is reflected the two aspects of male and female.

In the past, it may be that people granted God a masculine image because man's physical power often exceeded that of woman's and therefore he seemed to be the leader. In other words, man created God in his own image.

But within the kind of androgynous Spirit we've just considered, both sexes are afforded equal status.

So perhaps we should cease calling this Presence 'He', for the Power has now become a father/mother principle, and might more correctly be referred to as 'It'.

However, to avoid confusion, and purely for convenience, we'll continue using the pronoun 'He', even though our reasoning has indicated that the Infinite Spirit cannot possibly be a glorified finite male.

Let us now consider that if God's Spirit is pulsing within everything that *Is*, and His conscious manifestations are linking up with and mysteriously channelling His own flowing and Creative Will, then surely only He would know what their final objectives would be?

But this now raises the important issue of man's much-treasured free-will – where is it now?

Well, if nothing can exist without God, then man's free will must also contain aspects of God's Will within it, and what seems to be man's autonomous action, now becomes a reflection of the Creative Will of the One as it moves through the lives of the Many.

Could this be what Jesus meant when he said 'Thy Will be done on Earth, as it is in heaven'? Some might strongly disagree and find a different interpretation, but my purpose here isn't to strengthen established values, but to question and discuss them.

One of the main objections to the loss of man's free will in favour of all actions being the Will of God, is the obvious, and often very painful, dark energy as expressed through violence, hatred, anger and 'evil'. This train of thought has now brought us to the eternal problem of suffering and the reasons for it. But this dilemma could be more easily accepted and intellectually resolved if man thought of God as *an evolving Consciousness*: the One Spirit slowly evolving through the living experiences of the Many which He has created.

If accepted, this concept makes perfect sense of the ceaseless struggle to develop and unfold the mind, character and soul through the daily trials of existence, and its recognition fills Life with some deeper meaningfulness and purpose.

But if all our assumptions are so far correct, what then would be the point of praying to this Power; for if the Kingdom of God is within, in effect wouldn't we be praying to ourselves? Such inward-turned attention would undoubtedly enable us 'to touch base', so to speak, where we may reinvigorate and refresh ourselves by freely drawing upon our vital Essence.

It is claimed that prayers seem to sustain religiously minded people, as well as reaffirming their Faith; plus, they feel that 'linking' with God brings them closer to their Maker. And it must be remembered that prayer isn't always self-centred, many petitions being given for the good of others, or world peace, etc. But let's take a deeper look . . .

Prayers are subjective desires, born of emotions and firmly rooted within the conscious mind of personality, through which we believe this Infinite Spirit vibrates. But Infinite Omnipresent Consciousness would not only intimately foresee the rising of each soul's request, but also know the out-working of the desired actions, and the eventual result.

So our question, now, is not 'Does God hear prayer?' (for clearly He would: recognizing it before, during and after its mental birth), but should be: 'Will God take any action to answer our prayers?'

I believe the answer to that is: yes.

The Presence could attend to each supplication through other manifestations of His Consciousness — mainly discarnate spirit personalities in the Beyond, ordinary people like ourselves whose minds are existing, or vibrating, at roughly the same frequencies as the person who is praying.

This, then, could be God's way of 'personally hearing', and then 'impersonally answering', each prayer — a theory frequently confirmed by the Other Side, which explains why 'answers' are often so slow in materializing because our spirit friends have to work through many complex spiritual laws governing communication between the two worlds. I well remember an instance of one of my own prayers being answered in such a way.

It happened one cool August evening, at the end of a hot summer during which I'd felt soul-dejection, and was at a loss as to where my next steps on Earth would take me. At such trying times I've always turned to seeking within, often walking on the gentle Welsh hills and mountains to be utterly alone with myself, totally alone with God.

That summer night, the verdant landscape and its stillness beckoned me like a silent hand and I ascended to the top of a mountain, just as sunset was falling. Strolling quietly amongst the wild flowers, I let my thoughts run free, then I settled on an ancient grey rock set deep into the terrain, and closed my eyes in thoughtful prayer.

To truly pray, I believe we must sink deeply into the soul-nature of ourselves, seeking a spirit fountain of never-ending healing strength which springs from the Source, and reaches us through our higher mind: inspiration is waiting to pour into the soul from the wellspring of God's Spirit, whenever we touch the Living Flame within us.

Floating within cool velvet darkness behind my eyes, I quickly lost touch with earthly thoughts, and yet could still hear the distant calls of skylarks mingling with the evening breeze. Then, after sending out my requests, I became absolutely still, and I mean *really* still: the kind of deep inner peace that escapes those whose minds are ceaselessly filled with the sort of confusion that impels them from one anxious, psychological displacement activity to another.

But not so me; I was utterly tranquil, within, and had quietened the chattering of my conscious mind.

Then, in the twinkling of an eye, I saw the mists of the spirit world quietly rolling aside. As the thin gossamer veils between heaven and Earth began to vaporize, all about me there came a shining, golden light.

Fascinated and full of expectation, with my eyes still tight closed, I watched the glowing cloudbanks gradually gathering together in a circle about me – and within them came the shining hazy forms of spirit men.

Five white-robed beings, shimmering in the radiance of their self-luminous light, were approximating to my vision, tuning into my mind from the next realms.

These beings had the appearance of grey-bearded elderly sages, and with them came the most incredible sense of soul-stillness and powerful wisdom it's been my privilege to experience.

Mesmerized by their magnetic presence, from within the circle they'd formed around me I heard one of these wise beings break the peace. He spoke to me with his thoughts, yet his words were clearer to my hearing than the distant cries of the skylarks.

'You will not be left comfortless,' he said, in warm and compassionate tones, 'for the way ahead will shortly be made known to you.'

Then suddenly my anxieties were instantly released from within me, while the glowing forms slowly faded from sight – as though someone were dimming a light switch – and I was once more physically alone, back on the violet mountaintop.

The sage's prophecy was fulfilled within a few days when my pathway became clear, and my prayer was answered.

In touching the Essence of the God within, I not only imbibed personal spiritual healing and strength, but also gained the guidance of wise souls from worlds beyond Earth; and I fervently believe this kind of comfort and reassuring aid is available to everyone.

Such immediate results, however, don't always occur; experience has taught me they usually arrive in their own good time, and not in ours. This could be because the God-Power operates through channels of His own choosing, according to His own Creative Will, and within the scope of His own timescale and natural laws – Divine Rules which are an integral part of Himself, and which therefore govern us in every aspect of thought and feeling, no matter what we might think of them.

Such a Supreme God, who monitors and 'controls' every life via His dictates, would have no need to judge us in some final celestial court of law; but rather, judgement is now revealed as an on-going inward process, personally involving God – and undertaken by each individual life, according to the inner voice of conscience. This 'still small voice' could well be a vocal reflection of God's laws, the authority of which is coloured by the state of our own soul-evolution and personal moral standards.

So, having now explored some of the major ideas of what we think God may not be, with what are we left? Is there anything we can see, feel, know or experience which would substantiate, or indicate to us, the nature or existence of such a Divine Spirit; an All-powerful Consciousness or sense of Beingness which could be aware of us, has also created us, and seems to be evolving within each and every thing?

I think there is.

Gaze up into a dark night sky at the millions of twinkling stars invisibly held in their places by mighty forces unknown, and then try to imagine the immense distances between them, within the far reaches of what we know as outer space. All the brilliant suns visible to our naked eyes are glimpsed through our own amazing galaxy, the Milky Way, which might contain upwards of a hundred billion stars – and this is just *one* single galaxy in a universe which has a possible hundred billion other galaxies within it.

Pause for a moment, and allow the immensity of that incredible thought to register . . .

Now hold in your arms a newborn babe and look into its clear eyes and marvel at the beautiful light glinting within them. Feel and sense the movement of its wonderfully complex little body as you embrace it; caress its soft skin, and then contemplate the miracle of its conception and birth: how the amazing foetus with its plasma, blood, sinews, bones, nerves, organs and tissues, formed inside its mother's womb – seemingly without her conscious aid – and then how the child made its entry into this world. And how, after the passage of time, it will develop into a separate personality, uniquely its own.

It's amazing to think that no two people have ever been created the same, not since the dawn of time . . .

Then stand on a cliff and stare in humility at a deep red sunset, or at the purest violet dawn, appreciating the wondrous beauty of their radiant colours, and the fact that – as clever as we think we are – we can't touch them, successfully reproduce their vivid hues on canvas, or even attempt to personally create such magnificent vistas. We can only ever be passive observers, caught in voiceless rapture.

The very thought of how these scenes can be perceived by the human eye is incredible. After receiving millions of vibrations of light, the nerves and cells of the eye convey them into the brain which (when linked to something mysterious called the mind) is able to translate them and present them to our sight. Such intricate processes almost take our breath away.

And the next time we sit down to eat, let's remember where our food came from: visualizing our mighty Mother, the Earth, as she ceaselessly turns on her unseen axis, revolving to a mathematically precise timescale while remaining invisibly suspended in mid-space, and all the while being lit by an ever-radiant sun which has burned its energies for countless millions of years, without mankind lifting one finger to aid these natural phenomena.

Then – if these wonders aren't enough to indicate to us the Presence of an unseen Power – as the seasons follow one another with unbroken regularity, let us dare to comprehend the origin and blessing of life-sustaining rainwater as it quenches the grateful crops we've planted.

Even with all his current scientific prowess, man cannot manufacture the raw materials from whence water, or the seeds of our foods, originated.

Nor can he sculpt the living forms known as trees, or mould with his hands the multifarious oxygen-generating plants, perfumed flowers, or even one single blade of bright green grass. These wonders exist completely independent of man's will, and it's certainly beyond his power to create or bless them with that strange and mysterious pulsing gift called Life.

Then stop awhile and marvel at the unbridled energy of Earth's great oceans with their incessant ebbing and flowing, the tides that have perpetually moved through countless millennia; these waves were lapping sandy shores long before we came, and they'll continue to bathe this little planet, long after we've left it.

And since time immemorial man has been puzzled by, yet still he contemplates, such immense issues as the origin of his conscious awareness, the mysteries of time and thought, and even what could be the force that keeps his heart beating; but final conclusions seem just beyond his grasp . . .

And, when someone holds you so very close that you can feel the warmth of their breath on the nape of your neck, and experience the beating of their heart as it mysteriously and spiritually conveys to you its deep and wonderful power of love; when you sense these inexplicably thrilling emotions, these ecstatic feelings that resound somewhere unseen inside the centre of your soul − in the very heart of your innermost being − even then explanations as to how they are occurring, will evade you.

Nevertheless, let us be thankful for the shining jewel of consciousness which so freely grants us awareness of these experiences.

And so . . .

Is there someone amongst us who, simply by taking thought, could bring into being, out of thin air, any one of these remarkable manifestations?

Stand up the man who could snap his fingers and instantaneously create a similar parallel universe, and immediately fill it with multifarious forms of life and radiant energy.

Name the clever scientist who can bless inanimate forms with the mystery of a Living Mind.

And who among us could fully explain the depth of our feelings as experienced in the presence of freedom, truth, beauty and power?

Which one of us is capable of eternally governing

– with seemingly perfect, mathematical precision –
a universe so vast that human beings cannot see
the 'end' of it, this arena so full of the complex-
ities and manifestations of life?

Man remains silent. There is no-one who can
accomplish any of these incredible feats.

Man, who considers himself to be intelligent, is
unequivocably governed – and silenced – by the
majesty of every one of these miraculous powers.

*Man can only try to understand the living reality
of Pure Consciousness and Spirit residing within
him, and seemingly also 'outside' of him. But, in
truth, man cannot of himself create anything.*

These are humbling thoughts.

However, these wonders must have originated
somewhere: life-forms must have first been 'born'
before they could 'die' and thus transmute their vital
forces into other creative forms, setting up an endless recycling chain of energy that can never be lost.

Against this background of impossible challenges
and astounding acts, it's easy to see why man –
who realizes his relative position when measured
against these mysteries of Life and Meaning – has
willingly, and often with great humility, embraced
the existence of some kind of Creator-God.

Yet, because of the immensity of the concepts
we've been discussing, man has often felt unable
to fully understand such a Cosmic Power, which is
perhaps why so many religions have misrepresented
It.

The Great Spirit of Life has been frequently

belittled and grossly degraded by man's tiny imagination.

Perhaps man has covered the Essence of God with futile rituals, stifling creeds and unnecessary dogmas; perhaps he has attempted, by using his limited thought, to 'image' a 'universal human father', in order to satisfy his own self-centred desires.

But behind all this, the Presence has unerringly continued the unfolding and evolving expression of His Consciousness-Being: untarnished, unbroken, *unchanged* by the feeble imaginings of man, forever operating His omnipotent Creative Will, regardless of what human mentality has ever believed or done.

Countless mortals have been 'born', have 'lived', and have then transformed their energies and 'died' – but God, the Supreme Power, and His magnificent vast universe, have remained in existence, slowly evolving, functioning in perfect balance and blissful harmony . . .

I'd like to finish now with a part-mystical, semi-scientific, personal view of what I consider the true nature of God to be; only this time, when referring to the Presence, I'll be addressing Him more correctly, I believe, as It.

The Great Spirit is an eternal all-pervading Life-force: omniscient, omnipotent, omnipresent, Pure Consciousness.

It is not bounded by time or space, for It has 'created' these illusions Itself.

God is the One Life, the One Power, the One Mind, the One Energy; the One from out of which have sprung the Many, which are forever contained within the boundless Infinity of the One.

God is the Everything: the Absolute.

It exists within, through and around everything that we know, and all that which, as yet, has eluded our discovery.

All universes are held within the Mind of the One, and they, plus everything else which exists, or vibrates, and manifests Life within it, are thought-forms 'created' by Its evolving Consciousness, and are held within Its Imaging Mind and Feeling Spirit.

No life-form could exist anywhere, in any universe, unless it had first been 'born' within, or had 'evolved' itself out of, the Spirit of the One.

God conceived us: we belong to God; we are children of God.

The Great Spirit is our Father and our Mother, and is personally involved in our lives, beating within our very minds and hearts.

God is an androgynous power, holding within It the thought-forms of both sexes, the male and the female; the positive and negative aspect of each of Its manifestations have sprung into existence only because their origin is in the Essence.

God is vibration and movement: sound and silence; stillness and activity; all darkness and all light; all beauty and ugliness; depth and also shallowness – all duality.

Destruction and Creation are held within Its

Power, for all positive and negative forces have their origin within the Essence.

God is a Living Experience.

Our Primal Source is filled with sensation, sensitivity, awareness, emotion, thought, mind, and can best be described as Pure Consciousness – as can all Its manifestations, which are but paler reflections of Itself. Even seemingly insentient objects have life.

The Pure Consciousness-Being is in a state of perpetual evolution and unfoldment.

All life-forms continuously function within the Infinite Presence and are therefore slowly helping It to evolve Itself by developing their passionate natures through experiences granted to them by the All.

It gains Its evolution through the personal circumstances of every life – through all the suffering, as well as the joy, which each soul contributes to the Parent.

Such character-shaping experiences encourage Its creations to diligently seek, and eventually find, Its central Divine Spark; a Power that is embedded deep within them – a sense of Being-ness from which they were fashioned, and back towards which they feel drawn, back into what they mistakenly consider to be the Perfection of their Creator.

Man is constantly travelling towards self-realization, and it is only through this that God may be made known to him; for God can best be realized within ourselves, through a deeper link with conscious awareness.

Throughout eternity we will express this Supreme

Spirit in each of our existences, plus forever seek a closer union with It, and a fuller understanding of Its Parenthood and Its beneficent Healing Power.

The Great Spirit is the governor of all worlds, within and without, visible and invisible, and the arbiter of all destinies, achieving this guidance through Its own immutable natural laws which govern every facet of existence, everywhere.

These all-embracing, unalterable rulings are so mathematically precise in their operation that every Cause will undoubtedly bring its exact corresponding Effect, which becomes – in its turn – yet another cause, and so on into Infinity.

Through the Law of Attraction (Like Attracts Like), It ensures that the circumstances for conflict, challenge, and therefore soul-growth, are drawn within the orbit of each of Its creations, attracted by Its consciousness within the life-form – in order that It might evolve. (For example: Love attracts Love; Fear attracts Fear.)

Similarly, alignment with the universal laws produces harmony (ease) within our composite being, but misalignment results in disharmony or disorder.

These laws cannot be defied, abrogated or overruled. The Infinite Central Mind cannot be persuaded through any kind of 'vicarious atonement' to comply with finite human desires which are merely smaller expressions of Itself; but our prayers may be answered by some of Its other discarnate, spirit-world denizens, or other life-forms, or by us ourselves, according to Its all-powerful Creative Will.

God's Creative Will constantly manifests Itself by operating through these laws in every plane of life: physically, emotionally, mentally and spiritually.

The One expresses Its Will and manifests Its Power by continuously pressing through the thoughts and feelings of man, and of all other forms of consciousness in all worlds.

Its Will will be done on Earth, as it is in heaven.

Man is forever linked to the One First Cause, the Great Spirit of Life, and opportunities to spiritually evolve within the Parent Itself are ever available to each of Its creations.

We are in God, and God Is in us – in every one of us.

We are Children of the One Light.

The Infinite Spirit of Consciousness-Being is our First Cause and our Last; the All that ever Was, Is now, and everything that ever Will Be.

The Spirit of God is our One Reality: the Everything, and the Nothing; our Fullness and our Emptiness.

We cannot be where the Divine Presence is not.

The Great Spirit Is the Alpha and the Omega; the Beginning and the End.

And this is the One Living God.

We Belong to the Stars

From ancient stardust we are made:
     galaxy-children birthed afar;
     mentalities castawayed,

invisible to the naked eye,
uncountable, unweighed,
yet beating like the heart of an avatar
as every life-note's played.

We belong to the stars, you and I,
fashioned by Living Breath long-since:
from a timeless nothing
sprang liquid thought
which breathed and burned
genetic fingerprints.

An Infinite Spirit exploded Its Mind:
dispersing suns and sentient clouds;
warming blood and sprinkling souls
as stardust gifts
through hands of stone
and hearts of flint.

From only One came the All that Is:
an Oversoul breathed out Its Thought;
and back to Alpha we must return –
heartaches,
journeys,
starlight dreams –
from beginning to end
the soul will yearn.

15

Heal Yourself with Light and Colour

'The Great Spirit God is Light and Vibration which will heal your complete being,' said the spirit doctor's gentle voice, late one evening as I sensed several Other-World visitors standing around my bed. This happened at a time when my nervous energies were depleted by excessive touring and too much mediumistic work.

And the healing guide was perfectly correct. After carefully following his instructions and drawing upon the coloured Light-force exactly as he'd detailed, these powerful light vibrations penetrated every fibre of my being and replenished my body back into balance and health again.

You, too, can heal yourself with light and colour.

Regenerating light waves radiate from the vibrant Essence of the Living God and so they're ever available to us. Untold hidden Power resides within our psychic being and displays Itself in a personal radiation of dazzling multi-coloured lights, known collectively as the human aura.

Much has been written about these auras, these electromagnetic fields of energy surrounding all living and, seemingly, inanimate things. In fact, extraordinary photographs of everyday objects, ranging from loaves of bread to key-fobs, have revealed remarkable psychic images of forked-lightning sparks emitting from them. Such pictures are taken by the method known as Kirlian photography, and are so commonplace now that they've even appeared in popular magazines and daily newspapers.

Not surprisingly, when a spiritual healer's hands are photographed the Kirlian pictures are far more impressive: the brightly coloured sparkling lights extend much further into the surrounding atmosphere and are far more vibrant, reinforcing the idea that healers are tapping into, and then channelling, Cosmic Power.

One man who pioneered a way of seeing some of these soul-lights was Dr Walter John Kilner (BA, MB Cantab.) who joined the staff of St Thomas's Hospital in London in 1869 and worked there as a surgeon and physician. His main interest was in electrotherapy treatments, and he was appointed director of the then innovative X-ray department. But the world sensation he caused came by formulating the Kilner Screen, through which some of the lower-frequency human auric lights could be viewed.

His fascinating research was published in 1911 in a book called *The Human Atmosphere* and because of its success it is still available today.

Your local library will probably stock Kirlian photography books and Dr Kilner's discoveries if you want to further your studies.

Cosmic Light and Sound are *vibrations*, and therefore they're the very basis of existence upon which the Spirit, or Life-force, of all things feeds; and without such vital emanations, nothing could exist.

Perhaps the most visible of these universal power-supplies is our own sun. Its energy resources are immense and its vibrant light helps to give birth to and regenerate everything on Earth. It is the ultimate source of all our physical power (and part of our spiritual power, too), without which no life-forms could have evolved on Mother Earth. So it is hardly surprising ancient man worshipped this mysterious and glowing orb.

But hidden within the sun's health-giving, energizing rays are much more essential 'invisible' forces, which can be clairvoyantly seen. Furthermore, our bodies – both physical and spiritual – are continually absorbing these essential psychic emanations. There's a mighty reservoir of vibrating energy, freely available to us, if we learn how to more closely attune ourselves to it.

I'll be sharing a simple healing by light exercise later on.

But why do we need this alternative health therapy? Well in many respects, today's human being lives an unnatural life: twentieth-century existence has built thick concrete walls which surround us and keep out God's regenerating sunshine; and through the pursuit of money, many in the Western world feel trapped inside a hectic, hyper-stressful rat race that puts pressure on them to buy the latest luxuries as well as the basic necessities.

Added to this, there's the considerable stress of bereavement which adversely affects mental and emotional health because of man's ignorance of the laws governing life after death, a fuller knowledge of which would undoubtedly help him to cope with the painful loss of loved ones.

The psychic vibrations of grief (often seen as a dark grey cloud of gloom and despondency in the aura) throw the whole physical body into disharmony and turmoil by punishing the bereaved through self-pity, which, if truthfully examined – after all our tears and emotions have dried up – is exactly what a great deal of grief is revealed to be.

The certainty of eternal life allows people to wish their departing loved ones well, and gives them the freedom to graciously let them go, in the full knowledge that although the familiar physical presence can't be replaced, the soul lives on.

The problem of grief arises because its root emotion centres within man's ego-self, the part of the mind known as the bodily-consciousness, which, because of its sole interest in existence in the physical world, asks, 'What am I going to do now?' or states, 'I feel lonely and empty inside – I can't go on living,' etc.

Although these are quite natural emotional reactions, which anyone who's lost a special person knows only too well, when objectively examined, none of these anxieties has any real truth in it.

These fears are centred around the ego-self, or the 'I-thought' – which is the major cause of nearly all physical, emotional, mental and spiritual disorders.

The I-thought is the most easily registered portion of the conscious mind, which springs out of, and belongs to, the material body. The I-thought gives rise to physically-centred emotions and desires such as: I want, I must have, I am happy, I am sad – and a multitude of others, including those felt during the grieving process, as mentioned above.

The I-thought is an illusion that tricks the soul into believing that, I, the soul, am actually this physical body – when, in fact, I most certainly am not.

We are much greater than the body, we are limitless Consciousness, so none of the I-thoughts apply to the fundamental parts of ourselves – the Spirit and Soul which are our eternal aspects that transcend all the impermanent phenomena of the physical world.

An important point to remember when seeking health is that any disturbances in the mind and emotions will undoubtedly mirror themselves in the physical body as illnesses.

Mental and spiritual soul-conditions are the causes of either disharmony (illness), or harmony (health) in the body.

Man needs to balance all the subtle life-forces of his body, mind and spirit.

Just look at what we punish ourselves with today: our foods are chemically grown, unnaturally prepared, fast-frozen, or boiled so much that every ounce of goodness leaves them long before they reach our stomachs. They also contain several questionable additives which health-conscious people avoid like the plagues that they might very well be.

On deeper esoteric levels, 'dead' meat contains the numerous toxins from the slaughtered creature's system, *plus* the psychically impregnated horror of its frightening death which is powerfully impressed within every cell – and this remains psychically 'alive' in the tissues, and can subsequently become 'programmed' into the very substance of the human body which consumes it.

For the same psychic reasons, the wearing of animal fur is not advised. But even man-made clothes today are woven to foolishly block out from our skins as many revivifying sunrays as possible.

The common tap-water we drink is chemically treated, and the air we breathe is so badly polluted in some countries that it showers down yellow acid rain strong enough to rust iron lamp-posts and mark the paintwork on cars.

On top of all this, billions of people worry needlessly over things which shouldn't concern them at all, causing themselves deep soul-anxiety which prevents rejuvenating and restful deep sleep.

And all over the world, each morning clanging alarm bells rudely awake millions and propel them into a highly stressful, helter-skelter rat race to undertake jobs they really don't want to do, but feel they must, to earn their daily bread.

Then there's the misery and suffering of all those who've been made unemployed because of struggling economic systems, and many folk are left wondering how on earth they're going to financially support their families.

Further complications are caused by poor diet, bad hygiene, sluggish constipation, plus gluttony and overweight. Another two problems are smoking and drinking, both recognized as life-threatening habits, but they're still indulged in despite government health warnings on the dangers.

There are also other areas that create serious disturbances within the human animal, such as the stresses within emotional relationships. These are far too numerous to list, but worthy of mention here is sexual frustration: a vital life-force which, if not adequately expressed, can cause serious imbalance in our lives.

All these problems (and many more) are created directly, or indirectly, by us – and then people sit back and wonder why they don't feel too good!

It's a living wonder some people still have the strength to draw breath, let alone be healthy in today's crazy society which, I'm afraid, is sick; some have even said rotten, and I wouldn't disagree with them.

And when illness strikes people down, they then tootle off to the doctor begging, 'Please make me well,' when in fact gaining and maintaining well-being is our own personal responsibility. But, sadly, we seem ever ready to lay the blame at anyone else's feet, except our own, and not only in matters of health either.

So what's the answer? What can we do to start realigning ourselves with health and harmony again?

Well, we might start by studying all of the above-mentioned points, and then correcting them.

Of course, I must emphasize that physical exercise is also a great health boon. As readers know, I take a good deal of it, both in a multigym and at rigorous aerobics classes. There's nothing like working up a sweat two or three times a week for a few hours, trimming off the fat and building up the muscle, and getting fit at the same time. Exercise is one of the body's natural ways of cleansing itself.

Even if you're elderly, or don't feel as mobile or able-bodied as others, gentle movement helps the blood circulation and keeps the body more efficient: I know a few people who are wheelchair-bound, but they keep themselves trim by gentle daily exercise of the upper torso.

My own routines, plus a vegan diet and no alcohol, have kept me in radiant health; I'm now at my ideal weight, with no excess fat, my lungs and heart are strong, and I've never smoked in my life.

Just two of the nasty side effects of being too heavy for your height and build are heart disease and blood pressure difficulties, and if we're honest, most of us eat far too much for our everyday needs. But vast numbers of people ignore this and keep digging their own graves with their teeth.

I feel sure everyone would benefit by taking a one-day liquid fast every so often, or by going on a short liquid diet to help purify the body's toxin-laden tissues.

So why not be sensible – ask your doctor for advice and then get started on a healthier life style.

I wonder: if your body could speak, what would it say to you? In over ninety per cent of us it would probably scream for mercy at the top of its voice.

But are we listening?

Your body is the temple of your spirit, the vehicle which you need to express yourself in this world; but, at the end of the day, it's *your* temple and the upkeep of its health rests exclusively with you.

There's plenty of self-help literature available from your physician, so I'm going to concentrate now on alternative corrective therapies, ideas you may not be able to get at your local surgery – some of the simple esoteric (or hidden) aspects of health contained in the wonderful healing properties of light and colour.

Spiritual healers like myself have placed implicit trust and faith in the curative effects of light and colour, simply because we've had them proven to us so many times. But we're not alone in this: today, even the medical profession recognizes that light, and hence its reflection – colour – radiate amazing healing properties, previously ignored by modern medicine.

For example, scientific research has shown that

people suffering from angry mental disturbances, or deep-seated emotional complexes, when placed in a room which is bathed in violet light, become strangely calm or even fall asleep.

Whereas this might surprise many people, healers have always advocated the use of violet light for quietening the mind, for these rays vibrate at the top end of the visible light and colour spectrum and are known to induce a light-headed 'silencing' effect. This is why sunbathing with an ultra-violet (UV) lamp can be harmful if undertaken in prolonged doses: people can easily fall asleep under the violet rays and get badly burned from over-exposure.

I remember after one stressful British tour that when I got home I stripped off, put on a violet-coloured, knee-length T-shirt and wore nothing else all day. By the same evening, its powerful colour effect had calmed me down and fully 'balanced' my systems.

Nowadays, even hospitals are getting the message of healing by colour, and are redecorating drab grey or white wards in much brighter shades to cheer up the patients' senses. These livelier energy-vibrations have been proven to encourage speedier recoveries, and this is good news, for, as with any spiritual healing or other alternative therapies, light and colour treatments should go hand-in-glove with conventional medicine, and not be exclusively replaced by them.

But before we can heal ourselves with light and colour, we need a basic understanding of exactly what they are, and only then can we correctly use them to promote health.

Light

Light is a wave form of energy radiated from luminous bodies, and these vibrations are communicated to the invisible ether of space in waves which spread out and travel at the phenomenal rate of approximately 186,000 miles per second.

The seven colours of the rainbow are frequently called the primary colours, but in a stricter sense the primary colours of light are really three: red, green and blue-violet. However, if you mix these shades of light in the right proportions they'll produce white light.

The print on this page can be seen because light is falling on the paper which then absorbs every kind of light wave *except* that which 'vibrates' at the same rate as the vibrations of the particles forming the creamish tint of the paper, plus those of the black ink: these two light wavebands are then reflected away – which is why you can see their colours and read these words.

Colour

Colour is the name given to identify the various sensations with which light at different rates of vibration affects our eyes.

Think for a moment of one red rose: it's a mass of

vibrating atoms of physical matter which is absorbing every kind of light except the lower-frequency red vibrations – so these are reflected back off its surface and into our eyes, and we recognize these wavelengths as the colour red.

In terms of colour pigments, there are again three primary colours, but this time they are: red, blue and yellow – and these can't be produced by mixing together any other colours you can think of. However, by blending these three primaries, many other tones and shades can be obtained.

The crux of understanding light and colour is that: *everything vibrates*.

Light and colour can heal us because, just like them, we are also 'spirit life-force' – soul-matter which is in a state of constant vibration – and this is the common connection linking all things together. Colour and light, sound and vibration – they're all basically made of the same moving and 'alive' spirit essence.

Also in common with light and colour, each part of our physical bodies is a group of atoms vibrating at varying frequencies: flesh and bone are two different types of tissue possessing different consistencies because they're vibrating at slightly different speeds.

Everything that is us – the mind, the soul, the body – is continuously vibrating, and therefore other vibratory fields can, and most definitely do, affect us.

If you doubt this, just think again of how the sun's

rays can burn your naked skin; and what is sunlight but *energy-rays in vibration* which, when shining on your body, affect the rate of vibration of the particles of your skin at the point where the two meet: we feel warmth because our skin particles have been quickened by the atoms of the sun's energies.

And the same principles apply to colour: if you stand in a room painted in a deep-red rose colour you'll be substantially bathed by the light-frequency known as red, and this low rate of vibration will certainly affect you when it meets the vibrations of your body.

Everything is interconnected and nothing is really independent of anything else.

Both light and colour influence the vibratory state of every particle of ourselves, and therefore they can dramatically affect our state of health and well-being.

Light can either aid or hurt us. Sunlight, in sensible doses, is beneficial; but concentrate it into laser light and it can kill.

'Post-operative shock' is a rather nasty side effect caused by the misuse of light during major surgery – but I can offer the medical profession some simple, light-therapy advice. The intense white lights in operating theatres are the main culprits. White light is so highly active – so full of powerful energy vibrations which contain all the colours of the visible spectrum within them (as a simple glass prism experiment reveals) – that it has the effect of regenerating and exciting the protoplasm, which

265

can psychically disturb the delicate balance of tissue-structures and sensitive organ cells in the body's darkest recesses which have never before 'seen daylight'.

If surgeons illumined their patients in green light, post-operative shock would be reduced: the colour green falls right in the middle of the known spectrum and therefore promotes a balancing, harmonizing effect.

To me, it's all common sense.

Intrinsically, we human beings are, in essence, light, sound and vibration, and these energies can therefore be our saviours or destroyers. Rightly understood and correctly applied, light will stabilize all aspects of our physical and psychic being. But wrongly intensified and incorrectly applied – as in the case of a Star-Wars laser warhead – it can physically destroy us.

That's why it's so important to choose the right colours to wear next to your skin each day. The wrong colour-frequencies will lower your vibratory fields (and possibly aggravate any medical condition you might have), but sensible and carefully selected colours will convey more positive radiations which can correct or promote general good health.

Chromotherapy (colour and light treatment) has a profound and direct, esoteric (hidden) effect on all the visible and invisible bodies of man.

The cosmic properties of light, colour and sound will penetrate the psychic being to its deepest levels and create harmonious vibrations within the spiritual matter making up the complex set of inner soul-bodies that every one of us possesses.

By mentally visualizing selected light rays and then psychically drawing them to yourself through willpower, you will not only recharge your soul, but also harmonize your body, mind and spirit.

Harmony means health and ease. Disharmony means disorder and dis-ease.

Here are some general guidelines on what kind of effects colour and light might induce when either light rays or coloured clothes are placed within the vibratory fields of your aura (see overleaf).

The seven colours of the visible spectrum are placed in rising order: from red, which has the lowest vibratory rate, ascending to the violet rays which possess the highest frequencies.

A quick glance shows what each colour might bring, it's then a simple matter of wearing that shade, or shining that colour of light over the areas where treatment is necessary. For long-lasting benefits, why not redecorate your surroundings and allow yourself the daily healing of colour therapy? But pay particular attention to your bedroom because half of your body's life will be spent in being bathed by its colour vibrations. (Remember – even in a totally darkened room the colours will still psychically vibrate.)

Choosing your colours, of course, is a very personal decision, and what works for some might not for others; so try a little gentle experimentation. For me to give this subject the breadth and depth it deserves I'd need a complete book on its own. (While it's true to say that each colour can have a different effect in the realms of emotion, soul, and mind, etc, the basic meanings of each are roughly the same.)

I'd advise you to stay with your chosen shade until you feel the benefits of the treatment for yourself.

Remember that each colour also possesses a *negative* side, and this usually resides in its darker and muddier hues, so it's quite important to choose the brighter, more positive and pleasant shades for your treatment, but nothing too garish or brash.

Here are some of the main, widely accepted qualities of the positive shades and their possible beneficial effects.

The Principal Light and Colour Shades and their Possible Effects

red: stimulating
orange: vitalizing
yellow: quickening
green: harmonizing
blue: peace-inducing (pain-healing)
indigo: purifying
violet: silencing
white: regenerating

Other Popular Colours

black: strengthening
grey: neutralizing
rose-pink: soothing
brown: stabilizing

Imagine for a moment that a man has one broken leg. Under the plaster cast his muscles will be losing their strength through lack of use. The encased muscles are nothing more than a mass of physical matter vibrating at lower frequencies than the normal leg's muscles which are more active, fitter and healthier, and therefore their vibratory rate is faster.

To clairvoyant vision these two sets of muscles will show marked differences in the psychic colours (vibrations) that they are radiating around them, out into the patient's aura.

In order to regain an efficient vibratory rate the weaker set will obviously need exercise coupled with a sufficient intake of proteins and vitamins, but they can also be helped towards regeneration by colour treatment.

The white plaster and bandages are in themselves regenerating, but, in addition, the man could wrap a red cloth around them (to stimulate tissue renewal), then after a while, change to an orange-coloured cloth (to revitalize).

The slower vibrations of the weak muscles would eventually 'attune' themselves, and thereby 'speed up' their frequencies to approximate to those of the orange light waves; this would aid the man's body to use the proteins and nutrients to rebuild his tissues, and then harmony would be re-established (and maintained by a green cloth or by bathing the injured area in green light waves), until full activity and health is restored.

There's a great deal we can do to help ourselves when ill.

Everything has an influence upon us, whether seen or unseen – it's as simple as that.

If you have arthritis in the legs, then why don't you choose some green clothing to try and balance out the vibrations in those regions?

Or if you suffer from a nervous debility, or are highly strung, why not select a light-blue garment to bring peacefulness by wearing it over the solar plexus, which is the seat of the central nervous system (a psychic power-point situated just above the navel).

The shades you select from the list, of course, must be alive and bright – not dismal and dingy, for the very dark and murky hues can often have an adverse effect on us, and they don't carry as much helpful power or vibration as the higher tones. As a general rule: the lighter the shade, the higher the vibration, and therefore the more beneficial the effect.

(By the way, you can work out for yourself what wearing red underwear might do for you!)

Negative colour shades can do us the grossest disservice. I once helped a young man who'd undergone a long history of mental illness and nervous breakdowns. When another healer and myself called at his modest flat we were appalled; the confined rooms were dark and dingy, daubed with low-frequency, miserably drab and murky colours: there were muddy browns, blacks and depressing clashes of cloudy purple-reds. None of the colours in the apartment mixed, matched or complemented each other.

The overall effect was one of confusion, garishness and misery – and every day he was being bathed by these disharmonious vibrations.

The state of this man's mind was unquestionably projecting itself outward and reflecting itself in the depressing colours he'd chosen to surround him.

(I now have an amusing picture of readers lowering their books and furtively glancing at the walls out of the corners of their eyes!)

And why not? As a matter of interest, how do you think you and your home fare?

Before taking a critical look, here's another general rule which, if actioned, will help promote harmony and well-being:

A tranquil, calm and balanced mind is the cornerstone upon which contented and healthy living is built.

For all aspects of health it's essential to maintain an inner serenity – a peace of mind, a mental stillness – and also to have equilibrium within the emotions; after all, the mind controls the body, and each area of being will reflect the other.

Many mystics have believed that the Essence of God, the Great Presence, can be located in many virtues, but the realization of God beats in Absolute Stillness, and since we are forever linked to this Eternal Mind our own mentality should harmonize with this essence of tranquillity, if we wish to know peace.

Show me someone who doesn't worry, who takes regular exercise, both physically and mentally, rests and eats well and sensibly; someone who loves the silence and also finely orchestrated music; someone who delights in the beauty of poetry and the challenge of new and invigorating thoughts, as well as in appreciating the majestic tranquillity of the psychically powerful countryside; someone who has a sensitive heart which has a true appreciation of the feelings and thoughts of others, and therefore acts accordingly with graciousness; show me someone who does everything in moderation and who is as happy in his own company as he is when in a crowded room; someone who is thoughtful and kind, and who is therefore rendering selfless service to others; someone who truly loves others unconditionally, enough to set them free if necessary; someone whose character contains the good soul-qualities of patience, toleration and compassion, empathy and sympathy for all, including the animal kingdom, and therefore doesn't poison his body and degrade his soul by eating flesh foods; someone who expresses a genuine respect for everyone's right to speak and think and act freely, and who has purged all negativity of bitterness, regret, anxiety and hatred from his own soul – and I'll be proud to shake the hand of a reasonably healthy human being.

But how many such people do you know?

More importantly, are you such a person?

Now here's the simple light therapy visualization exercise I promised earlier, to help alleviate the crippling effects of twentieth-century stress, or pain, and which safely promotes general good health and balance in the four main areas of being: physical, emotional, mental and spiritual.

The pressures in my own public life are sometimes so immense that I've often used this, or a similar, visualization technique to help harmonize myself and encourage inner stability and strength.

It's quite easy to do, safe and beneficial, and can be practised at any time of the day or night. It's best to study it well first to get a full grasp of its format – and then, why not try it out? You might be very surprised at the results.

A Basic Light and Colour Therapy Visualization Exercise for Promoting Balance in Body, Mind and Spirit

Sit entirely alone, preferably in a semi-darkened or comfortably low-lit room.

Whatever your situation, make sure you won't be disturbed; put out the cat or dog, cover the budgie cage and place the telephone in a far distant room, close the windows and draw the drapes, because you're going to relax . . .

When calm, affirm to yourself, speaking out loud: 'This time is for me; no-one else.' And then let it be so.

You can lie down if you wish because it won't matter if you fall asleep – in fact, it'll do you more good if you do. Many people choose their bedroom as the ideal place to dismiss the rushing, noisy world, because they feel more at ease there, better able to travel within to the tranquil mind. But it's up to you.

Loosen any tight clothing until you feel comfortable and, if you can, softly play some of your favourite classical or mystical music – very, *very* quietly in the background.

It doesn't matter what piece you choose, provided it soothes your mind and doesn't cause unnecessary aural stress; it should be relaxing and able to promote the wonderful feeling of being utterly at ease with life, yourself, and with everything and everyone – for this is the mental and spiritual state we're going to seek.

Now lie or sit back and listen to the beautiful strains and peaceful harmonies of the music; there is great healing power in sound vibrations, just as there is in light.

Then gently close your eyes, shutting out the world, and, if you need to, with vocal positivity reaffirm to yourself again:

'This time is for me and no-one else.'

Then be quietly aware that it's now time to bid all your unnecessary bodily tensions farewell – they must gently ebb away . . .

Recognize every tense muscle in your body, be fully aware of each area of tension that you can sense, and then quietly tell yourself:

'All my tensions are now floating away from me . . .'

Taking each part of the body one at a time, first gently tense your feet, then instruct them to fully relax. Then, after they've released their tensions, move on to your legs: tense them, relax them. Then on to your hips, waist, stomach, chest, shoulders, arms, hands, neck, head and scalp – one area at a time, repeating the same tension/relaxation techniques.

Take plenty of time to achieve this; and if you still feel tense afterwards, go over it all again until you're fully relaxed.

Pay particular attention to your stomach area (over the solar plexus), plus your neck and throat, where tensions frequently gather in abundance.

When each part of your body becomes perfectly at ease, completely swamped by peacefulness and rest, take some gentle breaths, deeper than normal – but only a few.

Then, for a few moments more, breathe much more deeply, indrawing the breath right down into the depths of your lungs.

Then relax . . .

Now quietly, but positively, affirm with your voice: 'My body is relaxed and at peace with itself. Stillness and peacefulness are pervading my entire mind and being . . . '

And then consider this visualization which will bring its healing, beneficial effects:

Imagine that your mind is a still pool of water, unmoved by the breeze on a hot summer's day.

Clearly see this – visualize it on the inner screen

of your mind's eye – watch this calm pool, and gaze into it. Look into its clear crystal depths and notice the small silver fish, darting to and fro at play. Put your hands into the pool and feel the velvet coolness of its refreshing waters on your fingers. Then say to yourself:

'Just like this still pool, my mind is calm, peaceful, tranquil and serene . . . '

Then, in your mind, lie back on a grassy bank near the pool and gaze up at the bright blue cloudless skies above you and especially at the white sun brilliantly shining in the electric blueness.

And with each gentle breath you take, breathe in this white and regenerating sunlight, just as if it were air.

Imagine the light as a breath of life, and breathe it deep into your lungs.

Indraw its strength, and fill your body with its vibrant light and healing energy.

And when you exhale, breathe out of yourself all anxieties and cares – *let them go*.

Mentally be aware of this happening as you exhale.

Once more be conscious of the blue sky and the coolness of the nearby water. Then breathe in the sunshine until you can visualize all your body is filled with its radiant and golden/white light.

See every atom of your body sparkling with the brilliance of the healing, regenerating light, and tell yourself:

'The white light contains every colour of the rainbow. The white light is healing me, refreshing me, energizing and cleansing me. I am all Light.'

Repeat this a few times until it becomes, for you, a reality.

And then languish back on the green, grassy bank and enjoy the sunshine, deeply sensing the quietness, tranquillity and serene calmness of the summer's day and the restfulness of your peaceful mind, feeling totally devoid of any of its incessant chattering thoughts.

Then affirm to yourself:

'I will remember this peace, and keep it alive inside me, it will live within my life, in every second of every day – and nothing will disturb its healing effect.'

Acutely sense this tranquil state, this peace which passes all human understanding; know it; enjoy it; be it, and again tell yourself that you'll retain it.

And then, when you feel you've had enough: open your eyes, gently wiggle your fingers and toes, and slowly sit up.

Come back to Earth and set about everyday life again, but trying to keep this inner stillness at the back of all your daily routines – no matter what happens.

(And remember, it doesn't matter if you fall asleep during the visualization – it will only do you more good.)

This is just one of the many simple but helpful and invigorating healing by light and colour exercises which have been with us since antiquity. Many basic

277

treatments like this have been passed down into the public domain, but others of a more profound, esoteric nature have remained veiled in secrecy, and were only revealed to personally-known initiates by their teachers, the Spiritual Masters, within the ancient mystery temples of long ago.

However, much of these great souls' timeless wisdom and spiritual knowledge has thankfully been preserved and is now coming to light again in what's been described as the New Age.

Man has moved out of the Age of Pisces, and into my own birth-sign: the Age of Aquarius, in which many of the old ways are reappearing, slowly filtering from the Realms of Light beyond Earth into today's world.

In fact, 'Light' is the term frequently applied to the spirit teachings we can receive when we're in mental attunement with evolved discarnate minds.

During my countless out-of-the-body astral journeys, although my physical frame was often sound asleep in bed, spiritually I'd be conscious while travelling far out, deep into several of the many Kingdoms of Light in the next world, and I can clearly remember – and am now about to relate – some of the many occasions when I met my spirit guide, White Owl, and benefited from such timeless wisdom . . .

. . . from the place where stars are born and die
     comes the light that infuses the mind of man

from the centre of the heart of a cosmic soul
     comes the breath of life which beats in all

from the fathomless depths of timeless space
     comes the shadow-dance of a future now

from the tiniest speck of planetary dust
     comes the birth of a world as yet unknown

from the middle of the human spirit
     springs eternal life . . .

Stephen O'Brien

16

Ancient Wisdom

I

. . . Gradually I became conscious in my spirit body somewhere in the next world, outside what seemed to be a place of learning. I instinctively felt this was going to be a fascinating astral journey when I saw hundreds of people moving up and down marble-like steps into a huge impressive edifice; they were all dressed in different coloured robes which were created from a self-luminous spiritual light, and which seemed to be a part of themselves.

Standing beside me was my spirit guide, White Owl, resplendent in violet-coloured raiments reaching from his shoulders to the green-and-blue marble-flecked floor, while I was attired in similar fashion, but my robes were an electric blue colour.

Everything in the vicinity was so very lucid and 'alive', especially the magnificent building in front of us.

'This is one of the many Halls of Learning in this sphere,' informed my guide. 'Let us go inside.'

'Delighted,' I smiled, and we moved up the pastel blue-veined steps and into the first of several massive halls. The walls and floor were made of some kind of cool-feeling stone, but, of course, I intuitively felt this material had never been quarried; the premises around us were the mental creation of many minds who'd 'built' them.

There were no ceilings, and as I passed underneath the vast archways – they were about five hundred feet high – I noticed the walls were open to a cloudless sky, but before I could question this, White Owl had instantly read my thoughts and answered in his own deep thought-voice which I clearly heard within my mind:

'There is no need of roofing in a sphere where rain is unknown.'

I understood, nodded and smiled, and we walked further into the heart of the enormous hall.

Decorating the walls on either side of us were large murals which seemed hand painted, or perhaps it would be more precise to report they 'felt' as though they'd been hand painted. The interesting scenes depicted a number of eras in man's history; some showed prehistoric times containing friezes of dinosaurs and other now-extinct beasts, the like of which I've never seen on Earth. And I remember thinking to myself: 'There must be many more old animal bones to dig up back home. Some of these species haven't been discovered yet.'

'Take care,' advised my friend, 'for too many thoughts of Earth will draw your spirit body quickly back there, and this journey will be over.'

I immediately checked and changed my mind.

'Who did these?' I asked, indicating the beautiful works of art on every surface.

'They are thought-pictures, moulded, or created, by artists out of the ether which responds more directly to our thought-power than your physical matter does on Earth. These scenes are progressing upwards in time through the various ages of man, as you can see.'

Then we seemed to walk along, or rather 'float', further into a pale blue marble-effect room, and I was immediately struck by the change of atmosphere projected by the pictures displayed there.

'But these have transcended our current time back home,' I said, surprised to view what seemed to be a part of man's future.

'And what is current time?' asked my bemused friend.

'Well, the twentieth century.'

'But you did not originate in the twentieth century. That is merely your current Present. You belong here, in this world, which exists in timelessness.'

'But I just left the 1900s to come here for some nightly tuition.'

'So it seems, but that is not how it really is. Your physical body belongs to a certain point in the stream of time, but your Spirit cannot be contained within one time-conscious personality.'

'Yes, but—'

'Your ego – the thinking part of yourself – that which identifies itself with the personality and fleshly body known as Stephen O'Brien, that ego

283

speaks these thoughts, but the Greater You seems silent! The real You is an intrinsic part of forever.'

I understood what he meant, but clarified it further by saying, 'So these pictures of man's future, are you trying to show how they were created?'

'Yes. The time-stream can be met by an incarnating spirit at any point it has earned the right to touch. But these artists are not fleshly, and are merely copying what seems to be to you man's future. To them, however, it is an ever-present Now because they can touch the time-stream wherever and whenever they wish: they are not limited by clumsy physical vision and their minds can span eternity.'

'We've discussed this before,' I said, 'that the future, past and present are all happening now, together, simultaneously, but people "trapped" on Earth in a three-dimensional physical world are only aware of a small portion of consciousness which they consider to be their Present.'

'Yes, and here on these walls is a glimpse of what, for you in the twentieth century, is as yet to come. But these images will imprint themselves on your mind, Stephen, because we'd like you to share some of them with others.'

I nodded, then gazed more intently at one of the horrific scenes projected on to the surfaces about me, a strange picture which seemed to have a certain movement and degree of life all its own.

'These times are terrible,' I groaned. 'The destruction and carnage are vile.'

'As you see, man has a great deal more to learn. Always he tries to dominate and destroy. Look there! See the annihilation of these lands before us . . . This is the result of greed and the misuse of political power. And here is the man whose selfish desires will be satisfied.'

And upon the wall came the form of an officer. His skin was olive-brown and his swaggering short body and gait were sickeningly arrogant. I took an instant dislike to everything about him. I noticed there was a large white letter 'S' on the back of his green fighting jacket, alongside some odd yellow serpent-like motif, and he carried a kind of pistol in his hands with which he was indiscriminately shooting dying soldiers all around him on a battlefield. The self-righteous smirk on his moustached lips, each time another man died, was frightening to witness.

'I've seen enough,' I groaned, turning my head away from the sickening bloodshed.

'Very well; let us move to the next room.'

And this we did – where, upon the walls, were projected much less disturbing times. Before my eyes now, it seemed to me the Earth had been so badly ravaged and polluted by man that I was witnessing some future scene of rural reconstruction: hundreds of people, almost peasant-like in their dress, were busy restructuring the peaceful but savaged countryside.

Men, women and children were tilling the soil by hand – I saw no machines – and then filling the earth with containers of what I sensed were harmless and helpful organic chemicals, a kind of advanced soil-medicine, administered to re-establish the ground's fertility – for all around them in this farmland (which must have stretched out for a good hundred miles) there wasn't at present a single blade of green grass growing.

I was acutely aware that the productive soil had been damaged by man's shallow scientific folly. His war weapons had raped Mother Earth, turning her into a wasted no-man's land of shell-holes and poisonous radiations, strangling much of her land until she became a dead place of no growth.

'When will all this occur?' I asked.

'After the devastation,' said White Owl, a note of deep sadness in his voice, 'the time when a manic lust for power and greed will run riot through the minds of a small group of tyrannical men who will seek the nations for their own. As you see, there are three key personalities involved.' And he pointed at another surface where I perceived these three officers in counsel: one was a fighting-on-land expert, one specialized in air warfare and the other in battle tactics of the sea. The land expert, known as 'the butcher', was the officer I described earlier.

I slowly shook my head in disbelief as I listened to their vile thoughts and strategies for further carnage and destruction, and how they would seize more land, on which they planned to 'create a new and streamlined genetic human being'.

I was stunned into silence.

'Man has much to learn,' commented White Owl.

'He does indeed,' I sighed, sadly.

'Come, Stephen; we will move to another area . . . '

II

We entered a large room nearby which was covered by some sort of transparent ceiling which, in itself, was another kind of projector-screen.

Placed neatly all around the five walls were colourful couches, chairs and chaises longues, and we sat on a yellow silky-covered divan and peered up at the translucent dome in silence.

Soon, another dozen or so students of all ages joined us and a stillness descended, rather as though a film were about to start. In fact, it felt just like a night out at the movies, only there was bright daylight (as there nearly always is in the Beyond).

In this gathering of varied nationalities, I sensed there were some present who held a keen interest in science; also, many of them, I thought, had studied this subject on Earth, plus I 'knew' they were relatively new to spirit life.

'Correct, on all counts,' confirmed White Owl.

Strangely enough, I was also aware that some of the students were not yet 'dead': like me they were out on astral excursions while their physical bodies slept, and this was another lesson in their spiritual education. In fact, I perceived among us several guides with their mediums, and even one robust young man about whom I psychically sensed that his fatally-injured physical body was lying in a deep coma back on Earth.

Suddenly, the soft diffused light within the auditorium dimmed a little and our attention went upwards towards the dome. All at once we were looking not at a celluloid film projected on to the ceiling, but at a breathtaking dark night sky: a vibrant star-lit scene which was actually taking place, at that very moment, somewhere deep in outer space. All my psychic awareness told me this wasn't a staged reconstruction and that we were gazing at this magnificent view through a 'living telescope'.

'What you see is now occurring in a faraway galaxy,' said a man's deep voice, which reached us from out of no particular place; there weren't any speaker-systems, the voice just 'arrived'.

Then White Owl's thoughts addressed me personally, and I'm certain no-one else heard him say, 'There are souls out there whose mind-images and thought-transmissions are what you see before you. Are you fascinated?' he smiled.

'Yes,' I said, as we were presented with 'A Journey Through the Stars', where mysterious and fiery constellations of distant universes unfolded before our gaze. It was a highly educational and scientific programme, with no further spoken commentary being delivered, but many 'silent' facts, figures and statistical information inwardly communicated.

We learned how the galaxies and stars had been made, and how everything which exists was first conceived as a thought in the Mind of God, the

Great Spirit; and that each manifestation had Its Divine Spark within it, which consistently drew it back to seek Its Essence, and ultimately its destiny, something which – so the narrator's thought-voice said – would only be accomplished through aeons of spiritual unfoldment.

And each teaching point was conveyed to us by a living picture projected from somewhere in a distant universe, as perceived through the eyes of the band of spirits who were illustrating this lecture.

The educational instruction placed much emphasis upon spiritual progression being attained by mankind only by conquering his challenges and soul-hardships: those testing times when conscious entities have to plumb deep down into the soul to discover their latent strengths and abilities, to overcome each hurdle in the pathway of evolution, moving ever inwards towards ultimate spiritual Perfection, and God.

As well as being informative, this presentation was packed with living excitement, much better than a visit to a planetarium – more vital and far more interesting. This was no dry and arid theoretical talk – it was compellingly *alive*.

It was so interesting that I've no idea how long we stayed in the hall, but after the lecture concluded and we all filed out, I couldn't resist an amusing remark to my guide:

'Lovely film, but I didn't think much of the popcorn!'

White Owl grinned broadly, and we passed through into another area of the Hall of Learning . . .

III

We joined in with another group, this time of intelligent youngsters who were in an informal class, discussing universal religion, morality, philosophy and ethics.

Sitting quietly at the back of the tutorial we listened to their quite profound conversations which seemed to be far beyond the normal mental capacity of sixteen-year-olds; but then spiritual development in the Beyond can be much more rapid than on Earth.

As the bright youngsters threw some mind-boggling questions at their slim and youthful male teacher, White Owl must have sensed some deeper vein of subconscious thought about to surface within the group, for he leaned across and softly whispered to me, 'Listen very carefully to what transpires – it might interest you. You may not agree with all of it, but the experience could well be enlightening.'

Then a stocky, short-haired lad (his hairstyle resembled a newly-shaven, brown peach!) raised a new topic by discussing the spiritual teacher, Jesus of Nazareth.

'Surely, what he meant,' he continued with youth-ful vigour and conviction, 'is that if someone struck you hard on one side of your face and then you hit them back, you'd be behaving no better than they were: you'd be expressing anger and releasing more of it into the world. But if you resist anger, then you'll have learned more self-control.'

'And what conclusions do you draw from that, Shaun?' asked the olive-skinned teacher with the dark eyes.

'Well, that anger begets anger, and in the presence of this there can be no true peace and reconciliation between souls. It seems to me,' he added thoughtfully, 'that the important point here is self-unfoldment.'

'I agree,' chipped in a blonde girl nearby, a very serious and studious-looking type.

Then the lecturer, whose youthful looks belied what I sensed was an ancient mind, added his own comments:

'The Nazarene's teachings had nothing to do with any set religions of the day, and neither were they intended to create new sects. His teachings were of the Spirit, inspired by what some men have termed the Holy Ghost.'

'It was a barbaric age,' said the attentive blonde girl.

'And the people needed a concept of God to counteract these traits,' chimed in the short-cropped youth, 'and an invisible Father who was loving, rather than a wrathful deity, suited their minds and helped them to progress towards a fuller realization of what the Great Oversoul Is.'

'Yes,' agreed the affable teacher, 'but the bulk

of the Nazarene's teachings have barely survived on Earth; emotional dust and crippling mental dogmas, creeds and rituals have been woven so tightly around them by some, that modern-day man often misinterprets his spiritual teachings, blotting them almost from view.'

'I agree,' said the boy, as his teacher continued:

'But as I told you last time when we discussed these issues there will shortly come a "find" of several ancient documents on Earth which will bring to light more of these pristine truths.'

'When exactly will that be, sir?' asked the blonde girl, stealing the question from my mind.

'Quite soon,' he answered calmly. 'Specialist guidance is currently inspiring Earth-minds to uncover these relics, but it takes time to influence the slow mentalities of incarnate men and women, as you know,' he said, 'and also the time must be right, as fixed by higher authorities. When man is ready, they will be discovered.'

A classroom giggle rippled through the students because I sensed they knew full well that if this 'find' were to be made too early, certain men with vested interests might try to obliterate the wisdom contained within it.

The lecturer continued his theme with quiet authority:

'All of Jesus's teachings were about developing the self and realizing the God within. He spoke, did he not, of learning to know and govern the character and the mind – the importance he placed on motivation and soul-intentions shines out of all of his parables. By achieving soul-growth, he said, one would become aware of "the Father" within.'

'But God as a father is such an outdated concept,' said the questioning girl.

'Yes, but spiritual teachings must be acceptable to the cultural history and mode of thought of the generations receiving them, so that they're palatable,' answered the dark-eyed man. 'But humanity is now ready for much wider views, greater and more accurate revelations of the truth. You cannot teach a toddler the kind of pure mathematics you've learned here.'

'Well, you could,' said Shaun, 'but it's highly unlikely it would sink in and make sense.'

'Quite.'

Then another hand shot up at the back of the room. It belonged to a quiet girl of possibly fourteen, who had jet-black curly ringlets and deep brown eyes.

'May I ask why you refer to truths,' she challenged, 'because truth surely only has an absolute reality within the mental constructs and understanding of its perceiver?'

'Now there I'd have to disagree with you,' said the affable lecturer, 'because we can all hold *opinions*, but absolute *truth* is something very different – it exists no matter what we might think of it. There's a world of illusion separating these two. All the spiritual truths I've taught you in these classes have come from the Nazarene himself; I was a follower of his. In fact, he helped me rather a lot, but that was a long time ago now.'

There was a respectful silence amongst the group; everyone glanced at his neighbour, impressed by the humble way in which the teacher had expressed himself.

I was going to ask my guide a question, but he anticipated it and raised a silent finger to his lips and then pointed it at the man. So I stayed patient and listened intently, sensing more interesting points were about to emerge, as the lecturer continued:

'It was never the intention of the spirit known as Jesus in that particular incarnation to create an organized religion, or gather together a set of dogmas and creeds. What he revealed were spiritual truths, and these are what must be extrapolated from the many myths and mysteries which have been built up around him by some over-zealous followers throughout the centuries.

'As an ordinary man, born in the normal way into a large family, but descending from the royal line of King David – and hence his title "the King of the Jews" – he became a powerful prophet and mystic.

'He was an exceptionally evolved soul, born to achieve a remarkable spiritual mission.

'Of course, Judea of that time was under an iron-fisted Roman rule, and the Jewish nation continually prayed for a messiah – a deliverer – who would be its prophet-king; one who could wield the might of legitimate royalty and also the Teachings of Righteousness.

'To these ends, Jesus was trained for both roles; but his mystical and spiritual education among the Essenes, who were a band of white-robed healers living in semi-closed communities at that time, set him well on course to be hailed as their Teacher of Righteousness, which title he was eventually given.

'As an acclaimed leader of the peace-loving and scattered Essene communities, he encountered several problems with another band of political activists – the people we discussed in our last class, who were known as the Zealots and whose prime aim was to overthrow Roman rule by brute force, with the spilling of blood if necessary, in order to cleanse the holy land and return it to God and righteousness.

'Naturally, the Zealots wanted Jesus, of David's royal line, to be their commander-in-chief – a position he refused because his highly evolved soul set him against such barbaric acts.'

'He preferred the Way of Peace,' said Shaun.

'That is right. But amongst these Zealots was one named Judas, a dissatisfied mercenary who eventually became his life-threat, as I'm sure you know.'

'But what about the miracles, sir?' asked the curly-haired girl.

'Such signs and wonders must conform to the natural laws, and the Master perfectly understood these. We must remember that when we speak of the Nazarene, we are talking of an ancient being whose spiritual progression is legendary in these spheres.

'His body may have been that of an ordinary man, but he was certainly not an ordinary soul. He often referred to his physical temple as "The Son of Man", and his spirit as "The Son of God".

'And his immanent Spirit of Love is still here, in these very spheres around us. It also still lives within compassionate hearts on Earth, in souls who desire to serve any of their fellows who are in need.

'The Christ-light is ever available and willing to touch and aid those who attune themselves to it by trying to help unconditionally any other beings who might feel as though they're struggling along their difficult roads of spiritual progression, out of the darkness and into the light.

'The Christ-like beneficent healing guidance and inspirational power can reach the hearts of these people only because they've set their feet firmly on the path of service to all, for Love's sake alone.'

The whole class quietened, and drank in the depth of his implications, the respectful silence lasting a minute or more.

As for myself, I was enthralled, and so impressed by this lecturer's obvious and transparent honesty, and with the sincere way he delivered his truths, that I wanted to stay longer and hear much more.

'But come,' said White Owl, 'there are more places I wish you to see.'

So we quietly retired, leaving the group of

youngsters engaged in vigorous, healthy and open-minded debate, centring on whether or not religious organizations were needed on Earth.

I commented to my guide as we left:

'Their teacher was a very kind soul,' I said, 'and he seemed to know a great deal about the Master and ancient Judea. What's his name?'

'They call him Paul,' said White Owl, as he walked on to our next port of call . . .

17

Silent Sentinels

I

... From within an all-engulfing blackness, suddenly my psychic vision faded into consciousness just as my guide, White Owl, and I were standing together in a bright spirit sphere somewhere near the foot of a magnificent blue-grey mountain, down which clear crystal streams were freely running.

Gazing all around me at the majestic views of the spirit world, I had my breath taken clean away by their sublime beauty.

During this astral journey I'd regained awareness after a pause in one of our many discussions, as we'd walked along a river's edge that was lined with rising banks of brightly coloured wild flowers.

'This is lovely,' I remember saying, gratefully breathing in the scented air.

'Yes, these borderlands between the astral worlds and the higher realms are particularly pleasant,' responded my guide. Then, after we'd drunk in more glorious sights, White Owl resumed his previous topic of mankind's gradual progress through evolution.

'For many centuries man has been losing a sense of priority. By taking refuge in self-created religions, his insecure emotions have clung for too long to a dusty and outdated past. In science he has advanced quickly, but yet his soul lingers in the backwaters of spirituality, and there is still much of the realization of his origin and his eventual destiny veiled from him, by none other than himself.'

'Is there anything I can do to help?'

'Oh yes; there is always service to perform,' he smiled, after which his brown eyes were strangely stilled, as though contemplating something profound, so deeply that I wasn't skilled enough to read his thoughts.

'Name it,' I said.

'First, walk with me a little way,' he replied, 'for there is something I'd like you to see.'

And we moved out over the verdant riverbank as though we were 'floating' in the air like a gentle summer breeze, over the stream. We drifted quickly towards the opposite bank where we stood under the wide, spreading branches of a very old and friendly oak tree. I say friendly because it held within it a sense of great age and, strangely enough, a feeling of wisdom; as though it had seen and touched the countless human minds which had rested beneath it, both experiencing and absorbing their many interesting life-stories.

'This is one of my favourite places,' said White Owl, leaning his bare back against the wide trunk. He brushed his black hair from his forehead and then gazed up into the clear blue sky, as I gently sat beside him. Both of us were wearing dark blue loincloths which allowed the sun's rays to vitalize us.

'Many people have walked and talked here,' I said, reporting my awareness.

'Many,' he echoed, 'and this ancient tree knows every one of them. I often sit here when I need to contemplate. I find these surroundings ideal when I wish to read the records.'

'What records?'

'The collective thoughts of man, the sum total of everything that has ever been, from the beginning of time as we might know it through to the end, they say – though I have never been able to mentally reach that point. Amongst such beauty as this, which lightens my soul, I can fully relax and glean what men once were, what their desires for their tomorrows might be, and, indeed, some details of their future pathways. I have done that several times with your own life, and mine.'

'But how? Is it something to do with the tree?'

'No, we two are just old friends, Stephen, and this area is conducive to making such a mental effort,' he replied, patting the rough brown bark as a man might congratulate his faithful dog for retrieving a thrown stick.

There was a long, thoughtful pause while we took in the breathtaking beauty of the landscape all around us and listened to the soft breeze rustling the oak's leaves above us.

'May I read these records with you? Will you show me how?'

He turned his compassionate face in my direction, and in a very quiet voice said:

'Just close your eyes, and think of the sun.'

I obeyed, leaning back as we both dismissed visual contact with the countryside – and straightaway within the screen of my mind I was looking at some kind of huge and mighty multi-coloured whirlwind, rotating at a very slow speed.

It was so frighteningly powerful and absolutely magnificent that the very sight of it thrilled and silenced me. I was mesmerized by sensing its awesome living energies, lights which contained every known rainbow colour, plus dozens of others I can't even describe because I've no words to convey their sight and feeling.

Although the tremendous cyclone seemed to be moving in ethereal slow-motion as I watched it swirling, suspended in space a huge distance away, I intuitively knew its true velocity was incredibly fast.

Overcome by its magnitude, I was acutely conscious that it contained every thought that had ever been born, acted upon, spoken or dreamed of since the beginning of time as we know it.

This revolving power was filled with the evolution of man's mind and every one of his feelings, as if thoughts and ideas had been attracted to each other by magnetic forces, or gravitation, and they were now endlessly spiralling around and around,

302

living, and full of sentience and meaning.

As it thundered and sparked with intermittent explosions of light, it seemed to instantly convey to me an immediate sense of the countless heartaches and losses, laughter and dreams, hopes, desires, black hatred and bitterness of mankind, as well as all the unbridled anger and the pulsing of profound human and divine love . . .

All at once I was humbled, exalted, overawed, and then struck dumb and captured by its eternal omniscience.

'Do you feel the power?' whispered my guide.

'Yes I do . . . Yes, I can see it . . . '

'Then gently join your mind with mine, and I'll help you tune into these energy-fields, because there is something I want you to experience. Be still, now. Be as still as you dare, then blend with me.'

With reverence, I eagerly obeyed his instructions to the letter, releasing my willpower into his care while watching the vast cyclone, and at the same time calming myself within. I seemed to occupy two states at the same time – I was a deeply fascinated, yet somehow indifferent observer of the hypnotic lights.

'What must I do now?' I questioned.

'Just be still . . . for not everyone possesses this skill; I shall make the effort for you – but stay with me, mentally, and you will see what I will see.'

So I remained absolutely quiet, exercising the kind of perfect trust that spirit guides request of us at such times. And then, it instantaneously happened: I was no longer viewing the whirlwind – for it had immediately vanished, and in its place there appeared some strange scenes.

At first it seemed I could see a distant part of man's past, but then I realized my mistake, for into my mind came an overwhelming consciousness that the miserable pictures rolling out before me were a part of the Earth's future, and not its history at all.

Before me there sprang into view an island, surrounded by grey and lifeless shallow waters. There was no blueness in the seas, and the sky was coloured fiery red, with a dense and murky yellow atmosphere pervading everything in sight.

The sun looked like a huge, bright, red balloon, large but swathed in misty cloud formations.

Then I instantly knew there was no more life on this planet; it was a sudden realization that man had long since become extinct and all that was now left was what I could see: the fragile, crumbling ruins of some shattered cities scattered here and there at short distances from the seashore.

Then out of nowhere a man's deep voice seemed to say:

'It is finished: it is over. He is foolish; he is gone . . . '

And without warning, these scenes quickly shifted away and I saw nothing more . . .

I found my eyes wide open and White Owl and I were once again seated under the benign oak tree. I rubbed my forehead, stunned at the tragic end I'd viewed.

'Come,' said my guide, breaking my sense of isolation, and standing he then took my hand, which immediately dissolved all trace of my sadness as I recalled the mighty cyclone of Collective Thought, and replaced it with joy. 'Now we can go on our journey,' he said.

'Where are we going?' I mumbled, brushing invisible cobwebs from my face and standing erect beside him.

'To meet some people – if indeed I can call them such – who are not from Earth at all, not its past, nor its regrettable future which you have just glimpsed . . . '

When he squeezed my hand the freshness of the flowering riverbank swiftly disappeared like early morning mist in bright sunlight, and I was immediately caught up in the spirit, and the next thing presented to my vision was the familiar background of deep outer space.

We were both suspended, yet moving forward at an incredible rate, travelling onwards, way up into a black night sky, planets and stars all around us. It was such a welcome change from the great melancholy I'd just known and, thinking back on it now, that's probably why he had planned this short flight.

'The Universe is so silent,' I marvelled at last, utterly overcome by its peaceful grandeur, as I always am when taking these journeys through space.

'Yes . . . ' he replied thoughtfully, 'stars are

born and then they die; planets rage with power, unleashing mass destruction in atomic explosions; and yet, behind all this there remains Tranquil Stillness, apart and away from everything that moves – and this is God.'

'God dwells in silence,' I agreed, 'and there's nowhere to escape Its all-encompassing embrace.'

He smiled and we 'flew' on – if that's the right way to describe two beings horizontally flat out with their heads pointing forward towards a myriad glittering constellations.

For quite a while words were unnecessary and silence was all we needed; silence, and moments filled with visual splendour. We simply watched and experienced, observed in wonderment the vast night sky, the transcendental beauty of the stars set in infinite blackness.

It was quite beyond description.

Then I pointed a finger towards a distant galaxy where a supernova explosion was taking place. It seemed so close I felt I could have touched its dazzling power; but I said nothing, just indicated, and White Owl's gaze followed my arm and we beheld the disintegrating sun. Its sudden burst of energy was immense, streaming forth light, gas and debris all around it; and yet there was nothing to hear but silence – not a single physical sound reached my ears, as the sight stirred my soul . . .

'See there! To the right!' called my guide, and I noticed another cluster of faraway stars within clouds of gas shaped like a horse's head, and inside this atmosphere there seemed to be a feeling of 'life' as we understand it on Earth.

'We have arrived,' he said.

And the next instant we were swiftly descending through a yellowish cloudy atmosphere above a planet. No-one, I think, could accurately convey the peacefulness which surrounded everything there.

Quite quickly, we approached the firm mustard-coloured soil which easily bore our light weight, and we breathed the crisp fresh air, which seemed more vital than that of the higher worlds we'd recently left.

Gazing around us, I could see impressive, high green mountain ranges on all sides, and we seemed to be standing within what could have been an enormous crater; it was several hundred miles across, and we were located near its centre point.

'Where are we?'

'To give a name would be meaningless,' he said, 'its phonetic sound would not register properly in your mind.'

'Try me,' I joked; and he did – and he was right! I can't even remember it correctly now, let alone pronounce it.

'I am taking you to meet a group of souls who have been friends of mine for a long, long time,' said my guide.

We then walked forward towards the dead-centre of the cavernous crater where I could see there was some kind of glass-like shaft, leading down to beneath the planet's crust. It seemed about 50 feet across, and upon arriving at this translucent, rainbow-coloured 'stepway' – memory fails me.

Either I was put to sleep for a while, or possibly my mind has been blanked of information which mustn't be recorded . . .

II

. . . My consciousness returned when White Owl and I were in the middle of an impressively large, glass-like cavern lit by a diffused but bright peach-coloured light which seemed to have no central source from which it was created. We were both standing beneath what I knew to be the surface of the same planet's crust.

Bathed in this odd light which also filled the air, the atmosphere, everything, I sensed that this, too, contained all things in it: like the whirl-wind of Collective Thought, the very essence of hundreds of thousands of minds and characters, many lives, multifarious life-stories, innumerable souls swimming amidst a vast pool of experiences from countless beings, seemed to be 'living' around us in the atmosphere. That's the only way I can describe it.

'Their collective thoughts are strong, are they not?' smiled my teacher, who'd been carefully monitoring my reactions.

'Yes; but I don't know where I am,' I returned innocently, 'or what I'm registering.'

'Though this is a new experience, you have drawn the right conclusions,' he enlightened, obviously aware of my quandary.

'Be still, and tell me what you feel, Stephen.'

So I gathered my awareness and sensed the fine vibrations – and my findings startled me.

'Oh, I . . . I'm in the presence of . . . great wisdom,' I said, all at once humbled by the strong impressions.

'So it is,' he replied, his eyes moving forward where, just in front of us, something odd was occurring . . .

About six feet away – it sounds silly to give such a finite measurement, but that's what it felt like – a short distance ahead of us there came a glowing, bright yellow-and-blue cloud of self-luminous light which started to gently condense and swirl, undulating like the soft rippling of a still pool of water after a pebble has been dropped into it.

Within this cloudy mist I could see no visible form of a man, but nevertheless I sensed 'he' was there: this seemed to be a male presence, and someone very old and wise indeed. He was also someone for whom speech was unnecessary, I felt, and I assumed the light-being with whom we might converse, couldn't actually speak.

'Correct,' said White Owl, 'but watch, and listen.'

And then, quite by surprise, a deep and resonant voice issued forth from the glowing cloud:

'Greetings again. It has been some time since we last communicated so directly with one another.'

'Far too long, my friend,' returned White Owl in his distinctive but gentle thought-voice.

The cloud-personality, on the other hand, sounded like an ancient sage whose tones were low and tremulous as though quivering from great age. My guide spoke by thought, and yet this tremendously evolved being – whom I'd incorrectly felt *couldn't* talk at all – was producing perfect objective sound.

Then it suddenly occurred to me that what I was hearing was, in fact, the cloud-being's mind, and not his voice at all – yet his thoughts were so much clearer and better formed than my own or those of White Owl.

Then the voice seemed to 'turn' in our direction and the column-like mist was now about two feet in front of us. It was about eight feet tall and two feet in circumference, but at the same time softly blurring all around its indistinct edges, so that it didn't really hold one constant form.

Each time it spoke small explosions of peach light flashed and then instantly dissipated, in the region where the head and shoulders would have been, had it been a human form. It addressed my teacher again:

'I am glad you have come; I knew you would, and have transmitted my thoughts to that effect,' it said, and then out of the blue it suddenly *changed its voice* to that of a cultured woman's low and mellow contralto tones.

'We knew your curiosity would get the better of you.'

And then *a third voice* of a younger male spoke from it, as if answering my evident confusion:

'We are Many,' he said, 'and yet we are only One.'

Thoroughly nonplussed, I held my silence while studying this luminous mist as the column seemed to gather itself up from off the ground to a height of about five feet, and then form a rough circle of itself, a complete, three-dimensional, yellow-and-blue hovering sphere, suspended in the atmosphere, measuring about six feet or so across.

'I'd thought you couldn't speak,' I ventured, somewhat hesitantly.

'We cannot. We radiate thought,' said the warm-voiced woman. 'Your own mind clothes it in symbols you can comprehend.'

'We have no language,' said the deep-voiced resonant sage, 'we have no – '

' – means of physical communication,' interrupted the young tenor-male tones. 'We are Many and – '

' – yet we are only One,' completed the sage.

'Is there something you wish me to know, or do?' I questioned, conscious that this kind of spirit experience usually has a purpose behind it.

'They' obviously sensed my preference to hear the cultured warm tones of the woman, for that was who replied:

'Yes,' she said, 'we have watched you for many centuries now . . . '

I knew she meant *mankind*: the Earth and its people, and not me personally.

'How interesting it has been to see the rise and fall of so many nations,' she continued, 'the vanities of great ruling powers, and man's scientific strides forward towards his ultimate destructions – only to rise again like a giant flame from the ruination of bloodshed and despair.'

I maintained a humble silence, but my thoughts wouldn't keep still and I wondered if she was referring to the legendary lost continents of Lemuria and Atlantis.

'How valueless are names,' she exquisitely intoned, obviously aware of my thoughts. 'But the rise and fall will be repeated.'

Then I wondered why on earth she was communicating this to me, and whether or not some 'secret' implications had failed to register in my mind.

More peach lights flashed in the centre of the cloud as her gentle voice broke my train of thought:

'The rise is slowly climbing towards its zenith, but the fall this time will be great . . . Man has not learned. He has not – '

' – learned,' finished the young male's sad tenor tones.

Gathering my senses, trying to understand, I leaned forward and addressed the living mists.

'Have you – any of you, or all of you – an identity?' I asked.

'We are many,' replied the resonant old sage, 'and yet we are so few.'

By this I took the cloud of voices to mean that

they were one individual made up of multitudinous 'separate' personalities.

'We are in the presence of intelligence,' the woman said smilingly, as if she were really grateful for some mild amusement.

But my vanity was short-lived when White Owl said: 'There is a greater purpose for our presence,' after which the cloud of knowing resumed speaking in the woman's tones:

'We have visited your planet many times, and sent our guidance to numerous prophets and seers. Millions of inspired men and women have been encouraged by us to march forward and progress,' she said. 'But what now concerns us most is harmony. Humankind is in a state of deep disharmony.

'Man must first be in harmony with all aspects of himself (in body, mind, spirit and soul), and only then can he ever hope to achieve harmony with the rest of the universe and other forms of consciousness.

'As with us here, consciousness can only truly exist and be totally aware of itself when there is one harmonious accord between the many intrinsic parts of all of ourselves. Although we seem to be Many, we are but One – and this is and has always been our message.'

And in that moment a thought-flash lit up my mind: she – *they* – meant that all nations on Earth should join together until every mental, emotional, spiritual and physical barrier which currently separates them is utterly dissolved. Then peace would be born.

I felt privileged to instantly sense the mission of this luminous cloud of knowing.

'There is no separation or diversity,' she intoned, 'in Reality, All is One. And we are but Silent Sentinels,' she added, as if reading the questions in my mind, 'unseen on Earth, except for the rare manifestations of our presence and power; unheard, except within the minds of our chosen ones. And now we require further access to man.'

'I think I follow,' I said, 'but what can *I* do?'

'Tell man the way has already been made known,' she replied in her warmest response yet – conveying to me an acute awareness that their Mind and Its presence had 'appeared' innumerable times in Earth's past history where many glowing clouds and voices had accompanied other marvellous signs and wonders, frequently recorded in religious and mystical writings through the ages. 'But they failed to understand us, and made us into a God,' she said, rather forlornly.

'And worse than this, a vengeful God,' joined in the resonant sage, echoing much of her pathos.

'But we are not,' said the young male. 'We are somewhat more aware of God than they, but we are not God Itself; and we are not vengeful, but thoughtful and loving.'

The sage continued:

'Tell our friends on the material plane to seek advancement firstly in all the inner sciences – in the

314

study of the inward path of the soul: soul-discovery. Remind them of our message which speaks of seeking self-realization, seeking the God within themselves. Ask them to love themselves, to care for others and to think seriously of their tomorrow's consequences resulting from their actions today,' advised the deep-voiced ancient.

Then the young man added:

'Again we state that purification of thought and sensitivity to feeling is the way of progress – but most of all, create a heart which loves,' he said compassionately.

Then in perfect unison their three wonderful voices blended and intoned:

'Yes: the pure heart which loves can prevent the fall, after the rise.'

'I'll tell people,' I said, with quiet conviction.

And at this promise, the spherical cloud of voices shimmered like a dazzling, living pink light, shot through with peach-coloured sparkling stars: there were hundreds of tiny explosions within it as its electrical substance seemed to bristle with joy.

Then White Owl gripped my right hand much tighter, and suddenly my spirit sight left me – it vanished like a feather pulled into a whirlwind . . .

18

Psychic News

(Feature interview by Rita Smith, published in
Psychic News
London, Saturday 8 August 1992.)

Medium Launches New Book and Tour

Medium Stephen O'Brien is all set to embark on his
sixth UK tour this month, which coincides with the
publication of the third volume of his autobiography,
In Touch with Eternity.

His two previous books – *Visions of Another World*
and *Voices from Heaven* – sold over 10,000 copies in
the first two weeks of their publication.

Following what the medium described last year as
'worrying contract disagreements' with his previous
publishers – he claimed that they were denying
him 'editorial control of the text' – Stephen's latest
paperback is being published by Bantam Books
(Transworld).

Speaking on behalf of the publishers, Transworld
editorial representative, Brenda Kimber, said,
'Bantam was absolutely delighted to acquire Stephen
O'Brien's latest book. Although his many gifts

inevitably bring him many pressures, Stephen is always the complete professional. He is devoted to the people he serves. It has been a great pleasure to work with him.'

The book describes Stephen's work as a medium and contains many fascinating glimpses of life in the spirit world, including vivid accounts of visits to the higher realms with his guide, White Owl. The book also contains a pastel portrait of the guide by artist Lin Martin.

'These visits to the spirit world took place over the years,' said Stephen. 'Education is the key. Mediums are called upon to uplift and educate. It is an ongoing process. As you uncover one truth, so others are crying out to you to be found.'

The medium also tells how on one occasion his consciousness 'touched the past', and he was actually able to see his mother and himself as a child in Swansea. 'It was a time-slip,' he said. 'I was able to be present while the family day was going on. I believe if I had spoken to my mother she would have been aware of me.'

The volume throws new light on Stephen's controversial television appearances with Terry Wogan, and on the Granada programme, *James Randi, Psychic Investigator*. The medium commented, 'All my life sceptics have been pitted against me. It doesn't matter. A fact is a fact whether you believe it or not. I don't believe there is a life after death, I know it.'

Asked how spirit guides reacted to working with the media, Stephen responded, 'The spirit world will work with anybody who has got a willing heart and whose motivation is right. We are the limitations to their power. They would basically prefer conditions for contact to be absolutely perfect. I have been working publicly now for about twenty years,' he commented, 'and have never had those conditions yet!'

Stephen said he wrote his books, 'in order to share my experiences with people', especially those who knew little or nothing about mediumship.

'I have never believed in preaching to the converted,' he explained. 'I cannot see the point of it. The good news we have is for the people. Spiritualists already have it.'

The message relayed by his spirit helpers would, he added, 'remain long after the messenger is gone: and that's the way it should be.'

'Mediums,' he maintained, 'have the power to change lives. The purpose of mediumship is to touch and awaken the soul of mankind. I think once the power of Spirit has touched the heart and mind of a human being he can never, ever, be the same person again. A magnetic link has been made and they are reminded of their true source and essence. Slowly and surely it opens up a channel of power through their Higher Selves to the spirit world and to God.'

The medium's tour manager, Jeff Rees Jones,

told *Psychic News* Stephen would be 'travelling to twenty major cities across Britain, demonstrating mediumship in city halls and theatre complexes.'

On this latest tour, lasting from August to November, Stephen will be visiting venues in England, Scotland and Wales.

'These tours are very gruelling affairs,' Stephen commented. 'Living out of a suitcase is really no fun. It is often a quite lonely, work-filled time. The intense stresses from both public and Press can be quite crippling, especially for such a quiet man as myself, who prefers solitude to concentrated media attention.'

Describing himself as 'fit as a fiddle', the medium said he had 'undertaken concentrated physical exercises and a special vegan diet', which helped him shed 14 lbs. 'I now weigh just under a neat 10 stone (9 stone 12 lbs),' he added. 'It's all worthwhile when you see, perhaps, a mother's smile as she receives a meaningful message of survival from her young child on the Other Side.'

Asked whether he expected harassment from born-again Christian fundamentalists on his tour, the medium replied: 'I expect a few. My life wouldn't be complete without them!

'Nothing is forced on anybody,' he pointed out. 'We should never think that we're in the business of converting anybody. We are here to serve. My meetings are all about love. They're also about encouraging people to develop the good soul-qualities of peace, harmony, toleration and brotherhood.'

'Personal sacrifice,' he explained, was involved in 'delivering the message of the Spirit. If you have promised the spirit world you will serve, you have to give whatever you can and not dwell too much on your own feelings.'

19

'I Heard a Voice from Heaven Say . . . '

My bags were packed, my suits were pressed and Sooty was left with friends while my super-fit, brimming-with-vitamins body crouched in readiness on the starting block, facing another round of national tours. My manager, Jeff, had the starter-gun and – bang! – we were off!

Rushing headlong at full pelt, city followed city and meetings flew past in a continuous blur as I rocketed from one end of Britain to the other, stopping briefly only here and there to make some guest appearances on TV and radio.

The first surprise came when my telephone item on Britain's popular daytime TV show *This Morning*, transmitted live from Albert Dock in Liverpool, broke the national record for the series. I'd done the usual talk and a nationwide phone-in on psychic happenings, and within twenty minutes, so much interest was generated that the switchboard was jammed with over one thousand eight hundred personal calls.

This was my second appearance on *This Morning*, hosted by popular presenters Judy Finnigan and Richard Madeley (known to all as Richard and Judy). I'd been invited back because after my first visit, as well as viewing figures being quite high, something unusual had happened. On that occasion, interviewed by alternative hosts Ross and Sally, the studio had encountered 'some weird goings-on'!

I was conducting the phone-in when out of the blue one of the callers, a young man, suddenly accused me with: 'You don't believe in the same God as the Christians.'

I looked into the camera and said gently, but emphatically, 'There is only *one* God' – and upon the instant, millions of television screens blanked out right across the country! For the next four minutes vision and sound were lost throughout Britain, and to this day Granada TV technicians are unable to account for the power drain.

Next morning, of course, the tongue-in-cheek *Daily Star* provided the answer by declaring to its readers: 'Medium Steve spooks up the TV works!'

'Your spirit people certainly know how to handle a difficult situation and turn it to their advantage,' said a friend.

Incidentally, the *Daily Star* tabloid also ran an amusing feature asking readers to choose their 'Perfect Christmas Guest', and a wide selection of celebrities frolicked amongst the columns, including actress Joan Collins, about whom a man from Derbyshire penned, 'Her steamy presence would keep everything on my table hot.' There were invitations to such famous singers as David Essex and Dame Kiri Te Kanawa; and Susan Hampshire made an appearance, as did Nanette Newman – plus, one of the public had unexpectedly mentioned yours truly. Miss E. Mallaband from Sheffield had written, saying, 'My ideal guest would be medium Stephen O'Brien. We could have a three-way conversation with my late beloved mother, to ease this painful year without her.'

I was most touched – and I'm sure your mum *was* with you Miss Mallaband; at least, when I read your letter I prayed that she would be, and that she'd make her presence warmly felt.

The impact of both television and the written word is enormously powerful, and an interview with Frank Bough for Sky TV – which was apparently repeated several times – illustrates my point. A friend's brother, who was working forty miles offshore on an oil-rig in the North Sea, saw me and Frank chattering away about psychic matters at four o'clock in the morning! Just think: while I was tucked away fast asleep, oil-riggers, along with thousands of other insomniacs and late-shift workers, were listening to my dulcet tones. What a spooky old thought!

In the same programme was Jack Wild, who as a young man had played the Artful Dodger in the musical film *Oliver!*. While he was on air promoting his role in a new film, *Robin Hood, Prince of Thieves*, with Kevin Kostner, his fiancée and I were yattering away in the green room, and it turned out she'd been very taken with my work and was so thrilled to meet me that we missed Jack's contribution – so I consoled her with one of my autographed books!

Then I was off again on to a seemingly never-ending road: more cities followed in quick succession; and at another TV station I met one of the newest young British pop groups. Our paths crossed and we shared laughter, plus a little professional advice! They were called Take That – very physically motivated, often semi-clad singers – and they were being filmed frantically dancing to their latest release, but they just had to stop to catch their breath after such energetic routines to guzzle some coffee. Quite new to the British television scene at the time, one of the boys seemed rather anxious.

'Don't worry,' I said, 'the public'll lap it up.'

'Do you really think so?' he asked enthusiastically, interested in what he probably thought was a clairvoyant prediction!

'Oh yes,' I said, 'just keep shifting it all about and shaking everything back and forth: jiggle it all up and down and smile a lot, and they'll love it!' And of course, they did: the group got to Number One with their song 'It Only Takes a Minute, Girl,' whereas, in fact, the record itself was nearly three minutes long, as one of the boys pointed out! But my comments broke the tensions of filming and we all had a good laugh.

But there was quite a different backstage reaction when I appeared on Ulster TV with author David Icke, singer Michael Ball and popular comedian Terry Scott, who was undoubtedly fascinated by psychic abilities. No sooner had we met in a swish hotel over dinner than Terry, then sixty-five, grabbed both my hands tightly, pulled my face to within a few inches of his (our noses were almost touching), while he stared at me and commanded:

'Now – look into my *eyes*! Go on – look into my eyes and you'll *see*!'

'Yes,' I said, a little nonplussed, 'the eyes are the windows of the soul,' I added, somewhat confused.

'I know as much as you do,' he stated with obvious conviction, as he instantly released my hands and left me dumbfounded.

However, I felt more sympathetic towards David Icke, who'd received much unfavourable publicity because the Press claimed he had said he was 'the Son of God'. David maintained he'd said nothing of the kind, and took this media opportunity to clarify his statement that he was *a* son of God – as indeed we all are, for God's Spirit is within everyone. Of course, some bright spark at a newspaper had caught whiff of a possible sensation – and Bob's your uncle.

David Icke, who'd been a footballer and political environmentalist, and was now an author on New Age themes, had just released a book called *Love Changes Everything* which, funnily enough, was also the title of a hit record from *Aspects of Love* recorded by Michael Ball, another guest on the show that night.

Michael was a pleasant young man, and we chatted over drinks about his British entry for that year's Eurovision Song Contest which was to be judged the following week. He seemed a shade apprehensive about having his every reaction screened live to millions of people across Europe as the votes were telephoned in, but I was amused to hear:

'I've got it all worked out, Stephen: when the juries start ringing, I'm off to the toilet! And I'm not coming back unless we're winning!'

(I didn't have the heart to tell him I intuitively felt the British song wouldn't come top: but, to be frank, I think he'd already suspected this.)

People often write to me about my mixing with celebrities, gushing things like, 'Oh, it must be *wonderful* to meet such famous stars, Stephen!' But honestly, they're just ordinary, pleasant, flesh and blood folk like ourselves: I'd even go so far as to say you'd walk past many of them in a supermarket if they didn't have their make-up on.

Mind you, it's sometimes hard to accept that many of these glittering celebrities of the small screen – that candle glowing in the dark corner of your living-room – who'd always seemed so far removed from my everyday life when I was a lad, are now my company in the media spotlight!

Ain't life peculiar?

Even though I've really enjoyed meeting the 'stars', I must confess, there are some luminaries I'd *never* like to see face-to-face; and ranked among this élite are the infamous pair – Rod Hull and Emu. That bedraggled, stuffed puppet's razor-sharp beak has grabbed the deliciously white and unsuspecting neck of many a prim presenter! I think there must be countless celebrities who, every Sunday, lick their vegetarian lips at the wicked thought of Emu stew for lunch!

Mr Hull himself (when detached from the arm he so deftly conceals within his large and cheeky feathered friend) is a most agreeable chap, but as for that dreaded bird! Everyone knows I'm an animal lover but – I'm sorry, readers – you wouldn't get me anywhere near that creature in this universe, not for love nor money! I'd disappear down a black hole first!

Rod and myself – and the other thing – were booked to appear on BBC1 television's *Summer Scene* programme, but thank God we didn't actually meet, or should I say clash (?), our interviews being filmed at different times of the day. My joy at learning that Emu had sprouted a pair of miraculous purple wings (and had then legged it before I arrived at the studios) couldn't be contained!

Consequently, my own relaxed contribution to *Summer Scene* caused quite a stir in the country, especially when, after an interview, I gave a live spirit message, as requested. It went to an elderly lady in the studio audience, when her 'dead' father made contact.

'He tells me quite emphatically,' I said, 'that there were family connections to the Rhondda Valley.'

'Yes, years ago,' she confirmed.

'And he's come here today with Liz.'

'That's my mother-in-law,' and she raised an eyebrow.

Then the next snippet could have proved quite

embarrassing; we were on live national transmission and I really didn't know how to say what I was hearing, so I just trusted in God and launched it straight from the shoulder.

'He says you're into your second childhood,' I ventured.

'Oh yes! I'm *there*!' answered the delighted woman, happily agreeing with her father, who then sent his love and told her never to feel lonely because of his caring presence at her side.

As well as many whistle-stop TV appearances – some of which I'm afraid I refused because of what could have been their disrespectful content – I've lost count of how many radio stations I must have whizzed in and out of in the United Kingdom.

On the airwaves, dealing with awkward telephone questions, sceptical interviewers, and an often grateful listening audience, are all now part of my public persona. I must report that the media have received me favourably over the years; autographed copies of my books are frequently offered as radio competition prizes, and one cheeky disc jockey has even used *In Touch with Eternity* to balance the uneven legs of his favourite chair! But then, it is a rather bulky book, and what am I here for, if not to serve?

One amusing incident happened at an unmanned, down-the-line radio studio: a padded room where the guest sits alone, forlornly staring into a single huge microphone while he wears a set of headphones and waits (hopefully) to be connected live to another radio station in a distant part of the realm.

I say hopefully, because I've done many which have sent faraway producers into sudden panic attacks when national communications broke down! The incident that makes me giggle, even today, happened when I was plonked in front of the ominous black mike, patiently praying for a link down the headphones with the BBC in Ireland, when everything (as usual) went wrong!

I wanted Ireland, but the mysteriously clicking line suddenly produced a male, posh-sounding English accent, pompously addressing the person he thought was a famous British newscaster:

'Hello! Calling Michael Buerk in London!' he announced triumphantly.

'Foiled again, Moriarty!' I returned. 'This is Stephen O'Brien in Swansea, waiting for a line to Ireland, and listening to Radio Scotland on his headset!'

'Oh gawd blimey!' came the surprised reply. 'Hang on, mate, and I'll see what we can do!'

Thankfully, I eventually did get through with just a few minutes to spare before the live slot. (Well done, Moriarty!)

Radio, of course, relies solely upon the voice, and sensitive people can register much of a man's soul by listening to him speak. After my talk to the Irish people, the renowned film actor Peter Cushing followed on with an account of how he sincerely believed his beloved wife Helen would be waiting for him in the next world. Mr Cushing struck me as a very sincere man, and I hope my words about the certainty of an afterlife for everyone helped and comforted him – for he was quite right: I'm sure that he and his beloved wife will one day be reunited in a much better world beyond death.

My own voice, however, took on much jollier tones when I vibrated my vocal chords on the new BBC Radio 5 channel. The *Rave* programme had asked me to gauge my comments for a teenage audience who wanted 'to be entertained, so keep it light'! 'I'm such an old fogey!' I quipped – but I did the best I could – quite a feat, really, considering the youthful host kept referring to me as 'Stevie-poohs' throughout the interview.

And a similar delivery was requested for BBC Radio 1's top show *Steve Wright in the Afternoon*. The infamous 'posse' of cackling regulars, who frequently clap, whistle and jeer at the guests, were most amused when I told Steve survival was for everyone, even for one of his programme's cranky, senile and forgetful characters, 'Sid, the Manager'!

As a matter of fact, on that day the 'posse' were a few members short owing to influenza, so I even ended up being asked to frantically clap and whistle at myself with the best of them, just to make up the noise!

After every TV or radio appearance, of course, the public's interest is considerably regenerated and, as a result, Press features are frequently requested. When the *TV Times* ran a story on psychics and mediums helping the police, I was very pleased that as well as using some of the interesting parts of our interview, they were gracious enough to quote one very important point which doubly underlines the private nature and sanctity of communication:

Stephen O'Brien said that while he has helped people holding high office in this country he would never disclose who or why.

Asked how mediums can help the police Mr O'Brien explained, 'We may be given an article of clothing or a missing person's watch. That article is the psychic key to the person, rather like a housekey. Or we may be taken to the scene of the crime, where we pick up a psychic snapshot of the circumstances surrounding the event.'

Stephen ended by saying that once, at a sitting, a girl who had been brutally murdered manifested.

'She didn't want me to contact the police so I took no action,' he said. 'It's like a doctor's confidentiality – you don't betray a trust.'

A high media profile, of course, has its price: hundreds of work offers continue to arrive from UK organizations, plus from other countries, too. Interesting suggestions to tour Rumania, Hungary and India have all been recently requested. A few months back I was even asked to fly to Germany where my hosts would accommodate me in their castle on the banks of the Rhine, if I would demonstrate survival evidence to a group of twenty Catholic priests who were working in a hospice for the sick and dying.

But my time in Britain is usually so taken up with writing and travelling that I have been forced to refuse most offers. 'I'm afraid there's only one of me,' I've replied, 'but so many of you.'

However, I did accept one evening engagement at Waterstone's Booksellers in Canterbury, Kent, the night before one of my public meetings. Interest ran high and all the tickets went a few weeks in advance. I followed in the footsteps of such notables as Labour MP Antony Wedgwood Benn, and fiction horror-writer James Herbert! But from the moment I entered the building, strange things started happening to the electrics: they dimmed and flickered and then the entire top floor where I was to lecture was suddenly plunged into darkness!

The assistant manager came pelting through the crowd.

'Is this something to do with you, Stephen?' he gasped.

'Not that I know of,' I apologized, innocently, 'but it *has* happened before!'

So down to the ground floor we all trooped, where the staff hurriedly cleared away book-tables and I stood on one of these while a hundred and twenty people sat down on the carpet, up on the stationary escalator, and the stairs – and a lovely time was had by all!

I gave the audience a test to ascertain their personal psychic abilities, as well as what I hoped was an interesting talk on the very marked differences between psychic work and mediumship, all followed by a book-signing session.

I've personally signed thousands of my books in the last four years (I only ever sign 'Stephen'); and I still get lots of practice at the end of every theatre meeting! But I've done other autograph sessions, too, such as the one at the renowned Atlantis Bookshop in Museum Street, London, being invited there by the new editor of *Psychic News*, Tim Haigh.

I've also been known to spring the odd surprise on sales assistants when I've made off-the-cuff visits to local bookstores around the country while on tour. The staff, albeit stunned, were always pleased, especially when they could plainly see how tired I already was! 'Whoever said a medium's life was glamorous?' I said.

After *In Touch with Eternity* was released upon an unsuspecting world, even more letters than normal poured in from everywhere you could think of, by land, sea and air. My weekly postbag swelled with hundreds of interesting epistles. People said they were spiritually moved by it, grateful for it, and then asked when the next volume (this one) would be published! So many wonderful letters of kind support and encouragement arrived that I was overwhelmed by the love of the public, and soon found I couldn't cope with the amount of replies.

It took months to clear the backlog, and if some readers received short answers, please forgive me, but I'm only one man and the demand seems to increasingly outweigh the supply.

Letters ranged from praise to acerbic wit, and from the hilarious to the deadly serious – and I even had offers of marriage or 'delicious and tantalizing cohabitation', from people of all ages and backgrounds – and of both sexes, I might add!

One perfumed envelope looked rather promising: it was a very nice letter from a lady somewhere in England (modesty prevents me from naming her town). On reflection, I think I must have one of those 'Please will you take me home, feed me, and then put me on the mantelpiece' faces, for she – like several others before her – was offering 'a lifetime of unbridled passion and wedded bliss'!

All very well, you might say, but the poor soul made the silly mistake of enclosing a recent photo of her ample, but cuddly self. I couldn't help smiling as I remembered the late comedian, Dick Emery, reading out some similar fanmail on television once, and how wittily he'd dealt with it; it went something like this:

'And here's an interesting note from a leggy Miss Fanshawe of London: "Dear Dick, you'd better marry me or else! – snapshot enclosed". Well, Miss Fanshawe, having seen your photograph, I think I'll marry Else!'

Other parcels contained gifts from all parts of the world and arrived at regular intervals. Even my cat, Sooty, now has a weekly dose of her own adoring fan mail: I'm sure she's most touched.

She's been _delighted_ to receive scrumptious 'delicacies' from the Orient, kitty toys, and even her very own personally hand-knitted woolly pillow with silver stars, bright cloth flowers and colourful little plastic animals attached to it. The splendid array of creatures had amusing stickers glued on to them, such as 'Clairvoyant moo-cow', 'Psychic alligator' and 'Over-sensitive hedgehog'!

She was absolutely thrilled with it, especially when she realized her edged-with-fringes, tinkly-bell dream-pillow had been stuffed full of sensuous catnip! Madam thought she'd either died and scooted to heaven, or else it must have been her birthday!

But the funniest thing about this gift – sent by Sooty's greatest admirer, Kay – was what it was actually described as: 'Please find enclosed one intergalactic space-flight and activity mat. Would passengers please belt themselves in and refrain from standing while the mat is in flight!'

I found this hysterically funny, and even more so when another note came saying, 'Thank you for the photos of an ecstatic Sooty on her space-mat. I shall treasure them always and I'm now frantically knitting her a launch-pad, cockpit and joy-stick!'

(I didn't tell Fleabag that last piece of juicy news, for they say too much excitement in the feline population gives them worms.)

Anyhow, I had plenty of my own excitement to contend with. My whistle-stop public appearances continued to exhaust me, but they also presented the message of survival to many thousands of newcomers to the paranormal; and for these opportunities to serve, I'm very grateful.

It seemed strange for someone like me to be appearing at such bastions of the British entertainment industry as the much-loved City Varieties Theatre, Leeds, one of the world's most famous music halls, where I've happily worked to full houses on several occasions. The building has a charming Edwardian presence all its own, which was best captured by BBC television's *The Good Old Days* music-hall programme, when compère Leonard Sachs greeted colourful audiences, who were attired in old-fashioned clothes, by introducing the world-renowned show with some very flamboyant phrases.

So, when the stage manager told me at rehearsals, 'The chair you'll be sitting on was the late Leonard Sachs' seat,' I had an amusing idea. When the evening began, I delighted the audience by mentioning Leonard and heartily imitating his gusto and loud delivery as I loudly declared:

'Perhaps I should start by saying: Good evening, ladies and gentlemen! And welcome to this phenomenal and supernormal extravaganza of mediumistic and psychic impressions which involves – chiefly *yourselves*!'

And the audience loved it!

The City Varieties stage is quite tiny when compared with some of the opera platforms I've appeared on and other stages like the vast Wembley Conference Centre in London. Backstage at Leeds you have to keep doing gymnastic double-bends and constantly ducking your head while ferreting your way through a rabbit warren of small corridors, where the ceilings are incredibly low. How on earth the popular female impersonator, Danny La Rue, manages to get through such minuscule stairwells in full bustle and furs without losing a few sequins or a feather boa must be one of the modern miracles of the British entertainment industry!

It's spooky to think that while delivering spirit messages at my Voices Management demonstrations there, I knew the very boards under my feet had been previously trodden by the famous feet of such stars and entertainers as Gracie Fields, old-time comedian Max Miller, and the eternal saucy songstress Marie Lloyd; as well as modern-day names like Ken Dodd, Larry Grayson, and practically anyone else you can think of who's famous!

Voices Management doesn't organize all of my venues, however. *Psychic News* asked me to appear at their special charity events called 'Mediumship 91 and 92'. These were public meetings to celebrate the newspaper's sixtieth anniversary, as well as to raise funds, and bid a sad farewell to its departing editor of ten years, Tony Ortzen – while at the same time welcoming its new, younger man, Tim Haigh.

A glittering array of notable lecturers and popular sensitives assembled in London theatres, too many names to mention; but I thought it a pity that Mavis Pittilla, an excellent medium and teacher of paranormal studies, couldn't be with us, probably because of her hectic work schedule. Mavis and I have shared several meetings and some teaching seminars, and it's always been a pleasure to work with her.

One of the *Psychic News* venues was London's Mermaid Theatre in Blackfriars. Every seat in the house was taken, and a plane-load of sixty people had jetted in from Denmark, just to be there.

No sooner had I arrived than a bright bouquet was pressed into my arms from 'Grace and Dorothy, with blessings of light and love'. Such kind gestures of flowers, gifts and cards from the public are often left at stage doors, and are really very much appreciated. (My sincere thanks for the thoughtfulness of everyone who gave them.)

At these London events, I worked alone, and also with my colleague, psychic artist, Coral Polge, who drew the communicators' portraits which were then projected on to a large screen. The following compilation of *Psychic News* reports brought a sense of the evidence to its readership in seventy countries, and they begin with the spirit return of a young lad called Steven.

During the afternoon a double demonstration of clairvoyance and psychic art was given by Welsh medium Stephen O'Brien and well-known psychic artist Coral Polge.

Coral began to draw the portrait of a young man. 'He had hair like thatch, very thick,' she said. 'He died with a head condition. It would have been quite sudden.'

Stephen then picked up the link.

'A terrible tragedy,' he stated. 'He passed quickly. It involved a car and four people. I think I'm with someone up in the balcony. Who is Brian?'

Mrs Bloomfield, the recipient, recognized Coral's drawing. 'It was the name Brian that clinched it,' she said later. 'That is Steven's father's name.' (Steven was the lad Coral was drawing.)

Explaining why he had been presented in profile in his portrait, the communicator said through Stephen O'Brien, 'I'm giving you this side because the other side was so badly damaged in the crash.'

The medium said that Steven had chosen to be drawn in this position because there was a photograph of him just like this, belonging to his father, Brian.

'The communicator,' said Stephen O'Brien, 'has just said, "Susie almost joined us. She's still here: but she came into contact with the windscreen."'

Coral, still busily completing the portrait of young Steven, commented, 'Also, somebody must have had broken legs in that accident.'

'Correct,' replied Mrs Bloomfield. 'Susie had been hurt in the accident, she had broken her legs and nearly passed over. That was absolutely right!'

Stephen O'Brien then relayed this message for the communicator's father.

'Hold my dad; kiss my dad, and tell him I'm very much alive. And I'm sorry, Dad, for worrying you so much.'

Commenting on the accuracy of the messages

she had received, Mrs Bloomfield said, 'It was incredible.'

Another communication was given from a woman called Ellen who must have had great difficulty in getting about. Stephen proceeded to give evidential information about her to the recipient. Then came, 'She's telling me to remind you about the ferret. Do you understand? Did a ferret go down someone's trousers?'

'I understand,' said the recipient, amid much laughter, 'but the ferret went *up* the trousers, not down!'

Stephen then went on to relay the message, 'She's saying she has a baby that you lost with her, a boy.'

The mother was delighted to hear the words, 'Your son is really glad he belongs to you, and not to the lady who has recently betrayed you,' he added.

'I could wring her neck!' the woman exclaimed.

The mediumship continued as the drawing of a rather stern-looking, elderly woman appeared on the screen, and Stephen said that he could hear the hymn 'Rock of Ages' being sung. 'I feel she had strong connections with the Salvation Army,' he said. 'I hear the name of Mrs Powell. She's one of the old school from many years back.'

The woman was said to have had 'a big family, and just fell asleep when she passed over in her eighties.'

The recipient confirmed this and that the Powell referred to was her sister, not herself.

'She's still a Salvationist!' laughed Stephen. 'She's telling you to hold on to your faith even if someone tries to ridicule you.'

Another recipient was told by the medium that a Mrs Cooper-Williamson – 'the name is hyphenated' she emphasized – was trying to help her with some figures.

'She's talking about adding up a column of figures which comes to all but £400,' said Stephen.

'Yes, that's me personally,' said the woman.

During the double demonstration by Coral and Stephen, the psychic artist drew the portrait of an elderly man which proved to be the answer to a prayer for one member of the audience.

'I have a very tall, very angular man here,' said Coral. 'I get a great sense of loping along.'

Stephen joined in saying the next communicator had a link with the name Margaret Edwards.

'That's with me!' answered a young woman, after a pause.

'Will you watch the picture of this person as it progresses on the screen?' said Stephen.

Referring to someone named Lizzie on the Other Side – 'She always called a spade a spade' – Stephen told the recipient, 'to put your foot down.'

'Why are you smiling?' asked Stephen.

'Because I'm trying to do that, but not very successfully,' came the reply. Later, the recipient – she came from Lewisham but did not wish to give her name – told how she recognized the picture as that of her grandfather. Although she knew the name of Margaret Edwards, at first she did not claim the message because it was someone on Earth, until she realized her uncle's mother was also named Margaret Edwards.

The recipient later told *Psychic News* of her feeling of isolation and how she saw the world as 'a hard, alien, and uncompromising place.' She had even contemplated suicide.

Almost at the end of her tether, she told how the night before the demonstration she had said to the spirit world: 'I can't handle it any more. I want a message of reassurance from Stephen O'Brien.'

Her wish was granted.

The young woman explained she had never seen Stephen before, except on Terry Wogan's show (BBC TV), but after reading his books, she 'just felt he would be sympathetic.'

Of the message 'to put her foot down', she commented:

'It's true. If I'd done that two years ago, I wouldn't have the troubles I have now.'

That last example of how a spirit message averted a suicide attempt underlines just how private, meaningful and relevant the Other Side's evidence can be, *but only to the person receiving it*. The spirit people seem to know just what to bring, exactly what's required to comfort, uplift and educate those standing in the greatest need; but the mediums delivering these communications, of course, can frequently remain unaware of their important content.

There's one other very touching message of love and consolation that sticks in my mind. It came through recently, at Dundee's Caird Hall, Scotland, and I hope it may assist many people who have to face and cope with the difficult circumstances it mentions.

'I have your grandmother here,' I announced to a nervous young lady standing in the aisles, waiting at the microphone and listening to her spirit communication. 'And she's singing the old song "In My Sweet Little Alice-Blue Gown". Oh, that was her name – she was called Alice.'

'Yes, she was,' came the trembling reply.

'And she says she passed over in a hospital bed.'

'That's correct.'

'But she was semi-conscious, in a coma, before she went.'

'That's right.'

'And one night, you and she were the only two people in her side-room: and when you were all alone with her, you held her hand, just like this – ' and I copied the most peculiar hand-hold her spirit grandma was clearly showing me.

'Yes, I did,' said the tearful girl.

'And she tells me you sat there and thought to yourself, "I wonder if my darling gran can hear me, or see me?" Is that correct?'

'Yes . . . '

'Well, Alice now says, "You sang to me, too."'

'Yes, I did . . . I did sing to her.'

'She says: "You held my hand and smoothed my old, brown wrinkled skin, and you sang so softly and beautifully to me – *When you're weary, feeling small: when tears are in your eyes, I will dry them all*." You sang "Bridge Over Troubled Water" to your grandmother, my dear.'

'Yes I *did* sing it. That's *exactly* what I sang to her . . . ' she whispered emotionally through the microphones, wiping away freely falling tears as the audience was silenced by her grandma's touching recollections.

'Well,' I concluded, 'Alice says she loves you very much, and that your special song to her really meant a great deal "to an old body like me, girl." And she's ending her message with, "And please, Stephen, please tell my darling: *Yes* – I *could* hear you, *and* I could see you, too."'

And her grateful granddaughter was too emotional, far too overcome to reply . . .

Despite my joy in conveying such touching messages, delivered on stage in the quiet stillness of shadowy auditoriums, my life off stage has now become so terribly hectic that it often takes unexpected turns and sometimes gets quite exciting! I mean, how many chances in a lifetime does one get to visit Hollywood? After one TV chat-show appearance, a popular screenwriter telephoned me for advice about his latest project.

It was a script based loosely around the hugely successful psychic film *Ghost*, starring Whoopi

Goldberg, Demi Moore and Patrick Swayze – only his new script was to be a comedy.

So I dutifully read his plot and was offering my suggestions when he suddenly surprised me with: 'Listen, Stephen – if it goes into production, will you be our psychic consultant on the set?'

'Would I?' I said, raising my eyebrows. 'I'd be delighted!' – and I'm still raising them, and still waiting.

Well, we live in hope!

Speaking of which: one night back at the ranch – my old council flat where for nearly five years dreadful neighbours had tortured me day and night with their incessant noise and unruly bad behaviour – my personal hope of leaving the wretched place was fast flagging away.

As many readers will already know, at these premises I'd been beaten up as well as having had my car vandalized several times. On top of all this, there had also been police drug-raids directed at some troublesome young tenants. I was now at the end of my tether: my patience had all run out.

For the past eleven years, since I'd moved out of my father's house and into three different council flats, I'd suffered what seemed like a continuous horrifying nightmare from which I felt I couldn't wake up. Until . . .

In the early hours of one morning, just as I'd crashed into bed at around 2 a.m., dog-tired after the loud thumping noise of rock music from a tenant's record-player had stopped, from underneath my duvet-cover I suddenly heard a voice from heaven say:

'We want you to know: you'll be moving soon.'

'Oh good grief!' I exclaimed – sitting up in the night, and modestly gathering the sheets around my sylph-like form.

'Pardon I, but did you just say *moving*?'

'Yes,' whispered the voice.

'Well, thank the Lordie up above for *that*!' I replied, enthusiastically, flopping back down on to the bed and snuggling under the sheets.

Then, suddenly a momentous realization dawned: *freedom* – and I immediately sat bolt upright again and yelled back into the spirit world:

'*And it's about time too!*'

20

Wee Willie Winkie

One morning, Voices Management (that is, my tour manager, Jeff, and I) made an important decision about leaving the troublesome city flats where we'd lived next door to each other for five years.

'Between tours, we're going to get new houses,' I said, 'and now's a good time to buy – people can't sell property and prices keep falling.'

Jeff peered over his coffee cup, nonplussed.

'Oh, and where's the money going to come from? There's a recession on, in case you've forgotten,' he said.

'Don't worry about that,' I replied cheerfully, 'have some faith, and God will provide. The spirit world have predicted a move for me soon, and I believe them,' I said.

'Well, these horrible flats are getting me down,' said Jeff. 'Yesterday some of the nasty tenants shouted abuse at one of my friends outside.'

'Neither of us will be here much longer,' I added confidently, 'the Other Side will see to that. Anyway, I got a letter from a lady in Gloucester today, and she said that last week a spirit voice told her I'd now earned the right to have a quiet country house.'

Jeff raised a sceptical eyebrow and took another swig of coffee as I produced the note from my briefcase and read aloud:

'I'm sending my prayers for you, Stephen, because as far as I'm concerned, you've worked yourself into the ground for the good of others during the last twenty years, and you've suffered enough. It's about time that God gave you the peace and quiet you deserve, especially after helping so many thousands of people who are searching for truth, like me.'

'Let's hope she's right,' said my manager, adding: 'We'll both start looking for houses in the morning.'

'And I'll use my sixth sense when we visit properties,' I promised – for like thousands of others, I'm quite sensitive to the psychic atmosphere of houses. 'When I see the right place,' I said, 'I'll recognize it straightaway.'

This conviction was so strong because the secret history of old buildings has often revealed itself to me. I remember one such frightening experience happening when I was just twelve years old: our school went on a coach trip to an ancient Welsh castle, and we had a smashing day out – until my friend, Mark, and I wandered off from the crowd and found ourselves near a small dark opening at the top of what looked like a spiral stone stepway.

'Come on,' I said, being a nosy parker, 'let's have a look down here,' and we descended the slippery steps, not knowing what we'd discover; but nothing could have prepared me for the psychic terrors awaiting us at the bottom of the stairs.

With each step downwards, my young mind sensed the walls closing in on me, and a tight ball of fear formed in my solar plexus; then I suddenly stopped in my tracks and yelled out:

'Let's go back!'

'Don't be stupid!' said Mark, giving me a sharp dig in the ribs with his elbow. 'Go on, Stephen! *Get moving!*'

So further down we went, until the stairwell opened out into a high grey-stone chamber about the size of an average small house. The smell of damp moss filled the air and, as soon as I entered the room, I immediately felt ill, as though my lunch were about to make a sudden reappearance; the sickening atmosphere made my senses spin.

'Look up there!' said an agitated Mark, pointing to some rusty iron rings jutting out of the walls, about ten feet above the slimy floor.

As my eyes found them, I reeled against the nearest support, for all at once I could psychically hear the terrified cries of men and women, yelling out in anguish and searing pain, pleading for mercy and release; their blood-curdling screams were horrific sounds that seemed to resonate over my heart, thudding against my ribs.

I quickly tried to catch my breath.

'What's wrong, Stephen? You're as white as a sheet,' said my concerned friend.

'Oh God,' I whispered, still gulping to fill my lungs with fresh air, 'something terrible happened in here, I can feel it . . . people screaming, crying. It's awful . . . and it's something to do with those bars over there,' I said, pointing at the opposite wall where an old iron grid allowed some daylight into the chamber of horror.

'The people were petrified of that hole in the wall,' I said.

Then we were suddenly frozen to the spot, frightened by the sound of loud echoing footsteps descending the stairwell – but our fears quickly dispersed when our schoolteacher entered the chamber with the rest of the boys.

I did my best to regain my composure, but was soon stunned again when our history master explained:

'This part of the castle was reserved for prisoners who were tortured here.'

Mark and I glanced knowingly at each other, listening to his every word.

'High up, you can see some iron rings, boys' – and the class gazed upwards – 'and traitors were hung from these, facing that grid over there.'

Everyone glanced over casually at the small barred hole but when I caught sight of it again, my pulse raced away, recalling those terrifying screams I'd psychically heard.

'Outside the grid, there used to be a river,' said the teacher.

'But what was the hole for, sir?' I ventured.

'Well, it allowed the rising waters to completely flood this chamber and drown all the prisoners hanging from the walls.'

I was speechless, and didn't hear another word spoken by our teacher on that day trip . . .

Over the years, this kind of soul-power has intensified so much that wherever I find myself today, I know many hidden psychic impressions in the vicinity will be clearly conveyed to me – especially those permeating the atmosphere of any possible future homes.

Armed with such confidence, one day (seemingly on sudden impulse) I drove down into the beautiful countryside of Swansea's Gower Peninsula, passing through several little fishermen's villages and eventually ending up gazing into estate agents' windows at picturesque properties and 'dream-homes' for sale – but they all seemed way out of my price bracket; my wages would only allow a modest mortgage.

The Gower countryside had always attracted me because its spirit energies are so powerful: trees radiate extensive psychic auras and readily transmit their life-force to passers-by, and the country air, which is often more pure than that of the cities, is a great healer of the body, mind and spirit.

Then one day, while Jeff and I were browsing through pictures at an estate agent's, I suddenly caught sight of a small detached cottage in its own grounds.

'Oh, this looks lovely,' I cooed.

But I soon sighed heavily at the asking price, passed it by, then went to a café for a cup of tea when – quite suddenly I received an overwhelming psychic impression: 'I'm going to see it, Jeff!' I announced emphatically – and this I did, straightaway.

When I got there, I fell instantly in love with the house. Detached and full of character, it was surrounded by magnificent huge trees, some of them hundreds of years old. It was set in natural woodland, and I was further delighted to see plenty of active wildlife in the vicinity: squirrels, thousands of birds, cows, horses, and even a little brook, were all quite near.

But best of all – there were no noisy neighbours!

Even though I could see the quaint house needed some work doing to it, its potential as a haven of rest was obvious. Just like that time years ago when, as a boy, I'd been able to psychically feel the terror of those prisoners which had been impressed within the walls of that castle dungeon, now my sensitivity was registering the atmosphere of the cottage – and it had a profound tranquillity permeating it. My mind so clearly perceived this living vibration; even the earth that the house stood upon seemed to radiate spiritual quietness.

Overwhelmed by its serenity, I immediately thought, 'This place is mine.'

Everything about it felt so right and, as strange as it might seem, I instantly recognized every stone in the building. Each of the rooms was psychically familiar to me. What's more, the entire place was just as I'd always known it would be, deep within my soul.

I knew, beyond a shadow of a doubt, that White Owl and all my other spirit friends had helped me choose this house during several astral journeys taken in my sleep life.

I was also convinced that my inspirers had even prepared the way for this house to 'fall' into my hands. I was certain this place of peace had been specially set aside for me (coming, as it did, after so many years of hard work and struggle) and that both my spirit friends and I had been waiting for the right time to make this move – in between tours and after my father's death.

I also realized that if I added together my savings, plus the money Dad had left me in his will, and put down a deposit on the property, I'd just manage to buy this house with the addition of a phenomenally high mortgage; however, it would financially clean me out.

'Never mind,' I thought. 'Surely, it's better to be penniless and have such a restful home,' I reasoned, 'than to suffer any more trouble.' So my mind was instantly made up: I was going to get the house – somehow, *anyhow*; and that was that!

Furthermore, I wasn't in the least bothered about the possibility of facing the endless weeks of dreadful red-tape fuss that always precedes, and frequently delays, house sales in Britain, for within my soul

I had an unshakeable faith that everything would turn out fine.

So, a signature on the dotted line (which sent me up to my eyeballs in debt, but happy) bought me the house; and the first thing I did was plant some willow trees in the gardens, and I named the cottage 'Willowtrees'.

I'll never forget the first night my cat and I spent there; it was marvellous. Spring was in the air and the wild flowers had started to bloom, and summer was well on its way. As I lay in bed listening to the flocks of nesting birds giving their evening song, I smoothed Sooty's dear little person and said, 'We've come a long way, my girl. Whoever would have thought we'd be where we wanted to be?'

After so many exhausting tours, I was grateful to have found my new home, but also aware of the hard work in front of me, to try and meet the monthly payments. 'But at least we're here,' I said soothingly to Sooty, 'and God will provide. We wouldn't have been led this far without a purpose.'

And she looked up at me, rather quizzically, I thought, as good as to say: 'Well, you may be where you want to be, old man, but you're flat broke!' – after which I laughed myself silly, and then we both slept like logs.

In the weeks that followed, of course, both Fleabag and I began the long process of settling in and getting used to the old cottage and all its idiosyncrasies.

Our new home, because it's a mainly electric-powered house in the country, doesn't have its supply cables running underground as they do in cities, but here they run overhead on wooden poles, and this caused one minor emergency.

It happened one night during a freak storm when forked lightning and high winds suddenly brought down the power-lines, plunging me and Sooty into pitch-black darkness! It was then that I caught sight of my eerie shadow flickering along the walls, as I fumbled through the kitchen drawer, stepping on Sooty's tail in the process, until I struck a match to light a candle. After this, for the best part of two hours, I crept up and down the stairs with my candlestick in my hand, like Wee Willie Winkie until the power was restored!

The following day, when Jeff called round, he said, 'So the spirit world's prediction came true after all, Stephen: you've got your country house. You're very lucky.'

'There's no such thing as luck,' I replied, 'the time was right, and it's all part of my life-plan. And anyway, you'll soon be getting your own house,' I announced. 'I can sense it approaching.'

And within two months, this psychic impression was proven quite correct: one day while out walking, Jeff spied a nice place where the 'For Sale' sign had mysteriously fallen down and wasn't even visible from the street. However, *he* saw it.

This made him think that possibly 'some-one' invisible had knocked it over, preventing any prospective buyers being interested in the property.

He arranged an immediate viewing, and just as I'd experienced with my place, he instinctively 'knew' it had somehow been set aside for him. Visiting the property later, I fully agreed, and also recognized its distinctive oak-panelled hallway with its most unusual 1930s ornate brass lamp fitted on to the stairway bannisters.

'I've seen this fixture before, in my dreams,' I said with conviction. 'I've been here in the astral world, at night.'

'That's strange, so have I,' he confirmed. 'As soon as I saw that light fitting and, in fact, every single room, something inside me clicked, and I knew the place so well.'

'Yes, I told you it'd be OK,' I smiled, looking around his new house. 'Welcome home,' I said – and my prevision was completely fulfilled when he moved in shortly afterwards.

'But I'll have to redecorate it from top to bottom,' he lamented, on seeing the drab-coloured rooms.

'Well, it could be worse,' I said. 'At least you haven't got large gardens to cultivate – not like mine – they're vast and haven't been tidied up for years.'

This, in fact, was a gross understatement, for the land at 'Willowtrees' was so overgrown that you could have refilmed *Tarzan and the Apes* on it! Then I had a bright idea: my friend, Adrian, from England, was shortly to serve Wales by taking some mediumship services, so I got on the phone.

'How about giving me a hand with the grounds?' I asked.

'I'd really enjoy that!' he said, being a bit of a keen gardener.

So that summer Adrian came to the cottage for a week and, in addition to his spiritual work, in the sweltering June heat we cleared the terraces and dug the flowerbeds – and also basked in the glorious sunshine, as well as laughed, joked, sang and talked, in what turned out to be a great time, and one of the best weeks of my life.

The only bother we had was that whenever we tried to uproot old tree-stumps, suddenly – from out of nowhere – came hordes of horrendous prehistoric blowflies: they blackened the skies, then bit the living daylights out of us! We had lumps on our faces, backs, legs and arms – and, at the finish, poor Adrian threw his shovel in the air, despairingly, and we both ran for shelter indoors until dusk.

After a week's hard slog and a few dozen Kamikaze air-strikes later, my friend bid the razor-toothed midges and myself farewell, leaving me to finish the tasks in hand. But whenever I approached those tree-stumps, mysterious psychic signals must have gone out, and this time – out came the hornets! They were about the size of bumble bees and gave piercing needle-point jabs that felt like TB injections!

But curse as I might, they wouldn't forsake the taste of my sensitive blood, even though I'd sprayed every inch of my skin from top to toe with powerful insect repellent.

So there I was: bitten all over, and still left with only half of the gardens partly dug, during one of the hottest summers ever.

But I didn't moan or grumble. I had a big smile on my face, for one of my long-standing dreams had at last come true.

I was happy, and where I wanted to be; contented in calm and blissful surroundings: just me, Sooty, dozens of those thirsty bloodsuckers, hundreds of tall green trees, and thousands of nodding daisies . . .

. . . He maketh me to lie down in green pastures,
    He leadeth me beside the still waters,
        He restoreth my soul . . .

23rd Psalm

21

'Willowtrees'

It's high summer now. My gruelling tours and public appearances are thankfully over, and night breezes are gently wafting over the tops of the sixty-foot trees surrounding the gardens here at 'Willowtrees', my little home in the country, this place of my own, at last.

It's been a sizzling-hot June this year; the radiant sunshine's never let up for a minute and throughout today the stifling heat has scorched the grass all around. Dozens of bees have been flitting in and out of the wild flowers, and scores of birds have crisscrossed the sky in the bright sunshine.

I was glad when night fell, because it had been such an exceptionally long warm day: it was the summer solstice – the longest day – so for the best part of it I wandered around naked in the gardens, mowing the grass and giving the massive trees a serious haircut. Then I oiled myself from top to bottom (literally) with sun-screen lotions and creams, and laid on an old blanket, toasting myself on both sides until nicely browned. (It's been so good to relax and unwind, finally away from and out of the demanding media spotlight.)

After a catnap, when the grandmother clock in the library woke me by striking four and the breezes suddenly started to cool the air, I finished tilling the soil, put away the garden tools and called it a day as far as work was concerned, which was just as well, for by then my muscles were bronzed and my back was aching: all the bending, pulling, stretching, yanking and uprooting of unwanted shrubs and choking weeds had certainly taken its toll. So I gave myself a special treat.

I threaded the garden hosepipe through high branches in the big conifer tree, turned on the cold-water tap, and stood beneath the cool waterfall as it cleansed me of the long sweaty day and my gardener's pains. It was absolutely gorgeous . . .

Then I slipped into some white boxer-shorts, poured myself a lemonade and sat on the verandah, surveying the trees and thinking to myself just how fortunate I was to have such a peaceful sanctuary, at last.

At 'Willowtrees' I can meditate in the quiet atmosphere, perfectly undisturbed, and fully recharge my psychic batteries between hectic tours and engagements. The fresh air energizes me, so that I will be better fitted to go forward and serve others, as I promised the spirit world I would do, many years ago now.

A man has time to think in the country, its sights and sounds refresh his spirit: like this evening when, high above me, I laughed at Sammy and Sid, two acrobatic black bats who usually start their antics after the big owl in the woods has finished calling to his mate; those boys are a couple of good flyers; and I smiled at a chirpy greenfinch as he did his nightly skip from the willow trees into the stone bird-bath for his wash-and-brush-up, ready for the missis and bed.

This evening, I sat in silence and watched the last flames of the sun as they began dying away, at just past 10 p.m. As darkness was descending, the bright evening star appeared, piercing the blue night, high above my beloved hills and mountains of Wales, and it was an incredibly beautiful sight. The sun disappeared from view, diffusing the sky and the faraway mountains with brilliant colours, and I marvelled at the soft lights playing on the distant forests. Sitting quietly, awestruck by such astonishing beauty, my one pervading thought was: stillness.

I truly love the depth and serenity of twilight, when the country seems to generate its own unique brand of silence, its own unique spiritual presence.

It profoundly stirs the depths of my soul-sensitivity.

And tonight, just as the first glimmer of stars peeked through a deep blue mantle, there came this unearthly stillness . . .

It rolled in from the distant hills and gently swept across the fields like an invisible hand bestowing peaceful sleep on every creature in its path; then onwards it went, undulating over grasslands and moving through hundreds of rustling trees, leaving in its wake – deep tranquillity.

The birds were the first to sense it: dozens of them suddenly stilled their songs, almost simultaneously, then, as if responding to some soundless call of the spirit, they flew to their nests, ready for slumber. (After all, they've got to be up early to whistle their dawn chorus and greet the sunshine, and wake the man in the house.)

Whenever indigo night falls as beautifully as it did this evening, I can't help but think of the incredible aloneness of God, the vast infinity of timeless space, and the unfathomable depths of eternity . . .

But my reverie was broken by a noisy Sooty, who came swaggering out on to the verandah, all smiles and furry trousers, looking like John Wayne after pulverizing the baddies in a cowboy movie, rubbing her fur coat along my shins and mewing for all she was worth – for her supper.

'OK. I'm hungry, too,' I said.

I could feel the night-air temperature dropping, so I scooped up Sooty in my arms and ambled inside, thinking about the blessing of sleep, and also this book.

Then, in the cool kitchen, I sat at the table and became very still, and sent up a quiet prayer of thanks to the Great Spirit for having been given wonderful opportunities to share with so many people the spiritual truths I've discovered, during this, my intensely personal, spiritual quest – and I hoped my words would continue to comfort and help others.

I reminded my spirit friends that despite all the

hardships I've suffered in this life, I still feel very privileged to have experienced so many enthralling psychic adventures.

And I recalled that since a child, my inspirers have never failed to daily advise and encourage me every step of the way on my journey of self-discovery, this exciting search to uncover and fully realize the true Essence of Everything, whose name is Love.

Whenever I pray like this, as night falls, these silent voices from eternity still deliver their gentle inspiration.

And whenever these angels (who were once just ordinary people) see fit to convey to me their further helpful revelations about Life and its Meaning, I know it's because they want me to share their thoughts with others . . .

The Coming of the Sacred Night

Sunfall greets my quietest hour;
> stillworld,
> all around,
> inside, and out . . .

Shuttered doors
seal weary travellers aside,
as blessed day bows out to holy night.

Birds wheel against the purple lambent, painted sky,
heartsongs a-fly,
and nesting chicks summon motherlove
> for warmth,

'ere darkness freezes folded wings
and dries up tired eyes.

Country night, in silence bathed,
descends o'er fields of sleeping mice;
owls blink awake,
but feather-pillowed children dance in misty haze,
    as I sit before my window-glass
    and King Thought
    flights of fancy takes.

Behold God's night,
    serene in beauty coolness;
behold the tender drifting air
    through hushing trees
    and shivering corn.
God's night has smoothed the wild asleep
'ere dark gives way to violet dawn . . .

Privileged are we
    to sit and freely drink of this;
and blessed are we,
    as if He had lowered down His lips
    and kissed our sufferings.

Blue country twilight deep
has pressed its mouth on mine.
    Worshipped Nimrod,
    true loveliness is not thine –
    it births from the soul
    of some beneficent God.

So fold your hallowed wings upon me;
                enclose myself,
            utterly loved in sunset flight,
    by the deepest, holiest kiss of slumber —
            the Coming of the Sacred Night . . .

For further information on all aspects of the life and work of Stephen O'Brien, including obtaining by mail order his bestselling books, tape cassettes, autographed pictures, full-colour souvenir programmes, inspirational greeting cards and a full range of other quality items – please write enclosing a stamped addressed envelope to:

VOICES MANAGEMENT
(Dept B4)
PO Box 8
SWANSEA
SA1 1BL
UK

Voices Management regrets it cannot reply without a stamped addressed envelope, and correspondents are respectfully advised not to mail irreplaceable items, for neither Voices, nor Mr O'Brien, can accept responsibility for the loss or damage of any unsolicited manuscripts, poems, sentimental objects and photographs, or cassettes, etc. posted by the public.

Please keep your letters brief, and be patient when awaiting replies, as Stephen receives vast quantities of mail.

Thank you.

A SELECTION OF NON-FICTION TITLES
PUBLISHED BY BANTAM AND CORGI BOOKS

THE PRICES SHOWN BELOW WERE CORRECT AT THE TIME OF GOING
TO PRESS. HOWEVER TRANSWORLD PUBLISHERS RESERVE THE RIGHT
TO SHOW NEW RETAIL PRICES ON COVERS WHICH MAY DIFFER FROM
THOSE PREVIOUSLY ADVERTISED IN THE TEXT OR ELSEWHERE.

☐	13878 9	The Dead Sea Scrolls Deception	Baigent & Leigh	£4.99
☐	12138 X	The Holy Blood and The Holy Grail	Baigent, Leigh & Lincoln	£5.99
☐	13188 2	The Messianic Legacy	Baigent, Leigh & Lincoln	£5.99
☐	34539 7	Hands of Light	Barbara Ann Brennan	£12.99
☐	17512 2	It's all in the Playing	Shirley MacLaine	£4.99
☐	17239 5	Dancing in the Light	Shirley MacLaine	£4.99
☐	25234 8	Don't Fall off the Mountain	Shirley MacLaine	£3.99
☐	40048 7	Going Within	Shirley MacLaine	£4.99
☐	17201 8	Out on a Limb	Shirley MacLaine	£4.99
☐	17364 2	You Can Get There From Here	Shirley MacLaine	£3.99
☐	24452 3	Life After Life	Raymond A. Moody	£3.99
☐	40449 0	Closer to the Light	Dr. Melvin Morse	£3.99
☐	40534 9	In Touch With Eternity	Stephen O'Brien	£4.99
☐	11487 1	Life After Death	Neville Randall	£3.99
☐	13671 9	Mind Magic	Betty Shine	£3.99
☐	13378 7	Mind to Mind	Betty Shine	£4.99
☐	13046 X	Beyond the Occult	Colin Wilson	£5.99

All Corgi/Bantam Books are available at your bookshop or newsagent, or can be
ordered from the following address:
Corgi/Bantam Books,
Cash Sales Department,
P.O. Box 11, Falmouth, Cornwall TR10 9EN

UK and B.F.P.O. customers please send a cheque or postal order (no currency)
and allow £1.00 for postage and packing for the first book plus 50p for the second
book and 30p for each additional book to a maximum charge of £3.00 (7 books
plus).

Overseas customers, including Eire, please allow £2.00 for postage and packing for
the first book plus £1.00 for the second book and 50p for each subsequent title
ordered.

NAME (Block Letters) ....

ADDRESS ....

....